A DOCTOR'S OCCUPATION

A Doctor's Occupation

Dr. John Lewis

First published in Great Britain in 1982
by Transworld Publishers Ltd.

Published from 1983 to 1991 by
Hodder & Stoughton Ltd (NEL Paperbacks)
Seven Impressions.

This edition published by Channel Island Publishing,
Unit 3B, Barette Commercial Centre, La Route Du Mont Mado,
St John, Jersey, Channel Islands, JE3 4DS.
www.channelislandpublishing.com
Tel; (01534) 860806

ISBN 0-9525659-1-9

Printed and bound in Great Britain.

For my Ann,
whose unswerving loyalty, courage and love
have upheld me for five dark years,
and throughout our life together.
With every day that goes by,
I am mindful of our family motto,
'Think and thank.'

PREFACE

Many years have passed since the occupation of Jersey, and for a very long time after its ending I made a conscious effort to put out of my mind all thought and memory of those events which were associated with five of the most frustrating and miserable years of my life. For a decade or more, I did not wish to recall or speak of them, although from time to time friends suggested that I should leave behind a written record.

Apart from anything else, I felt that any time I could spare from a very large and demanding practice should be devoted to being with my wife and four children. Having missed the first five years of my eldest son's childhood, I was determined to weld us into as closely knit a family as possible.

But now that they are all married with children of their own, I decided, if only for the sake of the family archives, to put this story down on paper.

It does not pretend to be a rigidly accurate historical, political or military record. Forty years is a long time to keep things in one's head and, although some facts are as clear as on the day they happened, the sequence of others may be wrong by weeks or even months.

Most of the important facts were recorded briefly in my Medical Day Book, but I never kept a regular diary as such. Some of my friends (although a great many, alas, are no more) have helped with certain details, and I am very beholden to *The Diary of Occupation*, published by the Jersey *Evening Post*, for some facts and dates upon which I was a little shaky.

A great many items may strike the reader as irrelevant or trivial, but to us, at the time, they certainly were not. Those who went through that experience will remember how the acquisition of a box of matches, or two ounces of rice, was a matter of great importance.

A Doctor's Occupation is the chronicle of a man, left on his own, at the most important time of his life, who survived the Occupation with his health and sanity relatively intact—and of how he did it.

CHAPTER 1

When a man is faced, without very much notice, with the decision of whether to stay with his young wife and unborn child, or to leave them and take care of his patients, he is bound to have serious doubts as to the rightness and wisdom of whichever course he chooses to take.

As the result of my own decision, I had five years of personal loneliness, as well as considerable deprivation, during which there was ample time to ponder over the question. To this day, I am not sure that what I did was the right thing.

I first arrived in Jersey in May 1935, fresh from the job of Medical Superintendent at Westminster Hospital, London. During the three years up to when this book starts, I had learned to love the Island as deeply as any true born Jerseyman, and had settled down contentedly to a thriving practice, in partnership with Dr J. J. Evans. To complete my happiness I was engaged to Miss Ann Hulton, and we were due to be married on 8 October 1938. Jersey was beautiful, unspoiled and cheap, and life could not have been more wonderful.

I suppose we had our heads in the clouds too completely to take the political situation as seriously as we should have done, and when the black miasma of Hitler's war began to threaten we were overwhelmed, not so much by surprise as by a sense of the unfairness of it all.

The German threat to Czechoslovakia loomed, and we realised with sudden desperation that a declaration of war would probably coincide more or less with our wedding date. I took the precaution of ordering a Special Licence, in case our planned large wedding had to be cancelled.

As it transpired, none of this was necessary. Mr Neville Chamberlain went to Munich for a personal confrontation with Hitler, and came back with his delusory message of "Peace in our time". "Our time" proved to be all too short, but was at least immensely valuable in enabling our country to make hasty preparations for a war which was now plainly inevitable.

It also allowed Ann and me to get married in proper traditional style, and we set off for a month's honeymoon without a single worry on our minds. En route for Scotland, where, against all odds, we had only half a day's rain in one month, we stayed for four days at the Savoy Hotel in London, and it is interesting to record that we occupied the Bridal Suite at a cost of £5 per night. Similarly, the charge for supremely comfortable quarters at our hotel in Crieff, near Comrie, with superb food, was £1 per day, all found, for the two of us.

On our return to Jersey, as a married couple, we rapidly and easily settled into a routine of entertaining and being entertained, while I got down to the business of building up my practice still further. We were none of us, however, under any illusion that Munich was anything else than a very temporary pause in Hitler's maniacal bid for supreme power over Europe, and we lived our lives with this threat perpetually at the back of our minds.

On 1 September 1939, the Germans invaded Poland, and in accordance with our guarantee to that country, war was declared two days later.

For a few days our lives were completely disorganised. People began making arrangements for joining up, talked about black-outs, and had meetings to discuss Island defence, but when nothing at all seemed to happen, we settled down to what became known as the "Phoney War".

Island life returned to much as it was before, although some young men were called up, and certain commodities became harder to get.

The papers were full of awful things happening in Poland, Norway and Finland, but to us in our comfortable little paradise and to a lesser extent to those in England, the War seemed relatively remote and unlikely to affect us.

Later in the year came the sinking of the *Royal Oak* in Scapa Flow, followed soon after by the torpedoing of the *Rawalpindi* but, though appalled, we none of us felt the urgency of being at war.

Occasional snippets of good news, like the sinking of the *Graf Spee* and the capture of the *Altmark* with the release of all her prisoners, gave us the feeling that the enemy was not having everything his own way, but this was depressingly offset by the catastrophic figures of losses to the merchant navy of Britain and her allies.

Terrible things were happening in Norway where a frightening amount of Allied shipping was lost. Nevertheless, so much German shipping was also sunk that the Reich received damage from which it never really recovered.

On 10 May, Mr Winston Churchill became Prime Minister and within a few days the storm broke around our ears. Each day brought news of fresh reverses: Holland flooded large areas of her territory to no avail; Belgium overrun and surrendering; finally France, her Maginot line proving completely ineffectual, also capitulated.

The British Army, its entire European support melting away almost overnight, was forced to fall back on the channel ports—chiefly Dunkirk. Leaving all their equipment behind, the men were rescued by a fleet of small boats in a typically English display of heroism and panache. Even Jersey sent over all the shipping that could possibly be of any use in the evacuation, and brought back not one but several complements of British troops to the Island, for transhipping to the United Kingdom. Jerseymen performed countless acts of gallantry and expert seamanship which will never be acknowledged or commemorated.

As a nation, we suddenly found ourselves fighting for our very existence.

There was now no army or any other defence between Jersey and the rapidly advancing German forces, and the Island suddenly realised its own peril. Some said that Britain would never abandon us to our fate, and these were to some degree responsible for the dithering that followed; those who knew the real position acknowledged that we could never defend ourselves successfully and that our destiny was in our own hands, for better or worse.

Quite soon a few families began unobtrusively to leave the Island—they were almost all settlers of varying periods of domicile. Even earlier the wise virgins—not many it is true and not too obviously—had bought cottages in Wales or Scotland and got them ready for habitation. Some of the richer ones flew off quite blatantly to South Africa, America or the Bahamas, but those were only the advance guard and it was not till about the middle of June that people began really to take flight. Long queues started to form outside the shipping office and these were augmented by French and British civilians brought over from St Malo by private shipping in response to a request to the Island Authorities. All Italians (chiefly waiters) and any remaining Germans were interned in a camp at Grouville. Their stay there was not destined to be a long one.

On 19 June the British Government officially announced that the Island was to be designated a demilitarised zone. And there was to be a voluntary evacuation of a) women and children, b) men of military age, and c) any persons for whom there was room when a) and b) had been accommodated.

The suddenness of this announcement was a signal for the panic that followed. For several days the town resembled a stirred-up ant-hill with people running every which way—when they were not standing about in groups, talking, talking, talking.

My wife and I discussed the situation in all its aspects, and, although she was expecting our first baby in just over a fortnight, we decided to throw in our lot with the Islanders who had decided to remain.

Almost a year before I had applied for a commission in the RAF but beyond an acknowledgment at the time they had shown a marked reluctance to avail themselves of my services. I can only assume that, when things came suddenly to a head at the invasion of Poland, my papers were lost or mislaid; I never heard a word from them.

In this period, relations in my medical practice between the senior partner and myself had deteriorated and, although our timing could not have been more inopportune, we decided to dissolve the practice as from 30 June 1940. In this my wife Ann was stoutly behind me.

My entire capital had gone into my half-share of the practice, and if I left it unattended the chances of finding any of it left after an absence probably of several years was extemely remote.

My partner had announced that come what may he would remain in Jersey and no doubt he was already gloating over the probability of my imminent departure. He grudgingly agreed to take on the care of about a dozen maternity cases that I had specifically promised to attend, but refused point blank to come to any kind of arrangement for the duration of the War except accompanied by conditions which would completely cripple me financially for the forseeable future.

This hardened me in my resolve to stay and at once I took steps to lease a much smaller house at 105 Bath Street as from 30 June. We had previously occupied 100 Bath Street, a lovely Georgian house of nineteen large rooms with a big garden, but difficult to heat and keep clean, and ideal for having troops billeted on us.

105 Bath Street had twelve smaller rooms, was in excellent condition, could be easily heated and was perfect for our requirements. Owing to a suicide which had occurred there two years before, the owners had not been able to let it and when I sought a woman to dust, scrub and polish—which was all that was needed—there was an inexplicable dearth of applicants. However by offering wages somewhat above the odds and engaging two women together, the job was carried out, although the women stipulated that they should not be expected to work after dusk.

By this time the scheme for mass evacuation was well under way and whole families were leaving the Island on every boat. In four days five thousand cats and dogs were destroyed at the animals shelter, thus adding to the general misery and desolation—especially of the children.

The Island potato season also was in full swing, and merchant vessels were leaving daily with their cargoes. A small number of people were able to get aboard these, but their conditions of passage must have been fairly stark.

German aircraft began to fly over the Island in increasing numbers and at dawn especially they flew so low over the rooftops that they invariably woke us up.

At this time, due, I suppose, to a feeling that we wanted to be with our families, we took the habit of dining every night with Ann's parents at Beaumont. On the second such night an incident occurred which was funny, or tragic, depending on how one looked at it.

My father-in-law, Colonel Hulton, was Government Secretary for Jersey. In addition to many other duties he was *ex officio* the supervisor of the passport office which was run by Mr J. W. White. As far as I can remember Mr White had already evacuated, with his wife, and for security reasons the Colonel brought home each evening, in a suitcase, all the unallocated passport books as well as the official stamp.

Dinner was over; my wife and her mother had gone into the drawing room and the Colonel and I were enjoying a glass of port while discussing the situation, when suddenly there was a violent and repeated ringing of the front door-bell.

The bell was of the old fashioned kind, of brass or bronze on springs and rung in the inner hall by a wire bell-pull at the door. On this occasion the bell-pull was almost jerked from its socket and the tocsin-like jangling of the bell conveyed an indefinable feeling of urgency or near panic.

We heard the palourmaid open the door and the sound of voices raised in argument. Ella was obviously remonstrating with the caller and explaining that the Colonel was at dinner. Equally obviously this was all to no avail, for suddenly there were rapid footsteps in the inner hall followed by the patter-patter of Ella's heels and her shrill expostulating voice. The dining-room door burst open and the intruder entered with a rush as if catapulted.

We both recognised him at once as Mr Mervyn Cutler, a rich and prominent Island businessman, known to his friends as Merv, and to others as Vermyn. He had all the appearance of being either drunk or in a blue funk, and subsequent events inclined to the latter.

Without a word of apology he burst out: "Colonel Hulton, I must have a passport tonight!"

Those who knew Colonel Hulton will be aware that he was not the sort of man to view such behaviour lightly, especially as the gentleman was not one of his favourite people. I was aware of this and also knew that for various reasons a great many other Islanders disliked him.

With scrupulous politeness, but with a look of extreme distaste on his face, the Colonel said slowly and quite distinctly, "Mr Cutler, the passport office has been open the whole of today, and will be open the whole of tomorrow. I fail to see the necessity of this quite unpardonable intrusion into my privacy."

Almost with tears in his voice Mr Cutler begged his pardon and besought the Colonel to oblige him just this once. "I cannot tell you the reason," he said, "for it is entirely personal but I am booked on the first plane tomorrow before the passport office opens. I can't fly without my passport."

Before Colonel Hulton could reply to this impassioned plea, we heard a car swish into the short drive, and come to a halt with a violence which made me think of the gardener's comments when he had to rake the gravel in the morning. Mr Cutler palpably changed colour and beads of sweat appeared on his forehead.

Once again the bell sustained a violent attack, and Ella rushed to the door—but too late. The visitor was already in the inner hall and the next minute in the dining-room.

At this juncture I must fill in a few of the details of Mr Cutler's rather messy private life. Some years before he had left his very nice, extremely pretty wife and young family to go and live with a barmaid named Ruby. Whether he married her or not has never been established, but by the time I made their acquaintance in my capacity as *locum tenens* to their regular practioner, their relationship was considerbly less than cosy. Ruby was apt to throw things and unlike most women who are goaded into this expensive habit, she was endowed with a startling accuracy.

On one of my frequent professional visits to their home (for Mervyn was an abject hypochondriac) I arrived in the middle of a domestic fracas. Mervyn was already sporting a black eye which was spreading and becoming quite decorative in hues of blue and purple, and gave promise of being what is called by connoisseurs of such items "a four-penny one". But this was not why I had been summoned—although before the visit was over I felt bound in all human decency to prescribe for it.

Ruby herself was unscathed and retired breathing fire and smoke to the other end of the long room where I was discussing Mervyn's symptoms with him. From time to time she shouted a fishwife epithet at him, as successive waves of inspiration came to her, but it never occurred to me that active hostilities would commence till after I left. *Au contraire*!

We were standing talking on the hearth rug facing each other, when out of the corner of my eye I saw something coming through the air towards us. I ducked, as did Mervyn with a speed which suggested long practice, and the next moment a very nice, very heavy crystal vase smashed into a thousand pieces on the edge of the stone mantle, exactly between where we had just been standing.

Having now got whatever it was out of her system, the lady, giving a series of hoots like a train going into a tunnel, dashed upstairs, locked herself noisily into the bathroom, and proceeded to have a very impressive attack of hysterics. I left her to get on with it alone and concluded my conversation in the study. As usual Mervyn's illness was as the French say "a thing of nothing" but I made a mental note to charge a double fee, in lieu of danger money.

Now back to the Colonel's dining room.

The lady for whom Mervyn had left his wife was about 35, scrawny rather than slim, hennaed and brazen. Her husky voice, which I have heard described as 'sexy' reminded me more of a cinder under a door. Nevertheless, looked at quite dispassionately one could see where her attraction lay. She was what my fifteen-year-old son described to my horrified astonishment, as "alright for the rough work". He was probably right, but compared to Ruby, Diamond Lil of the old goldrush days was a shrinking violet.

This then was the lady who, with red hair on end and flushed with temper, swept into the room. I glanced at Colonel Hulton, who, grinning like a pleased shark, was enjoying the encounter to the full.

But she took no notice of either of us. Her eyes were all for her Mervyn, and sticking her face into his, she hissed through her teeth," I thought I'd find you here, you lousy swine. I knew your passport was out of date and I thought I was safe, but someone told me he'd seen you leaving a suitcase at the airport and I came here on spec. I also know that you've transferred all your assets to Canada. You were going to leave me here, penniless, while you skipped off!"

Turning to Colonel Hulton, she said, "If you have stamped Mervyn's passport, I must ask you to give me one too. He's not going off without me."

Colonel Hulton looked at Mervyn. "Is it your wish that I should give this lady a passport? She is perfectly entitled to one, you know, but it would be nicer with your permission. And of course you are liable for both fees."

Mervyn muttered something about the whole thing being quite preposterous, adding that he himself had taken the last ticket on that particular plane but that she could come on by a later one if she liked.

She gave a mocking, mirthless laugh and said "Do you think I was born yesterday, Mervyn Cutler? Make up your mind here and now that I am not letting you out of my sight until we are sitting side by side on that plane for Canada—and not even then, perhaps. And just in case you have other ideas, take a look at this."

With that she produced from her handbag, a small but very businesslike pearl-handled revolver.

"I have been practising with this ever since I bought it," she said, "and I never thought it would come in so handy. Even if you manage to give me the slip, I'll track you down and let you have it where it matters. I'm not likely to miss you either. Now will you ask Colonel Hulton for my passport?"

Mervyn nodded dumbly with a face the colour of candlewax.

Colonel Hulton, still smiling quietly, took out his pen and filled in the passport. I was intrigued to see that her second name was Minerva and thought how little flattered the goddess of that name would have been. The two passports were stamped and signed—Ruby thereafter putting both in her handbag.

Mervyn shambled through the door, too broken even to say goodnight, but Ruby said her farewells with a little smirk of triumph and twiddled her fingers as she went through the door.

Colonel Hulton sank into his chair and said, "Whew! I'd cut her throat before I'd take her to Canada, and if I couldn't manage it, I'd cut my own!"

CHAPTER 2

With each day the certainty that our turn was coming next grew stronger. Gunfire and explosions could be heard plainly from the French coast, and at night flashes and flames could be seen. Such a feeling of tension and dread expectancy grew up that many families who had decided to stay (and had therefore done nothing about disposal of their houses or goods) took fright and left the Island for the mainland, without any idea of where they would be able to find refuge once there. Some of these panic departures were so sudden and ill planned that families were split up and found themselves half in the West Country and half in Yorkshire. One woman even left a hot iron on the ironing board and rushed for the boat. The fire brigade had to be called.

One beautiful day, Ann and I took a picnic lunch up to Col de la Rocque, on the north-west coast, and lay in the grass on the cliff-top in the sun. We could hear the sound of guns, seemingly from several directions, and occasionally we spotted a German plane high above. But it was so peaceful and beautiful it seemed impossible that such a way of life could come to an abrupt stop at any moment.

We called in at Waldegrave in time for an aperitif before dinner, to be met by Colonel Hulton looking very serious, with a paper in his hand. I read it through quickly, and as I finished he said: "This puts an entirely different complexion on your situation."

The paper described a German scheme, which had already been started in Poland, for removing young boy babies and having them fostered as Germans in the Reich, presumably as replacements for their own men killed in the war.

I saw at once what was on his mind and said: "Do you think I should take Ann over?" He replied: "Yes, in view of this possibility I think you should–if you're not too late to get a seat on a plane. There may be no truth in the whole affair, but the Germans are so logical in everything they do, that I shouldn't like to take a chance on it. Even with the war hardly begun, they've already committed such unbelievable atrocities that when they see the tide running with them, which I am confident it will from the start, they'll stop at nothing which will bring any conceivable advantage to the Reich."

Then and there we decided to go. Both of us were haunted by the thought of our baby being taken off to Germany, and the virtual impossibility of finding him at the end of the war. And there was the probability—even if we did find him—that he would not take to us or we to him, after so long a time.

We did not stay for dinner, but went straight home and started to pack a few essentials.

We still had no idea when we should be able to get a passage and, next morning, as Ann had everything pretty much under control, I went round as many of my patients as possible, to tell them what was happening and to ask them to appraise as many others as they could. I telephoned all the obstetric cases to let them know what arrangements I had made for them, and then sat down to wait for lunch. At the same moment my secretary came in to say that there was an urgent case at Victoria Village. I went off at once.

I was just leaving that patient's house when the telephone rang—my secretary to say that we had two seats booked on a plane for Exeter at 2.15 pm. It was already after 1 pm, and I had to get back to town, collect Ann and the luggage, say goodbye to her parents and be at the airport in slightly more than one hour. At Baxter's mill I had a back tyre puncture, but I just drove on regardless. Our two maids had already left, in floods of tears, in the earlier evacuation, but our cook, faithful Mrs Ozouf, whose family all lived in Jersey and had no intention of leaving, promised to live in the new house and keep it going till our return. As we could not get possession till 30 June, she would see to the move also. Ann had a taxi waiting, and we were at the airport with about five minutes to spare.

A number of our friends were going by the same plane, and of one pair, the husband had a Picasso under his arm, the wife a sable coat—no other luggage, not even a tooth brush. I thought this was rather an off-centre piece of one-upmanship and said so, jokingly, but they replied that the telephone message had reached them only half an hour before, and they had grabbed the two most valuable things in the house and ran.

We landed safely at Exeter. Where there occurred as bad an example of hidebound bureaucracy as has been my lot to endure. To the utter fury and disbelief of everyone, including myself, the customs put us through a minute search for paltry packets of cigarettes, while anxious mothers with tired fractious children stood about, listlessly watching the precious moments, during which they could have been seeking accommodation, fly by. Nightfall was not far off, and many of them had nowhere to lay their heads.

All telephone booths had long queues and Ann—though all too visibly pregnant—could find nowhere to sit. I took my place in the shortest queue I could see, and stood there in simmering impatience, wondering if the Cardiff train would come in before I got to the telephone. But I got there just in time, and arranged to be met in Cardiff. In the slow train to Bristol, crammed to the doors, Ann started to have irregular labour pains, and after we changed to the equally full, equally slow Cardiff train, they became so regular and so strong that I began to pray that at least we would reach a hospital in Cardiff before the worst happened. If it had happened in the train, I shudder to think what we would have done. All the carriages were at bursting point, and there was scarcely room for a single extra person in the corridors.

But nothing did happen, and as we approached Cardiff I fought my way to a window; leaning out, I saw the dependable, reassuring figure of a good friend waiting on the platform.

No formalities here. A word of explanation, and in a few minutes we were away and speeding along the winding roads of Wales, leaving behind all the drama and nastiness.

On the stroke of midnight we crossed the threshold of my home, to a warm, heartfelt welcome. My mother took in the situation at a glance and forbade any questions. With a hot drink and a warm bed, and under a mild sedative, Ann was almost instantly asleep, but still whimpering with her pains.

I joined her almost at once, and we both slept soundly till late next morning, when the pains had subsided, and with them most of my anxiety.

We decided on the morrow to drive to Cardiff, to call at RAF Headquarters, to see what was what, and afterwards to consult the best obstetrician in Wales.

I had been uneasily aware for some time that the baby was lying awkwardly, and for its safe delivery would need the best skill available, in a modern, well-equipped nursing home, rather than an isolated farm in the wilds of Wales.

The specialist proved charming and competent, and the nursing home comfortable and almost aggressively up to date; but the RAF office was offhand and evasive. They said they would contact me in due course—no date—no promise—no nothing.

But on the June 26 the situation changed dramatically.

A long telephone call from some very good friends (and patients) still in Jersey, informed me that my ex-partner, without a word of warning to anyone, and without making any arrangements for our patients, had unaccountably panicked and left the Island.

In fact, had not some neighbours who had heard shots from his house gone to investigate, no one would have known he had left. His neighbours found in the grounds the bodies of their two magnificent bull mastiffs, and that of one of their gorgeous macaws. The other had escaped and was subsequently captured. Now was the time of the big decision. No one seemed to know exactly how many doctors now remained on the Island, or which ones, and there were still more than 40,000 inhabitants who had decided to stay.

Even without my notebook, I knew of at least eleven expectant mothers whose confinements I had promised to attend within the next month, and I felt honour bound to return at once, if only to arrange for some one else to take them over.

Ann was overdue, it's true, but as fit as a fiddle and insistent that I should go. As we said goodbye on Cardiff station, we both felt quite sure that I would be back within a week, and in good time for the baby. Neither of us could know that we would be separated for five years, and that my baby son would not see what should have been the Island of his birth until the morning of his fifth birthday.

CHAPTER 3

During the night crossing, which was easy, I got into conversation with an elderly man in the bar. He was a solicitor, coming over in connection with a will, and was returning the following day. Of course he never did, and was stranded without home, family, money, clothes or friends, on an Island that was new to him, for five, long, frustrating years. I met him several times subsequently, and admired enormously his courage and philosophical outlook.

When I landed on the quay, the place looked much as usual, with lorries and waggons loaded with potatoes strung out along the quay and stretching onto the Esplanade.

I made for my house immediately and was greeted with utter astonishment and some relief, by Mrs Ozouf. She told me that the afternoon surgeries were almost empty, but a long list of house calls had not been answered for several days. I decided to spend the day visiting the imminent confinements, and as many of the other callers as lived in the vicinity. All were delighted to see me, many of them with tears of relief, and I worked steadily all day without breaking off for lunch. I had already telephoned my in-laws to announce my arrival and to invite myself to dinner that night.

In the early evening I came to the end of my round at St Brelades and, homeward bound, was coming down Mount les Vaux, under a dark sky that presaged a heavy thunderstorm, when just below St Aubin's school I was aware of a rat-tat-tat which at first I took to be heavy drops of rain on adjacent roofs. German planes had been passing over all day, often very low, so that for the moment I did not connect the two sounds, until I saw flakes of slate flying off the roofs of nearby houses. It was obviously not a concerted attack—more like a pilot trying out his machine gun, for the bullets were not many, but a practice bullet can kill just as well as one fired in anger, I made my way in some haste to Waldegrave.

Before I got there I heard a series of explosions and concentrated machine gun fire from the direction of the town, and saw smoke rising somewhere near the harbour.

I found Colonel Hulton on the upstairs balcony, looking through binoculars, but by this time there was so much smoke and dust that there was very little to see.

More reports followed, now further away, and he suggested we should drive there and have a look-see.

Potato lorries waiting to unload around the weighbridge had received their share of attention, their owners having to take refuge beneath them, but in all eleven people were killed and nine injured. There was a good deal of blood about and people looked white and shaken. Colonel Hulton, used to such situations, said: "Get them to talk to you, it's the best treatment for this kind of shock." This we did, and after several had recounted their experiences, we left them considerably perked up, and drove out to la Rocque, where there had been another explosion, and a concentrated machine gunning of the whole length of the coast road.

We heard subsequently that Guernsey had had much the same type of attack, but had fared worse. They had 22 killed and 36 injured, among them people embarking on the mailboat which had brought me to Jersey that morning, and was on the return trip to England.

That night I tried to ring my home in Wales for about the fifteenth time. All lines were jammed, understandably, as we had been warned that telephone links with the mainland might be cut at any time. Frantic with worry and quite unable to sleep, I sat down by the telephone at 11pm and put through a call every fifteen minutes. At 2am I finally got through, to receive news which increased my anxiety tenfold.

No baby as yet, and the specialist had asked Ann to go into the nursing home for an induction the following evening.

But on the night of the message Cardiff had a massive air raid, and the home received a direct hit. Everyone in it was killed including the specialist's wife and four children. The specialist was on a night call and survived.

So in spite of all my carefully laid plans we were back to square one. After all, Ann had to face her confinement in the wilds of Wales, with only an inexperienced doctor in charge.

This was worse than anything I had feared and, had I anticipated any such thing, nothing would have induced me to leave Ann as I did. This was almost certainly the last telephone call I should be able to make, and I faced the prospect of months or years living in state of suspense.

While I was still on the line, I had to concoct a plan, off the cuff, and as my mind was in such turmoil I found it difficult to think straight.

At that time there was a regular request programme on the BBC between 5.30 and 6pm, and I asked my sister to request a broadcast, as soon as the baby was born, of "Sweetheart"—a tune to which Ann and I often danced when we were engaged. She promised faithfully to see that this was done, and no matter where on the Island I happened to be, I was always back home with the earphones on in time for this programme. But there was no broadcast of 'Sweetheart' and with hope fading daily I was almost physically sick each evening. Had something happened to Ann? Had something happened to the baby? Or were they afraid to tell me?

I kept at it for a month and than gave up. No baby could be that long overdue. Beside this worry, all the tribulations of the occupation faded into insignificance; and although I tried not to panic my in-laws, it remained a gnawing anxiety in the forefront of my mind. It was ten months later that I received the first Red Cross message, that all was well with them both. I subsequently learned that the BBC flatly refused my request, on the pretext that it might contain some secret code. How careful can you get?!!

I heard eventually that, by some miraculous luck, Ann had

got hold of a first-class, highly experienced nurse (her name would be Miss Lewis, of course) and went into labour on 13 July, knowing that the baby was still lying awkwardly, but would turn of its own accord if she could find the strength to hang on. She had been married to me long enough to understand that in such cases any premature interference, particularly with forceps, might easily endanger mother or baby or both. So whenever the doctor appeared with his ominous black bag, she waved him away, and finally told him she would send as soon as she judged herself to be ready.

Nurse Lewis stayed with Ann comforting and encouraging her for 72 hours, when in the small hours of 16 July the child turned of himself and shortly afterwards, with no anaesthetic or obstetrics, a fine boy of nine pounds made his own way into the world.

The whole of the rural neighbourhood erupted with joy, as all our friends and neighbours had been on tenterhooks for the past fortnight.

What my feelings were can be imagined. My greatest anxiety was now over, and no matter what else was in store for me my heart was like a singing bird.

But all this was yet to happen. Now I was back to my disturbing telephone call by a cable which was cut four hours later, preventing all further direct speech with the mainland for the next five years.

My only recourse now was to throw myself totally into the practice, and wipe out all the arrears of work which had built up. I remember very little about the next four days except that the following night, instead of occupying my comfortable bed at Waldegrave, I was sitting up with the first of my eleven confinements. It proved to be every bit as difficult and disagreeable as I had anticipated, but we had a beautiful boy. He grew up into a fine young man but after all the trauma of that night, was tragically drowned while swimming eighteen years later.

Early on the morning of 1 July, messages were dropped calling for the surrender of the Island, and cessation of any type of resistance. White flags had to be flown from all buildings—even private houses—and white crosses painted in prominent positions. I flew an old pair of white underpants on a broomstick, from the window of 105 Bath Street, but nobody seemed to take much notice of my feeble protest.

Late that afternoon, while driving towards First Tower, I was astonished—I don't know exactly why, because we were all expecting it—to see a young German soldier riding fairly slowly towards the town, on a small collapsible motor bike. He was followed, about fifty yards behind, by two more similarly mounted—all very young, grim faced, but at the same time incongruously self-conscious. I stopped the car to have a good look, and a passerby told me that they had landed by parachute on the airport. They brought their machines with them, and assembled them on the ground.

This was the first occasion on which I noticed how quickly news seemed to flash around the Island. Several times subsequently, when telephones had become a rarity, I noticed the same thing, and in most cases the information which was passed proved to be quite correct.

What the mission of the parachutists was, and where they were going, I never discovered, but they were followed soon after by several bodies of infantry, who had landed in troop carriers and who marched to St Helier in absolute silence. This was quite unlike their subsequent behaviour when they sang hearty patriotic songs in praise of the Reich.

The following day soldiers were seen exploring the town in twos and threes and, though it was "verboten", even making small purchases in the shops. Some strolled around the residential areas, peeping rather diffidently through windows or open doors. Most of them were young and shy, probably country boys, and one of these had the fright of his life when a girl of seventeen or eighteen met him suddenly in a side street and collapsed on the pavement in a fit of whooping hysterics.

Living fairly nearby, I was summoned by a purple-faced teenager, who had obviously run the whole way at top speed, I arrived hot-foot at the scene of disaster, and at once recognised the girl as a member of one of my more 'nervy' families.

The poor victim, looking better than most of the spectators, had a strong, regular pulse and a fine, ruddy colour;

with eyes tightly shut she was giving off hoots reminiscent of a caliope on a roundabout, at the rate of about twenty a minute. She was surrounded by a sizeable knot of sympathisers, mostly neighbours, and largely middle-aged ladies, but all experienced and practising members of the spectator industry.

As I knelt tenderly beside her, she opened one eye just wide enough to see what sort of effect her performance was having on the doctor, then shut it again tightly.

She nearly forgot, at this point, to give off another hoot, but recovered herself in time, and delivered such a volcanic one as to cause among the onlookers what the papers sometimes describe as "a sensation in court".

Had this happened in the bad, rough-and-ready old days, I would have borrowed a pin and sunk it to the head in her backside but, failing this dramatically effective cure, and in the present era of kid-glove medicine, I was reduced to prescribing the most nauseating draught I could think up.

The original messenger—a glutton for punishment that boy—was despatched *ventre-à-terre* to the chemist, and the girl's mother was told that, after its administration, the girl would soon sit up (probably to be sick) and could be taken home.

A babe in arms could have diagnosed it as a case of exhibitional hysteria but as I left one of the crowd, a noted busybody, well known to me as an enthusiastic participant in any kind of drama—the more macabre the better—took me confidentially aside and whispered that it was absolutely shocking that those swine should have so frightened poor Ethel—"What with her nerves and all." A nicer girl you could never wish to meet, and so large-hearted—why she would give you her last penn-y.

I am afraid I was rather perfunctory, but consoled her by saying that Ethel would soon be quite alright, and would no doubt get used to the sight of German soldiers in time. Subsequent events proved me to be all too right, for some months later Ethel was brought to my surgery by her mother. Large-hearted as ever, she had given to some German soldier, not her last penny, but something less easily replaceable.

She had the first German baby born in the Island.

As regards their attitude to the Islanders generally, and the womenfolk in particular, the Germans behaved immaculately. Most of the so-called fair sex seemed to have read, with delicious terror, what went on during the sacking of towns in Medieval times, and I got the impression that they were divided into two camps: those who were terrified that they might be raped, and those who were afraid that they might miss any fun that was going. In the event, the principles of the first category remained unsullied, and the second category underwent, if not something as exciting as rape, at least what, in military circles, is known as peaceful penetration.

Two elderly ladies, leaders of what was then termed the social set, marked the occasion by taking to large hats and heavy, dark veils. Presumably this was to conceal their fatal charms from the brutal and licentious soldiery. They needn't have bothered for one, still a spinster, was reputed to have been a beauty—about sixty years before—and the other had never been at any time. I never heard of anyone being tempted to lift the veils, or for that matter, anything else.

That same evening I decided it was time to take possession of my new house and, having dined with my in-laws, let myself into 105 Bath Street about 10.30pm. Mrs Ozouf was already asleep and I went straight up to my bedroom.

The house was on three floors with surgery premises, kitchen and scullery on the ground floor, dining room, drawing room and bathroom (with connecting spare room beyond) on the first floor, and four bedrooms on the second floor.

The two back bedrooms, one opening into the other, Ann and I had decided should be our quarters. This we did because the further room, though well fitted up as a dressing room, was where the suicide had taken place and we doubted whether any living-in staff would be prepared to occupy it. Neither room was large, but they were quite big enough for us, and being away from the main road—overlooking the back garden—were quiet and airy.

What with all the emotional turmoil of the last few days I felt anything but sleepy and, getting into bed under a good light, tried to bury myself in an interesting book. Without much success, however.

When three o'clock came, sleep was as far away as ever and in desperation I put out the light, hoping to drop off eventually.

No sooner was the room in darkness than a terrific row started in the dressing room. Not a scratching or a shuffling, but a full-blooded hullabaloo, as if two people were throwing trunks at each other. No human sounds or voices either, but a continuous bang, thump, crash.

I lay still for some minutes hardly able to believe my ears, and thinking that there could scarcely be anything left unbroken in the dressing room. Then, deciding to investigate, I turned on the light.

Instantly, all was quiet.

I entered the dressing room, switched on the light but to my astonishment nothing had moved. All was precisely as I had left it.

Let me at once make it quite clear that I am not, and never have been a "psychic" person. I have never believed in ghosts and have always pooh-poohed ghost stories.

In spite of being a doubting Thomas, I think that at any other time I would have been thoroughly scared but, situated as I was, I really did not care a hoot what happened to me. I was depressed and miserable and, while I was not prepared to accept it as some sort of psychic phenomenon, I was anxious to investigate the cause of it in a purely objective way.

Leaving all the lights on, I returned to bed and began evaluating the circumstances just as one would with a difficult medical problem. First of all I had to satisfy myself (a) that I had not been dreaming, (b) that I had not been suffering from hallucinations after the sleeplessness and mental stress of the last few days, and (c) that there was nothing strange happening, either in the spare room below or in the attic space above.

But before doing anything else I again put out the lights, first in the bedroom then in the dressing room while remaining in the latter. Not a sound. But the moment I quitted the dressing room, the hullabaloo started. Anyhow, I had not been dreaming.

Having a torch with me I switched it on and re-entered the dressing room. The noise stopped. Then I went downstairs to the spare room, directly below the dressing room. This was where we had stored all our surplus furniture, and there was no space to swing a cat or even a mouse. Nothing had shifted there.

Above the dressing room was the roof space, accessible only by a narrow trapdoor. Standing on a bedroom chair atop a trunk, I pushed up the cover and shone my torch inside. Nothing there except a quantity of blue china chemists jars, left by a previous tenant, and quantities of black dust with no footprints or other signs of disturbance.

I hopped into bed once more and started reciting Hilare Belloc's poem which starts, "Do you remember an inn, Miranda, do you remember an inn?" and got halfway through without a mistake. So I wasn't hallucinating. Then I switched out the light and again the noise started.

By this time I had established that the only time the noise occurred was when I was not in the room. It did not matter whether the light was on or off, but by now I was getting a bit bored with the whole performance and, strangely, a little sleepy. Consoling myself with the thought that the suicide, whom I had known though not well, was a quiet peaceable sort of man, I wondered why his ghost should want to frighten me. I put out all the lights, pulled the bedclothes over my head and to the continuing accompaniment of the hullabaloo dropped off to sleep.

When I awoke next morning, all was still, and in the bright sunlight the events of the night before seemed completely unreal.

After breakfast I went off on my round as usual, when I had plenty of time to do a bit of thinking.

I decided that, for obvious reasons, it would not be wise to mention the matter to Mrs Ozouf. In fact, I never told her, and she remained in the house as caretaker for twenty years after I left it.

The next evening, having had a maximum of three hours sleep the previous night, I returned early and read for half an hour. But the moment I put out the light, I experienced a carbon copy of the night before. By putting my head under the bedclothes I was asleep in minutes, and was oblivious to any noise there might have been till I awoke to another bright, and silent, day.

The third night was a replica of the previous two, and I began to think that this was something I would have to live with, but on the fourth night nothing whatever happened. I never heard a thing from the dressing room during the five years I lived in that house.

CHAPTER 4

Everyday we saw fresh batches of Germans, wandering through the town and looking with amazement at the selection of articles displayed in shop windows. Whatever the military strength of the Reich, it was evident that its people were kept very short of consumer goods. Very soon, although it was *verboten*, they began buying in increasing quantities, and a little later on I realised that anything one needed for the bleak days ahead must be snapped up quickly.

With prices already beginning to rise daily, it became plain that, if I bought everything I could conceiveably need, my credit at the bank simply would not stand it. Almost all my money was in England with Ann, and a visit to my bank manager was urgently necessary. Understandably, the poor man was as vague about the future as I was myself, but with my in-laws standing surety, I was able to get a substantial overdraft.

Being a cigar smoker, I bought a fair stock of what was left (which was not very much, for there had been a heavy run on them by the Bosches). I already had several hundred Burma cheroots, which I customarily bought direct from Rangoon at ten pounds per thousand delivered—and very good they were. In fact a new supply, ordered and paid for, was overdue, but I never got them.

Though I had never smoked them before, I also bought

a brace of pipes and a quantity of cigarettes, for the use of my friends. Had I realised at the time what a valuable form of currency cigarettes were to become, I would have bought all I could lay hands on.

I almost forgot about tobacco, but remembered in the nick of time; my friendly tobacconist let me have two pounds out of a rapidly depleting stock.

Next I paid a visit to my wine merchant, who at first said that he was already completely cleaned out, but subsequently weakened, under pressure, and admitted that there might be a few odd bottles in the cellars.

So we went down, and they were indeed a sorry sight, although the Germans had not yet been there. Many bins were completely empty, but one contained two bottles, another five, another seventeen half-bottles and so on. Most were first quality wines: Haut Brion, Chateau Latour, Chateau Lafitte, Chambertin, etc, but we turfed them out into empty cartons, all mixed together, and found that there were more than 250 bottles of various kinds.

There were also four unopened cases of Pommery and Greno pink champagne to add to the bag. I felt I had to have them as I was certain there would come a day when we should have something to celebrate. This hope was vindicated eventually. We opened the first case at the Liberation, and finished it when my wife and son arrived in the Island. The other three we drank at the christenings of my daughter and two more sons, born during the first three years after we came together once more.

The wines were marked thirteen shillings and nine pence, eighteen shillings, etc. Had I paid their face value most of my overdraft, or rather what was left of it, would have evaporated, but when I pointed out to my wine merchant that the Germans would shortly take them anyway, and pay him in Occupation paper money, if they paid at all, he charged me a flat five shillings per bottle. Just as I was leaving I spied a cask in a corner and asked what it contained. He told me it was a Greek wine (Chian, I think), which he had tasted and liked while on holiday in Greece some years before. In an expansive, possibly alcoholic, moment he had ordered several casks, but being very sweet they proved to be not to the local taste, and were left on his hands. The upshot was that I bought fifty gallons including a good oak cask for five pounds. This as well as the other wine was delivered at my house the same afternoon.

I spent that evening and most of the night taking up the floorboards in the dining room and drawing room and storing the bottles between the rafters. With the floor relaid and the carpets replaced I felt fairly secure from discovery.

The barrel went out to the shed and, in the summer especially, the syrupy wine was invaluable for stewing any fruit that was procurable.

Other household supplies I bought when I could and, had Ann been there to do it, I am sure we would have been better provided for. I had never been responsible for such a thing before, and found it difficult to imagine a situation where nothing, literally nothing, was to be bought in the shops. What I had laid in seemed an awful lot at the time, but events proved it to have been woefully inadequate.

Up to this time I was still using my large professional car, a new Oldsmobile Drop Head Coupe, custom-built, black, and with real leather seats and hood in dark cream—very smart, and in immaculate condition. One afternoon, drawing up outside my surgery, I saw two very slick airforce officers standing on the pavement, who at once showed great interest in the car. One looked at the other in a meaningful way, gave him a nudge, and then they walked away.

The next day I received a requisition order for the car, and the same afternoon, before I had time to make any sort of protest, I came out of my surgery to find that it had been driven away by an army chauffeur who just got in and drove it off, while I was seeing my patients. I rang up army headquarters who were polite but cool, and informed me in perfect English that my car was required for official use. Officialdom must have covered a multitude of sins, for in the subsequent few months I encountered it in various parts of the Island, usually carrying a hilarious pair of young officers, or an officer with a girl friend. Later I heard that it had been seen at a garage after an encounter with a granite gatepost. By all accounts the gatepost had come off best.

What eventually happened to it I never discovered but after the Occupation I received £110 pounds in compensation—probably a thousand pounds less than I could have got had I been able to sell it post-war.

Thereafter I used Ann's car, an aging Singer, in good mechanical condition and very reliable, but rather hard on oil and petrol. Eventually even this was requisitioned, but in the meantime I had the chance of buying, for £30, a rather dilapidated, but mechanically sound soft-top Austin Seven which served me faithfully for the duration, and which made the most of the steadily decreasing petrol allowance allotted to doctors.

For the first few months of the Occupation we were infested by the German air force. Most of them were officers, and we were told that they were here for a rest. After the thrashing they received in the Battle of Britain, I think this was very probable.

They were very young, many very good-looking, impeccably tailored, insufferably arrogant and carried themselves as if they belonged to an entirely different race from the ground troops.

It was their habit, especially when they were tight, which was often, to walk along the pavements in the town, three or four abreast, and to shove civilians off their path, into the roadway.

On one occasion a patient of mine who had never been afraid of her shadow, and was not far short of sixty, was pushed off the kerb and landed on her hands and knees in the gutter.

The officers who had lunched rather well, obviously thought this the cream of humour, and laughed up-roariously till she picked herself up, confronted them and dealt the nearest a very professional sock on the jaw which knocked him flat on his back. To add to the pleasure of the spectators, he went down with such force that he split the back of his scalp and a most satisfactory amount of blood was seen to spoil the collar and back of his smart uniform. Military police were sent for, and she was taken off to prison, where she served seven days—a lenient sentence, in the circumstances—but I imagine that whoever tried the case felt that she had a good deal of justification.

I called on her after her release to offer my congratulations, and she said that although the seven days in prison was no bed of roses, the satisfaction she got out of that punch was worth every minute of it.

One interesting aspect of the case was that the young man, who was made to look such a fool, continued to hold the stage. Admittedly there was quite a lot of blood, but it couldn't have hurt very much, and was only a superficial cut on the scalp. I cannot help thinking that a British air force lad would have clapped a handkerchief to the spot and, looking a bit silly, have got out of the limelight as quickly as possible. Whereas the German, deathly pale, with teeth chattering, allowed himself to be assisted into a nearby jeweller's shop, sat in a chair and comforted with restoratives. I think those lads were not as tough as they would like to have been thought.

This was rather borne out by a hairdresser patient of mine, who told me that these young officers spent hours in his salon, having their nails manicured, faces massaged, eyebrows shaped and hair permanently waved. This last I know to be true, for I often came across them in the town, wearing hair nets—presumably to keep the waves in place till the set was complete.

Suddently they disappeared like swallows in autumn. One day they were there, the next they were gone, and we heard that, like the swallows, they had gone to North Africa.

Only the "Jerry bags" (local girls who made no attempt to resist the advances of German soldiers, so attracting the loathing of fellow-Islanders) mourned their passing, and we civilians felt almost friendly to the humdrum ground troops, who at least, if not so decorative, had far better manners.

It was about this time we began to see occasional couples of Germans, in ordinary uniform or even civvies, wandering about in unexpected parts of the town. The two men of each pair were always the same ones, and although the authorities denied that there were any members of the Gestapo on the Island, that is what they unquestionably were. They spoke perfect English or American, and hung about on the fringe of any group of Islanders chatting together, or those queuing for goods.

Later, when wireless sets were forbidden, they would go up to any pair of civilians whom they saw in close conversation on the street, separate them out of ear-shot of each other, and demand to know what they were talking about. If the details of the conversation did not tally, both civilians would be taken away for interrogation.

Very soon we learned not to talk to each other in the street, and only passed the time of day, though we might be the best of friends. After curfew, when no one was abroad, the Gestapo even stood with their ears glued to the window of an occupied room, either to catch details of conversation or even, if they were lucky, the tones of an illicit radio. This cold, implacable surveillance induced a feeling of dread in many people who had any sort of guilty secret, and many radios were either destroyed or handed in.

Though we all hated the Gestapo and would have done them any harm we could, Joe Everett, a local dentist, loathed them with an intensity that was quite terrifying.

Whether this was due to a particular incident I never discovered, but Joe took to hunting the Gestapo between the onset of dark and the curfew hour.

He was wise enough not to do this every night or indeed every week, although he walked the side streets quite regularly—casing the joint as it were.

Thus he got to know the regular habits of his quarry, and also the small alleys or back gardens down which he could make his escape.

His task was made complicated by the fact that the Gestapo usually worked in pairs, but there were times when for instance one would be snooping in the backyard of a house, while the other waited outside on the chance that someone would break cover and try to leave the premises in a hurry.

This was Joe's chance. Superficially he seemed a very inoffensive, middle-aged individual, with no particular characteristics, but as befitted one who had been a welter-weight champion in his day, he was very quick and light on his feet.

When he encountered a Gestapo man, either alone on the watch or walking by himself, which was not often, he was on him like a flash, either with a bone-cracking smash to the jaw, or a heavy blow to the solar plexus. In any case the victim was out for a considerable time and Joe, depending on the circumstances, evaporated down some previously explored alley or sauntered off, whistling unconcernedly.

When most of the wireless sets were ordered to be handed in I gave up an old set which had not worked for many months, but retained my new one. I also had a small portable set, old but in perfect working order, which I hid for nearly a year in my midwifery bag; I kept it purely for the news, when I could not get back to town. But when the batteries gave out I destroyed it, partly because I doubted the possibility of obtaining another battery, but mainly because merely asking for a battery would advertise the fact that I still kept a set. Getting the English news regularly was one of the few things which made life worth living, and I was determined to keep my set at all costs.

The penalties for doing so became increasingly severe, and at last involved even the death penalty. But as so many who were caught were sent to German prisons and never returned, the end result was much the same. Furthermore, discovery in any house meant that everyone living there was sentenced, and when I decided to keep my set I had to avoid involving Mrs Ozouf.

I felt therefore bound to tell her of my decision, and to offer her the opportunity of returning home to sleep, and of coming in as a daily. This she categorically refused to do, and I have never forgotten such a wonderful proof of loyalty on her part.

Together, with hammer and chisel, she and I broke down the brick chimney breast in my bedroom, put a wooden shelf in the unused chimney cavity and fixed the wireless set firmly on it, covering the whole with a plastic sheet. Two leads were attached to long flexes: one had a plug to fit a lamp socket and the other a pair of earphones. These on their flexes were dropped down the chimney to reappear in the unused bathroom fireplace immediately below. Here I fixed up a ledge at arm's length, on which the earphones and plug, wrapped up in a cloth, rested, and from which they could be pulled down and connected with a table lamp when I wished to hear the news. When I was satisfied that it was working properly, I bricked up the hole in the chimney breast, plastered it over and, a couple of days after, repapered it.

Fortunately, the room had been done over in a pale-cream water paint so that matching of the new work was easy. With a large picture hung over the mantle there was no sign of anything having ever been disturbed. I imagine the set is there still.

This was my source of news as long as the electricity held out, and then I went on to a matchbox crystal set, made and given to me by Péré Rey, director of the Maison St Louis, who was himself a powerful partisan. By resisting any impulse to broadcast what little good news was coming through, especially at that time, I managed to keep my set until the end of the war. Many people blabbed to all and sundry, some it seemed in a spirit of bravado, but sooner or later they all ended up in concentration camps, and very few returned.

CHAPTER 5

Let me make it quite plain, before I go any further, that the Germans' broad policy was to preserve, as far as their own interests allowed, the basic individual liberty and welfare of the Island community. Shortage of supplies, and the consequent deprivation we suffered, were by no means entirely their fault, but rather that of the strip of sea which separated us from the French mainland. The considerable harassment (especially towards the end) by our own RAF naturally increased their difficulties and hence ours.

It is true that the occupying forces always had bigger rations, more fuel, more light and more privileges, but they were the top dogs, temporarily at least; in similar circumstances, I suspect that our own army could well have been as tough or tougher.

As a general rule, the private soldier behaved admirably, and the few ugly scenes which took place occurred mainly when the Germans were drunk, which was seldom. Cases of rape, for instance, could be counted on the fingers of one hand.

There were a good many reasons for this. Certainly, for the first year or so, every German was fully convinced that the conquest and occupation of Britain was only weeks away.

I myself, worried out of my mind about the fate of my wife, went to the occupying authority to find out if I could get a message to her, through friends in either Southern Ireland or Portugal.

The official I saw was a kindly man, well past middle age, speaking excellent English, and he patted me on the shoulder in a fatherly way, saying: "Don't worry too much. There is little doubt that we will be in London within three weeks, and then you will be able to see her for yourself."

This was before the Battle of Britain which was so decisive, and he radiated such complete confidence that for a moment I almost thought it might be true.

In such a climate of optimism, it was easy to see that the enemy would want to create as favourable an impression as possible, in what they openly described, in an early official announcement as, "Our first stepping stone to England."

But two and a half years later, the local German press was referring to us as "An outpost of the European Fortress"—a tacit admission that the occupation of Britain was no longer within the scope of their ambition.

But even when the three-week target had receded into the distance, and the Battle of Britain had been fought and lost, coupled with the bitter realisation that the Hun was not going to have a walkover, they did their best to remain tolerant and co-operative.

Provided you went along with their clearly defined rules, or were prepared to put up with the consequences of not doing so, you had no real grumble.

From what we heard, and occasionally saw, in French papers (smuggled over by crews of French cargo boats and passed avidly from hand to hand), punishment for comparable offences in France was far more rigorous, and this pattern continued to a large extent, throughout the Occupation. At the time, I put down the leniency we received as their way of currying favour with a people who could possibly become fellow citizens. Later, when eventually the war seemed lost for them, they were trying to earn a good mark in advance against ultimate punishment for war crimes. I think they genuinely looked upon us as belonging to the same race as themselves, and therefore liked us as much as they abominated the French.

Of course this was by no means the first occupation by Germany, of French soil, and with each defeat they have become increasingly bitter.

But in case we should begin to think that we were under a benevolent occupation, they never neglected an opportunity to exhibit the iron hand in the velvet glove.

One example was the quite unnecessary bombing at the outset of the Occupation, and another the ruthless execution of François Scornett. He was one of a party of sixteen young Frenchmen who had tried to join the Free French by escaping in a boat from the Normandy coast. They were captured off Guernsey, which they mistook for the Isle of Wight and brought here as prisoners of war on 3 February 1941. Fifteen of them received sentences of penal servitude, but François Scornett was condemned to death for "favouring the activities of the enemy, by wilfully supporting England in her war against the German Empire". Why Scornett alone? Had the others just gone in the boat for the sake of the ride? There was no opportunity or time for appeal. Just a few minutes for a priest to give absolution.

The poor lad was bundled into an open lorry, where, manacled, he sat on a cross bench, straight and dignified. His coffin travelled with him, plain for all to see. In the grounds of St Quen's Manor, he was put up against a tree, refusing a blindfold. As the firing party levelled their guns he called out strongly "Adieu! Vive la France!" and the fatal volley rang out.

At this time escapes to the mainland were just starting, and Denis Vibert was among those who successfully got away. So did John Langley and Barbara Hutchings, now happily married and living in Australia. But many paid with their lives or with stiff terms of imprisonment.

It also served to deter those hot-heads who were suspected of planning sabotage. The clearer thinkers were in no doubt that, in our closed conditions, any sort of sabotage was not only risky but completely unproductive. More important still, there would be instant repercussions on the civilian population who were very vulnerable to all sorts of reprisals.

Be that as it may, we heard no more about sabotage until much later in the Occupation.

Although the Germans dealt out punishment right and left, for what to us were very minor breaches, they showed astonishing forbearance in the case of my father-in-law, Colonel Hulton.

Within a few days of the Germans' arrival he received a note from a high-ranking official saying: "Colonel M. presents his compliments to Colonel Hulton, and wishes to inspect the Island Prison. Colonel Hulton will meet him there tomorrow, Tuesday, at 8.30am."

My father-in-law had had a very rough Kaiser's war, had spent a greater part of the time in trenches, and had twice been badly wounded. Furthermore, as he spoke very good German (although he never divulged it here), he had served on the Inter-Allied Commission at Frankfurt-am-Main from 1918—1922. There he had seen how the Germans behaved after a lost war, and when Hitler started his first bid for power he said: "Here we go again; one minute they're at your feet, the next at your throat".

Anyway he was not a man to be bullied easily and, had the note been a little less peremptory, would have answered differently, for his manners were impeccable. Instead his reply was:

"Colonel H. H. Hulton, DSO, MC, presents his compliments to Colonel M. and notes that he wishes to inspect the local prison, on Tuesday next at 8.30am. Unfortunately, Colonel Hulton is in the habit of breakfasting at that hour, but will be pleased to meet Colonel M. at 9.30am."

This exchange worried my mama-in-law no end, because she thought he had stuck his neck out unnecessarily, but she settled down when a curt reply from Colonel M. arrived to say, quite shortly, that he would be there at 9.30am.

On the Tuesday Colonel Hulton exuded charm. He ceremoniously presented Captain Foster, then Prison Governor, to Colonel M. and with the Colonel's ADC and the Head Warder they started their tour. As the short-term prisoners had all been released at the start of the Occupation, the prison was practically empty, and the visit soon over.

On their return to the main hall, the German, suspicious of the shortness of the tour, said, "Now I will inspect the political prisoners."

Colonel Hulton's answer to that was, "I am pleased to be able to tell you that we have no such things, and never have had."

The German, by now getting short of patience, struck the table smartly with his cane and rapped out: "Enough of this nonsense! I wish to see them this instant."

Patiently, Colonel Hulton, savouring every moment of the encounter, and speaking very slowly and distinctly, as if to someone of rather feeble mind, said:

"In a free country, we do not have such things as political prisoners." The German, fighting annoyance with disbelief, was silent for an appreciable time, then said wonderingly:

"Mein Gott. What a nation."

The ADC, who had acted throughout as interpreter, turned away to hide a smile.

Colonel Hulton died after a very short illness on 9 December of the same year, in his own home, in his own bed. Stricken as we were by our loss, for he was a tremendous character, it was perhaps just as well. He was incapable of compromising his principles, and would almost certainly have ended up in a concentration camp, where he would have died in squalor and misery. Those who knew how he insisted on all his comforts, would well understand that he would not have been amused by that.

To go back a little. I have already referred to the enormous flood of orders issued by High Command at the start of the Occupation. Some of these quickly died a natural death, but many left us in no doubt that we were under a bigoted regime.

The first announced an expurgation of the public library, by members of the propaganda office, and almost at once the place was over-run by little grey men with rat-like faces. All works decrying Hitler and his gang were removed, and presumably destroyed, as well as a much larger selection of works by Jews, about Jewish subjects, and even Jewish travel.

The second was more sinister. All Jews or people of Jewish origin must register and all their business premises had to be clearly marked "Jewish".

Later in the Occupation came an order informing employers that they were at liberty to dismiss any Jewish employee without fear of a case for compensation.

Most Jewish people had wisely left the Island at the evacuation, but about thirty still lived here, in fear and trembling. Of course, none of us altered our attitudes to the Jews, just to please the Germans. But the Germans, baulked of their prey in one way, managed to get most of their names onto the lists for deportation to Germany in 1942.

The only Jewish national left to me as a patient, was a middle-aged woman whom I had attended for some years. A widow, in comfortable circumstances, one met her occasionally at cocktail parties, and she was the living embodiment of a doctor's nightmare.

Although not exactly a hypochondriac, she always had something the matter, usually imaginary and, more often than not, triggered off by a medical article appearing in that month's *Reader's Digest*.

If she required me to visit, it had to be at once, or even sooner, but my bills, I may say, were not settled with equal dispatch, and were often queried. I was only the current incumbent in a long line of her medical advisers, and I prayed hard that she would soon find someone else to take her fancy. On the telephone she was brusque and hectoring, and always attempted—with conspicuous lack of success—to bully Mrs Ozouf (who was also my receptionist). Mrs Ozouf hated her guts, but this attitude was entirely mutual.

My patient was a big woman and, though not exactly fat, gave an impression of force and dominance, which was not belied by her behaviour. She also had the reputation of being a very good bridge player: hard on her partner, insistent on post-mortems, and a very bad loser.

Although as strong as an ox (but with considerably less charm), she would, in the waiting room, always try to jump the queue by playing on the sympathy of the other patients, and explaining that her health was so delicate that sitting up for long periods affected her heart, or her back, or whatever.

Mrs Ozouf nearly always managed to thwart her in one way or another, and although no words ever passed between them, it was amusing to see how like a pair of dogs they were stiff-legged and ready to start a fight.

When her name appeared on the second list for deportation, she appeared at once in my surgery, and the change in the woman was quite unbelievable. In place of her arrogant entrance, and her look around the waiting room as if all the other patients were lepers, she crept in and sat in an unobtrusive corner seat, in a state of near collapse.

When her turn came, she was weeping as she came into my consulting room, and sobbed for several minutes before she could speak. Then there was a torrent of words, most of them incomprehensible, but I did pick up "Belsen" and "gas ovens", and so gathered that she was listed for deportation.

Without much conviction, I comforted her as best I could, pointing out that she was a British subject, and therefore of the same standing as the other deportees. But she would not be convinced. "Once they get me to Germany," she said, "I will disappear without trace, I know I will, and you can't tell me otherwise."

I must say I rather agreed with her, but suggested that she should give me twenty-four hours while I thought out some plan, and still sniffing she departed.

Next afternoon, she was my first patient, having been there a full hour before surgery opened. This time, she was rather more composed, and I outlined my plan.

I would take her into a nursing home, and under a local anaesthetic, make a long incision in the skin of her abdomen—no deeper. Then sew it up with skin and tension sutures to simulate a large abdominal operation. This would prevent her being deported just then, and by the time she was declared fit, the whole scheme might well have come to an end.

I sat back and waited for applause and gratitude, but not a bit of it. She thought the whole plan was very far-fetched. Couldn't she just lie in bed at the nursing home, and would

I give a certificate to say that she had had a serious operation?

To this I gave a firm "no". If the Germans were going to be threatened with the loss of their prey, they would certainly send one of their own surgeons to the nursing home, and insist on seeing the incision.

If she would consent, I even offered to write up the most circumstantial bedside notes as to the extreme gravity of her condition, but she would not entertain the suggestion in any form. Like a great many bullies she was a physical coward, and the abdominal incision, under a local anaesthetic, was a hurdle she simply would not take.

I pointed out that if she really had suffered from an urgent condition, her abdomen would have to be opened, but she said that in such a case, she would be under a general anaesthetic and therefore quite unaware of what was going on. Could I not give her a general anaesthetic and get a surgeon to do the job.

I pointed out that I was risking my neck in any case, and did not feel entitled to ask another man to risk his. Any German surgeon, with his wits about him, might easily spot what had happened; in that case, she, I, and the hypothetical third party might end up in a German prison camp together.

But no. We argued to and fro for some time, but she was adamant, and I longed to tell her to go to the devil in her own way, but her terror was so abject and pitiable that I had to keep the subject open. She sat there with the tears dripping into her lap, without any attempt to wipe them away, suggesting all sorts of alternatives, each more absurd than the last.

Finally, and against my better judgement, I agreed to perjure myself still further, by a written report to the German doctor, enumerating all the terrible illnesses from which she had suffered, and the present precarious state of her health. In spite of the mental trauma to which she has been subjected, and a certain loss of weight, she was still a substantial woman, and I could not but wish that she had lost two or three stone, to make the story more convincing.

I even went to the length of presenting in person the

report at headquarters, but was met with the polite and rather enigmatic message that the report must be presented actually by the patient to whom it referred. This, I thought, is where we come adrift, and I was not wrong.

The Germans are no fools, and as I had feared, my report cut no ice at all. The German Medical Officer, with whom I had had dealings before, and who was the one member of the staff whom I should never have attempted to bamboozle, sent me a note in impeccable English. In a vein of wry humour, he congratulated me on my consummate skill in steering the lady so successfully through such a number of dire illnesses, and that doubtless due to me, she was now in such excellent health that she was fully able to take the little trip to the Reich. I felt an utter fool.

On receipt of this, I went to see her and found her sitting in a low chair dazed and collapsed.

She weakly suggested that she would consent to anything—anything I cared to do, even under a local anaesthetic, but I patiently explained that now she was known to the German Medical service, it was all too late. Then she disappeared, suddenly and without warning.

For a time, it was thought that she had committed suicide, and I should not have been surprised, but there was no sign of a body, and the Germans began to be suspicious. Two members of the Military Police paid a call at my surgery and questioned me closely. They even searched the house, without pulling it about too much, but naturally found nothing. There were a number of things I was a little anxious about, but knowing her whereabouts no better than they did, I was bolstered up by conscious innocence, and finally they left, convinced.

They made spot checks upon those of her friends with whom she had had most to do, again without result. They even advertised in the *Evening Post*, but all to no purpose. Finally they gave up, and presumably closed the file.

Nearly two years later, in the autumn of 1944, I was paying a routine visit to an elderly couple who lived near the centre of town. The old-fashioned house, with a lawn and shrubbery in front, was no more than fifty yards from a private hotel which had been taken over by the Germans, and was the scene of a great deal of their traffic.

Walking up the path, I saw, screened from the street by the bushes, a lady sitting reading in a deck chair and evidently enjoying the late sunshine. She was wearing a wide-brimmed hat and dark glasses, and the sight of her gave me some surprise for my patients were elderly, almost recluses, and I had never known them to be visited by relatives or friends.

As I came abreast of the lady, she raised her face from the book and looked idly at me. Recognition was instant and mutual, but she hastily went back to her book, and I gave not the slightest sign that I had spotted her. Nor did I at any time mention it to the old couple.

After the Occupation, I did bring the subject up; the old couple told me that their guest had left on the first available boat.

They said that they had never seen her before in their lives, until one night when, after dark, she came asking for shelter. In fairness to her, she told them the whole story, and they, to their eternal credit, took her in. "It was the only Christian thing to do," said the old gentleman, but the old lady (rather tartly, I thought) said: "Two and a half years is a very long time, doctor." Unless the leopard had changed her spots, I could not but agree with her most heartily. Although the old pair lived in a large house, which had once been very well kept, they had, even before the war, shown every sign of living in genteel poverty, and after the liberation I saw no sign that their circumstances had ameliorated. Nor did they ever refer to the subject in any way, but my bet is that the lady in question never dipped her hand into her own very considerable funds, as some sort of appreciation for their risking their lives to save hers.

Among the more tiresome of the German orders was one forbidding cyclists to ride two abreast. At the beginning this made sense but, even when the roads were practically bare of cars, offending cyclists were arrested and prosecuted.

In the quiet lanes, without a car in sight or earshot, single soldiers (not even on patrol) were apt to jump out of the hedge and challenge cyclists.

On one occasion, a soldier fined a cyclist fifty marks on the spot, but said he would waive the fine in exchange for the bicycle. In spite of protest he did just that, and rode away leaving the cyclist stranded.

Another cyclist, also fined fifty marks, refused to hand over the money without an official receipt. For that, he got a broken jaw and the certainty, shared by everyone, that few such fines ever reached central funds.

Most people were nervous of complaining, from fear of victimisation but, had they done so, such was the aim of higher authority to stand well with the Islanders, I am sure their case would receive sympathetic consideration.

On the other hand, a young woman mucking out her horse, and exasperated by the singing of a platoon of soldiers marching along the road, threw a forkful of manure over the intervening wall. Some of them were spattered, and she received a three-month sentence. She at once appealed, and it was raised to six months.

Another man spoke his mind in no uncertain fashion to a Jerry bag, who forthwith reported him. He received two months which on appeal was raised to six. After that, people decided to put up with whatever sentences they received in the first place.

The Germans' occasional leniency did not extend towards secret societies, which they regarded with implacable hostility. The Masonic building in St Mark's Road was raided and all the symbols, regalia, records, etc. packed off to Germany.

Steps were also taken to list the silver plate in churches of all denominations throughout the Island, but this aroused such an outcry that it was hastily abandoned.

Organisations like the Salvation Army were banned, and all clubs had to have written permission to carry on their activities. Applications from badminton clubs, darts clubs, sewing guilds, Mothers' Union and even more nefarious gatherings had to furnish particulars of activities and names of members. The various dramatic societies, seemed to be allowed more latitude than most, and they flourished. This was as it should be, for they helped enormously to keep up morale with their monthly shows, which were very well done. Dyed sheets, flour bags, mutton cloths and curtains, intricately hand-made by hundreds of helpers, looked marvellous from the auditorium and, unlike most other things during the Occupation, gave no impression of being makeshift.

The cinema still functioned, but so much propaganda was thrown on the screen that, except for Jerry bags and their soldiers, few civilians cared to go. They were, however, crammed with the German rank and file, for the very blatant propaganda kept up their morale too. I heard that some of the documentaries of fighting on the Russian front showed the Germans inflicting so many crushing defeats that it would have been no surprise to see the Soviet troops fighting with their backs to the Great Wall of China.

Every Saturday afternoon an army band—a very good one too—played in the Royal Square and attracted a large crowd of Islanders. They offered all sorts of pieces—well-known music from classical opera, English favourites like the Londonderry Air, tunes from musical comedy, traditional airs and even hymn tunes. With the band was a sort of disc jockey who called out to the crowd for suggestions, or made some of his own.

On this particular occasion he shouted: "Hands up all those who would like us to play selections from *The Merry Widow*." Instantly a forest of hands shot up from all parts of the crowd, and at the same time a movie camera started shooting. The resulting film was subsequently shown in cinemas all over the Reich, with the caption: "Citizens of the Island of Jersey, who are so happy under the protection of the Führer that they are seen giving an enthusiastic Nazi salute."

Two soldiers who raped a woman at St Martin were arrested, but there was no mention of it in either paper, nor were the men brought to trial on the Island. No one must know that the *Herrenvolk* did such things. They were quietly put on a boat for France, en route for Germany, and in all probability ended up in the front line somewhere in Russia.

Nineteen forty-one saw a general tightening up of everything. Rations were reduced considerably, and continued to be till the end.

From time to time the enemy seemed inexplicably to develop a fit of nerves. An inoffensive countryman, out after curfew, was shot dead without being given a chance to account for himself, and a German soldier was also shot dead by a sentry for forgetting to give the password.

The end of the year was cold, and in an effort to keep warm the troops installed rather makeshift, free-standing stoves in the houses they occupied. As a result, St Ouen's Manor had a disastrous fire and the oldest wing, including the big drawing room with all its historical treasures, was completely gutted. Another very beautiful house, Beauvoir, St Saviour, was also totally burned to the ground.

I shall always remember the early spring of 1941, when the first batch of Red Cross letters arrived but, miserably, none for me. I don't think that, in my adult life, I have ever been so disappointed. The next batch, however, did contain one with the news that I most wanted to hear, and I was able to send off an ecstatic reply to Ann.

I also sent a letter to a great friend, whose nice house had been requisitioned and occupied by a large German unit. My message ran something like this: "Think you ought to know that No. 11 now contains quantities of confidential domestic utensils. Amenable. Careful, so far. John." This evidently made no sense to the official censor and was transmitted as above; unfortunately, it made no sense to my friend either or to his immediate circle, who consulted others in turn. Plainly there was no crossword fan in the vicinity, and the solution had to wait until my friend returned to Jersey.

Later in the spring, in order to reduce the number of mouths to be fed, all Czechs and Swiss, and most Italians, and their families, were repatriated and left in a ship flying the Red Cross flag. This ship returned still flying the same flag, and was used for transporting not only troops but urgent military materials as well.

To save petrol, a horse-drawn ambulance was constructed

and buses restricted to a circumference of three miles around the town. One bus was converted to burn charcoal, and this plied at a sedate speed between St Helier and St Aubin. Again to save fuel, a number of bakehouses were pooled, and only a full oven of bread baked.

Robberies became more frequent and the German courts worked overtime.

Two women seen putting up "V" signs were sent to prison in France for nine months, and a man who insulted a German, found exploring his house in broad daylight, received a similar sentence. An elderly man who defended his wife, when a German officer snatched at an RAF diamond brooch she was wearing, had to serve twelve months at a prison in Germany. Fraternisation was wearing thin.

Towards the end of the year, relations between the two communities became even more strained. This was partly because the German's standard of living was constantly increasing as the Islander' fell. For instance, the enemy were using a thousand gallons of whole milk per day, while we queued for skim. They were eating our succulent pork or veal, while we were given a weekly two-ounce ration of superannuated, worn-out dairy-cow beef from France.

Relations were not helped when a batch of troops, already drunk, burst into the Oxford Hotel, long after hours, and started to raid the bar. The landlord was badly beaten up, but his wife waded in wielding a full bottle to such effect that one of the raiders was laid out cold. Nothing so blatant had occurred before, and it was hushed up as far as possible.

About this time arrived the first gang of Russian workers, much to everyone's surprise. Very early one morning, on an urgent visit to a patient at St Lawrence, I had just passed Meadow Bank, when I became aware of an extremely unpleasant smell—a compound of urine and faeces, but above all of mice. Rounding the bend I saw a column of men being herded (and "herded" is the word) by Nazi soldiers. They were of all ages, all bearded, some with shoes in various stages of decrepitude, but many with just rags wrapped around their feet. They all looked worn and emaciated, and one old man, propped against the hedge, would probably never reach the top of the hill alive.

The soldiers waved me to stop and indicated that I must turn at the next gap and go back. This I did and finally got to my patient by way of Ville Emphrie—a long way round when petrol was so scarce. I learned subsequently that this particular batch were inhabitants of a village in German-occupied Russia, where some sort of sabotage had been committed. In retaliation the Germans had rounded up every male between sixteen and sixty, locked them all in unfurnished, unheated covered trucks and sent them across Europe, as forced labour. Having never set foot outside the trucks, which were not opened until they were transhipped in France, and being completely devoid of any sanitary facilities whatsoever, it was small wonder that they stank the way they did.

I did not see them again, except working at a distance, but I gathered that they were put in a camp somewhere around Ville au Bas, St Lawrence. Subsequently I got to know a Russian from the same camp, although he had not come over with the group I saw then but some time later. He told me that a number of the original group had died within days of their arrival.

Many months after, I was called on at the Jersey Maternity Hospital by a German MO who wished us to enrol two Russian women in our Ante-natal Clinic. I arranged for them to come up periodically, and they were escorted by a corporal and two soldiers who sat in the next room while the women were being examined. This was only after I had had a heated exchange with the corporal, who insisted on being present while they were being examined, and said that his instructions were that they should not be let out of his sight. I refused point blank, and said that I would telephone the German Medical Officer—upon which he gave way. I was told that when all the men in the village were rounded up, two newly married girls, who were determined not to be separated from their husbands, cut off their hair and dressed up in men's clothes. Both girls were almost as broad as they were long, and with clothes many layered and bulky, it was easy to see that they could well pass off as a couple of sixteen-year-old boys. They worked side by side with the men at the heaviest labouring tasks, until their condition was discovered.

As we had no language in common, except dumb show, it was difficult to communicate, but at least I was able to examine them and found both cases completely normal. Whether or not they had to continue work as usual, between their periodic visits, I was unable to discover, but eventually they both went into labour, astonishingly enough, within hours of each other. I was notified by the staff that they had been admitted in the small hours, but that the pains were weak and not yet established, so that there was no immediate hurry.

I called in during the course of the morning and as I passed through the doors I was greeted by a high-pitched keening sound, which rose to a crescendo when the pain came, but was sustained, though with less conviction, throughout the resting period. This, if allowed to continue, was likely to be exhausting to the two girls themselves, and upsetting for the other waiting mothers, but nothing would stop them. Several nurses tried to indicate that it was quite unnecessary to keep up such a noise all through labour, but they had obviously learned in their Motherland that this was the thing to do, and they kept it up right to the bitter end. We were all deafened and exhausted when this came.

After completely straightforward confinements both mothers had fine boys and appeared to be blissfully happy, but after a few hours it was evident that something was troubling them. At length, a young probationer solved the problem—baby clothes.

Up to this point the babies had been put in the routine nighties, kept at the hospital against just such a situation, but the Russian mothers obviously thought them very strange and regarded their offspring clothed in them with apprehension and suspicion. We thought they were worried as to how they would cope when they got back to the camp, and already various members of the staff had organised a whipround among their friends and relations outside. But all too plainly the Russians didn't think very much of tiny vests and matinée coats, although they seemed tepidly pleased with booties and mittens. But these interested them more for their novelty value than anything else; they would hold them up in front of each other and burst into gales of laughter.

But the things which really delighted them were some old sheets and blankets. In dumb show they gave us to understand that they wanted needles, thread and scissors and, as soon as these were produced, set to, and cut up both sheets and blankets into strips about eight or nine inches wide. These they sewed end to end in lengths of three or four yards and proceeded, according to some age-old system, to wrap each baby into a cocoon, arms to their sides, leaving a small aperture for the face, and another at the back for changing. The resulting chrysalis gave the impression of the baby being twice its normal size, with the face at the end of one shallow tunnel and the baby's bottom at the end of another. The latter was covered with a piece of many times folded sheet and kept in place by a final strip of cloth.

The mothers were now completely happy and remained all smiles for the rest of their stay. They attended to the babies entirely themselves, stuffing their breasts down the tunnels till the babies took hold, and leaving them there till they fell asleep. How the babies got any air at all while feeding beats me, but it seemed to work perfectly, with no nonsense about bringing up wind, and no patting of backs. They changed to the other breast when the first was empty, and that was that.

Why the babies did not die of heat stroke I cannot imagine. I can quite see it would make sense in Central Russia, with temperature at forty degrees below, but at this particular time the Island was enjoying a mini-heatwave. I worried about this quite a lot, and tried to communicate my concern to the mothers who, I think, did understand in the end what I was trying to say, but were completely adamant and left hospital with their babies still tightly cocooned, seemingly still well and thriving.

We never found out what happened to them. Under occupation conditions we were faced with many similar situations of which we were not told the outcome.

Naturally, after due time, we started to have German babies. At first the girls were shunned by other mothers, but after a time were accepted with more tolerance, although when there were several in hospital at one time, of their own choice they asked to be put in adjacent beds.

Almost all these girls came for delivery to the Jersey Maternity Hospital, but occasionally, where the father-to-be was an officer, or the girl the daughter of well-to-do parents, the birth took place at one or other of the small private nursing homes scattered over the Island.

Some babies went directly from us to the crèche, but the majority of girls decided to keep them, although the relatives mostly agreed to this rather grudgingly. But no one can resist a baby for very long and, naturally and inevitably, they won their way into the heart of the family.

On one occasion a high ranking officer called to inspect the crèche and was shown round by the matron. Seeing a number of very bonny, blonde children he said rather patronisingly, in his excellent English: "Ah, I see some of my troops are beginning to leave their mark on the local populace."

"Not at all," replied the matron coolly, "those are all pure Jersey blood—it's the blonde Norman stock."

Rather annoyed, he replied: "Surely it is impossible to deny that children of German fathers can always be recognised by their superior physique."

"On the contrary," was her retort. "Most of the German illegitimates are definitely sub-standard."

"Nonsense!" he shouted. "How can you make such a claim when the whole world knows that our entire army is composed of carefully picked men?"

"Well, some hereabouts have not been picked very carefully," she said quietly, "and I can only conclude that the mothers of these children, who are largely the dregs of our community, have taken up with men who are the dregs of yours!"

Without replying, but red with temper, he stamped out of the building, leaving her to wonder what was going to happen. Fortunately this interchange occurred after D-day, when imprisonment in Jersey was not so frequent and exportation to France impossible—so she heard nothing further about it.

CHAPTER 6

During the occupation, there was a great deal to do and I had more than enough to keep my mind occupied.

Dr R. M. McKinstry, Medical Officer of Health for Jersey had asked me to take charge of the new Jersey Maternity Hospital which was starting up at what had previously been the Jersey Dispensary—a Cottage Hospital partly supported by endowments.

Soon after their arrival, the Germans had taken over the main block of the General Hospital leaving for civilian use about a tenth of the whole building. This included the Marie Louise Ward, a number of small side wards, the children's ward and the maternity wing. The last was immediately cleared preparatory to receiving general patients, and the mothers hastily transferred to the JMH.

Many of these admissions were in poor shape, and it rapidly became evident that they were suffering from a fever of the puerperal type. Penicillin had not yet been discovered and M and B was still in its early and very unpredictable stage. Nonetheless we battled on. We never actually lost a mother but, careful as we were, some of the new admissions became infected and the fight went on again.

At last I contacted Dr McKinstry, and we decided it was imperative to find alternative accommodation for new mothers.

Bon Air Nursing Home, at that time not running at full strength, was chosen and formally requestioned, and the existing patients were returned to their families, or to other private nursing homes on the Island. All new patients were taken in and nursed there. The old patients stayed at the JMH till all the mothers were free of infection and fit to go home; then began the Augean task of rendering the entire premises germ-free.

As the Germans had taken over the sterilising plant at the hospital and would undertake to deal only with a limited number of sterile drums for the civilian sector, we had no alternative but to do the work ourselves.

The JMH staff were magnificent, as were the Red Cross nurses and the large body of voluntary workers, right down to boy scouts. Fortunately the weather was warm and sunny, so that all doors and windows could be left open day and night.

Each bed was dismantled and carried out onto the lawns which were much more spacious then than they are now (today we have a big new car park). Each section of every bed was scrubbed meticulously with soap and water, and disinfectant, then left in the sun to sterilise further. Blankets were collected by volunteers and washed in their own homes. Fortunately we still had soap and fuel. Sheets went to the General Hospital laundry, which was still operating.

Scaffolding on free loan was erected, one ward at a time, and every inch of wall, ceiling and passage was washed with disinfectant, soap and water. Finally the parquet floors throughout the hospital were similarly scrubbed three times, and left to dry between each operation. All other furniture was washed in the same way, and the whole place left to dry for several days.

We then started to admit new patients only, Bon Air being kept on till all its patients had been discharged.

As a result we did not lose a single patient, and in spite of a shortage of almost everything especially towards the end of the Occupation, we had no serious infection of any sort for the rest of the time.

In fact, the JMH was a sort of holiday home and rest cure

for the mothers who went there to have their babies. The catering was in the hands of Miss Nell Brett, a capable and highly intelligent woman who in addition was a cook of genius. Admittedly, we had our own extremely productive kitchen garden, and certain allowances from the authorities, but she worked marvels with unpromising materials, and every meal would have borne comparison with that of a good hotel under peacetime conditions.

Some of the patients were in dire need of good food, for many mothers denied themselves proper nourishment so that their existing children could have a little more. Admittedly all children had a small extra ration of milk and occasionally a little something else, like an orange, cocoa or a couple of ounces of macaroni, but these benefits were irregular, and not of much benefit in households of three or four fast-growing, boisterous, ravenous youngsters.

Strangely enough the babies that arrived were almost all fine fat specimens, in spite of the emaciation of some of the mothers. One poor woman with five children under seven could scarcely totter from weakness on admission, and yet she gave birth to a lovely baby of eight and a half pounds. After ten days of good feeding with us, she herself had visibly put on weight, but was still several pounds short of six stone on discharge. Happily she survived and I saw her in the town some years after, plump and rosy, with a family now numbering ten. This makes nonsense of books and newspaper articles authoritatively advising pregnant mothers, and giving infallible diets for keeping the baby small.

The other interesting thing about occupation conditions was that many women who had long given up hope of ever having a baby suddenly found themselves pregnant. Some had been married as long as twenty years and most sailed through their confinements without any difficulty. All had lost weight, some a considerable amount, and I put down their good fortune to a diet mainly of vegetables, compulsory exercise—no petrol, no buses—and consequent loss of abdominal and pelvic fat.

Many single children, perhaps engaged or even married, suddenly found themselves with a small brother or sister, but the most extraordinary case occurred about halfway through the Occupation.

We had three admissions, all of the same family, within the space of one month. One was the grandmother, aged 53, who had married for the second time and became pregnant in the first month. She told me that she had married for company and at first thought that the change of life had been responsible for all the weight she was putting on. The second, her daughter was in her middle thirties and the third, her grand-daughter, aged eighteen. The grand-daughter had her baby first, and grannie hers last, so that the last baby arrived in the world to find himself already a great-uncle to a child older than himself.

Another woman aged forty, married for more than ten years, who had longed for a baby all her life, was in seventh heaven to find herself pregnant, and despite all the shortages had gathered together a complete layette and, wonder of wonders, a new perambulator. Just after she had passed the six month, a German unit called at their home and dragged her husband off to prison, because he had been seen to pick up a leaflet dropped by a British plane. The leaflet was intended for France and had been carried to Jersey by some trick of the wind, but at that stage of the war any excuse was good enough to harry the population.

The shock sent her into premature labour, and she came into the JMH and had a baby weighing one pound, ten ounces, the next day.

This was in 1944 when the regular electricity supply had given out, and of course we had no means of operating our incubator for premature babies. However, well greased, wrapped in cotton wool, and with two hot water bottles renewed every two hours, day and night, we kept the baby going. He was christened Glyn.

At the start, the mother had no milk, but we were lucky just then that there were several mothers who had more than enough, certainly for such a tiddler whose demands were so slight. Belatedly, the mother's milk came in, and everything seemed to be going splendidly, but we dared not yet unwrap the little cocoon to verify this. When we finally did so, after some months he weighed just over four pounds, was crying strongly and moved his limbs well. By this time the mother had gone home, and walked up to the hospital to feed the baby four times a day.

Suddenly one afternoon I had an urgent call. Glyn was bringing up his feeds, and had a small lump in his groin, which although I had never seen one in so small a baby, I diagnosed as a strangulated hernia. By applying hot compresses and gentle pressure, I persuaded it to go back, and for a week all was well; but it occurred again and this time I was not so successful. Our senior surgeon, Mr. Arthur Halliwell FRCS, was called in, and had no luck either. Immediate operation was imperative for, although the baby might well die during the operation, he would certainly die if it were not done.

With some trepidation I gave the anaesthetic, and marvelled at the deftness of Mr Halliwell's fingers working in such a tiny space. All through his working life he was noted for his speed and delicate touch.

When the baby was returned to his cot, still unconscious, he looked like a small, white, wax doll, but he was still alive.

When he recovered consciousness he took a half-feed at once and kept it down, but six weeks later he strangulated a hernia on the other side and a second operation was successfully carried out. After this he thrived visibly.

By the date on which he should normally have been born, he had reached six and a half pounds, but for safety's sake we decided to keep him for a further month. Then suddenly the Germans had one of those inexplicable panics which seized them, with greater frequency, as the Occupation wore on.

They imposed a total curfew for 48 hours, and the mother was therefore unable to come up for feeds. As she was then living about two and a half miles outside the town, she decided to take him home. There was no obvious reason why she should not, and when I visited them next day all seemed to be well.

But late in the evening of the following day he started to scream and would not take his feed.

There was no telephone in the house, nor in the immediate vicinity, and she was afraid of being shot if she was spotted breaking the curfew. Her husband was still in prison, and she had no one else to fall back on. She paced the room for hours in the dark, trying to pacify him, and finally he stopped crying so she placed him gently in his cot and lay down in her clothes on the bed beside him. She must have dropped off for some hours, and on waking immediately went to feel the baby for she had no artificial light. He was so limp when she picked him up that she knew at once he was dead.

A few months after this the Occupation ended, but she continued to grieve and, quite groundlessly, to blame herself.

However, in a short time she came to see me, and almost fearfully announced (she was now more than 42) that she thought she might be pregnant.

This time after two attempts to miscarry, and several other alarms, she carried to full term and successfully gave birth to a lovely baby girl—only a few days after my own daughter was born. That child was a brilliant student, as well as being extremely pretty, and understandably the centre point in the life of her parents, who are now living in England.

The main characteristic of the JMH at that time was the very high sense of duty and comradeship amongst the staff, led by the matron Miss Elizabeth Thornley who kept the same staff for the whole of the five years, with very few exceptions. All through that time there was no talk of hours of work or overtime. If a job was there to be done, it was done, and properly, no matter how long it took. Everyone worked for love of the job, and with very little thought of the remuneration.

Trained staff was not easy to come by One young English sister who had come over to convalesce and was trapped by the Occupation, joined us at once, and although still very delicate worked until the Liberation, but sadly died very soon afterwards.

Two others, semi- if not fully retired, returned to full time obstetric nursing, and lent their expertise to the less experienced staff.

As I was in the act of carrying out a difficult forceps delivery, one of these fell dead across the bed. The charge nurse was out of the ward for a moment filling a syringe, and

I could do nothing until she returned. Neither of us realised what had actually happened—unexplained faintings were not uncommon in those days—and it was only when I saw nurse's face go pale that I knew that sister was dead. The post-mortem showed that she had had a massive brain haemorrhage and had died instantly.

As time went on things got tougher, although as a hospital we had a few special concessions. Even with these, fuel was at a minimum, and central heating only turned on for snow or severe frost. Babies had to depend entirely on frequently renewed hot-water bottles—which, day and night, was quite a chore in itself.

We had an emergency lighting system, which we used only for operations, when the main electricity supply was turned off. In the last year even that failed us, and we fell back on candles and oil lamps, and getting the fuel for these was an almost impossible problem.

We were also forced to give pure chloroform as an anesthetic an obsolete and dangerous alternative to ether which was even more dangerous by its tendency, to explode in the presence of a naked flame.

Swabs for operations ran out, but a whipround the friends of the JMH produced quantities of cotton or linen rags which were sterilised in a fish kettle. Even these came to an end and we were reduced to strips of old underwear, and anything else not actually coloured.

Rubber gloves had given out some time before, and pre-operation scrubbing up of bare hands was done with the little real soap we had left (not the ersatz stuff) and these tablets were jealously reserved for this purpose only.

In spite of these makeshifts, the figures were excellent. We had no infections to speak of, and of approximately two thousand deliveries in five years, there were only three maternal deaths, two of which were quite inevitable. This was a record of which any fully equipped hospital in peacetime would have been proud.

Of the babies born, one hundred, at an absolute maximum, were of German parentage. A few more were born at home or at some of the small private nursing homes, but I doubt whether the very outside figure for Jersey exceeded one hundred and twenty.

On the second day of the Liberation I was waiting for a friend in the foyer of the Pomme d'Or hotel, when I saw an Island official talking to what was obviously a reporter. Suddenly, catching sight of me, the former said: "Here's the very man who can give you the correct figures," and bringing him over introduced us.

He proved to represent one of our most popular dramatic daily newspapers, and for the truths' sake I was glad to give him the figures I have just mentioned.

Imagine my chagrin when, in next day's article on the subject, he stated that he had been informed from a completely reliable source that four hundred German babies had been born in Jersey alone. This was bad enough, but I felt that popular journalism had reached the dizzy heights of absurdity when I read in the *Daily Mail* of a few days later that three thousand was the correct figure! This was one thousand more than the total of babies of any nationality born here during the five years of the Occupation.

All the German babies are now grown up and most of them married. To the best of my knowledge, whatever stigma was originally attached to them is completely forgotten, and those of them that I know personally are good, solid, well-respected Jersey citizens. A conquering army, from time immemorial has always brought a change of blood, and in Jersey's case this will I am sure have done no harm in the long run.

Now what of their mothers? A great many had a genuine love affair with their German boyfriends. Most local men of marriageable age had left the island, and as many of these soldiers were notably well favoured, what happened was inevitable and understandable. Many of these girls reared their own babies, which eventually were completely accepted by their families, and when the war was over married British men and forgot the unhappy past. Such girls kept a low profile, and certainly after the war, their neighbours forgave and finally forgot their little peccadillos.

But there was another group of girls, those with special

looks or charm, who caught the eyes of the upper ranks, and were enabled by them to flaunt their advantages before their less adventurous sisters.

These girls were entertained by day, and especially by night, in houses requisitioned as officers' quarters, and even in that holy of holies, Government House. While the rest of the population were living on boring and unappetising rations, these girls revelled in delicacies brought over from France and expensive groceries requestioned from Island stores, washed down with wines and champagne. A number of houses had been abandoned with all their contents, and I often recognised, on the backs of these girls, gowns, smart suits and furs belonging to our friends who had left the Island.

What the Island womenfolk most resented was the sight of these girls, their legs sleek in nylons procured from Paris, mincing along the pavement in French shoes of the highest fashion, while they themselves clumped around in wooden soled clogs, with bare legs or, at best, darned woollen stockings.

One girl, denounced her own father for keeping a radio, after he had thrashed her with a leather belt for arriving at breakfast one morning in a car driven by her German lover. Her goings-on were no secret to the neighbours, but up until then he had refused to believe, or perhaps did not want to believe, any reports about his lovely adored eldest daughter.

No one will know what her innermost thoughts were, when his rash but understandable action cost him six months in a German detention camp. Happily he returned alive, though visibly older.

At the Liberation, she and many like her disappeared from the Island, though nobody knows how they got away when many deserving cases had to wait six or eight weeks for release.

What was never explained was that most of them vanished without trace, but one, I was informed by a bitter sister-in-law, has married well and is living in the Birmingham area.

Another somehow got to South Africa and married there a

prominent and wealthy business man. She is living in great style at the Cape, and has been recognised by several local people holidaying there.

Of those who did not manage to get away, some were set upon, had their heads shaved, and were daubed all over with tar and feathers. These just sat tight and rode out the storm. Several are now in good positions, prosperous and highly thought of, by a generation which has no knowledge of their previous background.

The most condign punishment was meted out to the wife of a local tailor, who was certainly of an age to know better. Quite early on, she became mistress of a high-ranking, middle-aged officer who, as the French say, "put her amongst her own furniture".

He had taken for his own quarters one of the finest houses on the Island, which had been abandoned as it stood when the occupant fled.

The lady who had left the house was well known for her chic and her expensive clothes. Naturally her wardrobes, chests and cupboards became as Tom Tiddler's ground for Ginger Lou, who had a passion for clothes, combined with a highly developed dress sense. She was French by birth, though married to a Jerseyman, and was well up in her thirties, perhaps even her forties, but her figure was astonishingly good and she had very neat legs and feet.

The clothes she found waiting for her might have been made to her measure, and for five years she enjoyed the title of the best-dressed woman in Jersey.

While everyone else walked, or laboured around on bicycles, she sat elegantly in the back of a huge limousine, sometimes with and sometimes without her lover, in full regimentals but always with a military chauffeur. To look at her, you would never dream that she came from a second-rate tailor shop in a poor part of the town. Always expertly made up, with her beautiful red hair extremely well dressed, she never overdid the part, but rather under-accentuated it, with plain well-cut gowns, and immaculate matching accessories.

Her behaviour, however, spoiled this impression. Going marketing she kept an eye open for any shop where a queue outside betrayed the presence of some little extra, like a few eggs (one egg per shopper was the allowance) or perhaps a quartered rabbit. A word to the chauffeur stopped the car slap outside the shop, no matter what the state of the traffic and, going straight to the head of the queue, she would declare in a loud voice: "I will take the lot." The shopkeeper did not dare refuse.

The disappointed shoppers dispersed, but lined up like a guard of honour, on either side of her path to the car, hating her with their eyes in a dead silence that was far more menacing than shouts or insults. The chauffeur was ready with the door open; she slid in quite unconcernedly and drove off in an aura of expensive perfume. Similarly at the hairdresser. The majority of these had closed down for the Duration, and those still in business did so on materials smuggled to them by the crews off German-controlled French ships. As there were no telephones enabling her to do so, Ginger Lou usually sent a note by her chauffeur, commanding, not asking, for an appointment. If anyone else had booked that particular time, it was just too bad. She was also most exacting and pernickety in her requirements, and took up twice the time of an ordinary client. She paid only the usual fee, nonetheless.

The Liberation came at last, and with her lover on his way to internment in England, Ginger Lou very wisely went to ground, so thoroughly that those who were aching to get their hands on her feared that she might somehow have got away.

Whoever was hiding her must have been a very stalwart friend, or was being paid very well, for had that person been detected he or she would have had a really rough handling.

Understandably, Giner Lou had generated more hatred than all the other silly young Jerry bags put together. Others had been seen to accept chocolates, soap, cigarettes and nylons from their boyfriends, and this had annoyed many people, but she had assumed the role of a member of the Master Race with true Germanic thoroughness, and Islanders from every walk of life would cheerfully have killed her.

Before the War she had been a patient of mine (usually non-paying, I might add) and many people knew it, so that at this period I was approached several times: "You get about more than most people, doctor. Have you seen any sign of Ginger Lou?"

Whether such a situation would have been covered by my Hippocratic oath was never put to the test, for I was genuinely able to lay my hand on my heart and swear that I had not seen hide nor hair of her. Until one beautiful fine day when the Liberation was more than a fortnight old, and I was paying a visit in Plaisance Road, St Clement. Suddenly I heard something which sounded remarkably like a pack of hounds in full cry.

Ginger Lou, tempted no doubt by the gorgeous weather and perhaps thinking that the hue and cry had died down, had decided, as there seemed to be very few people about, to take the air in Howard Davis Park. Unhappily for herself, she could not resist dressing up for the occasion, and in a smart day frock, with a silver fox cape on her shoulders (part of the loot), she stood out like a sore thumb.

She was noticed at once, and a second later identified. Where a minute previously there appeared to be only two or three pensioners in the park, people seemed to spring out of the ground in all directions, and the hunt was on. More people, hearing the hullabaloo, came running into the park from the nearby streets and joined the pack.

Ginger Lou, twisting and turning to avoid the crowd, took refuge in a shrubbery, but was soon flushed from there and made for the rosebeds. Hands grabbed at her clothes but she tore herself away and rose thorns completed the havoc to her toilette. By the time she was caught she was almost naked. The rosebushes were festooned with tufts of fur, and looked like the scene of the plucking of a number of grey and black chickens. As no tar was available, someone produced a tin of sump oil, and after this was poured over her, she was rolled in the dusty soil. Finally she broke away, too slippery to hold, and went streaking down the passageway by St Luke's Church, into Plaisance Road where she sheltered in the porch of a house opposite. The occupants opened the door and, seeing what was outside, closed it hurriedly. In the meantime the police arrived, and having sent for a taxi, stood guard before the porch to hold off the crowd.

The taxi eventually drove up and the driver, after one look at his prospective fare, said: "Not bloody likely, not on my cushions!"

However, the police, after begging an armful of newspapers, covered everything that might be soiled and helped her in. Then they took her, for her own safety, to the prison. There she was presumably cleaned up, for a short time afterwards she appeared before the court, who ruled that she be given ten pounds and deposited on the quay (at Weymouth, I think) with a heavy penalty against attempting to enter the Island ever again.

Another of these illicit love affairs at least had a happy ending. Before the Occupation I had from time to time, while in one of the country parishes, seen an outstandingly beautiful girl, usually going to or coming from the village shop. The shopkeeper was one of my patients, and one day I happened to call just as the girl was leaving. I enquired who she was. I was told that she was known thereabouts as Lovely Laura, that she was an orphan and that she kept house for her grandfather. I was also told, with an acid twist of the mouth, that she was "stuck-up" and that although all the local boys had at one time or another made a pass at her, she would have none of them.

Some time later, when the Occupation was well under way, I came across her in the lanes, walking with a handsome young German officer. They made a strikingly good-looking pair, he well over six feet, she tall too, holding herself and walking as duchesses are supposed to do, but so seldom seem to.

She was not in the slightest self-conscious, and gave me a pleasant friendly smile as I cycled past.

Thereafter, I met her several times, sometimes alone, more often with him; she always smiled pleasantly and he saluted.

This went on for I should think the best part of a year and suddenly I never saw him again. I imagine he was recalled to the fighting line.

Some time later, I had occasion to visit my shopkeeper patient again, and was scarcely through the door before she, evidently remembering my previous interest, said: "Have you heard that Lovely Laura is in the family way?" Sniff. "So much for her airs and graces." Sniff.

Later still, I saw Laura again leaving the shop. She was well advanced in pregnancy, but carrying herself as gracefully as ever, smiling at people as she passed them, but not always getting a smile in return. She must have had her confinement at home, or in a nursing home, for she certainly never came to us at the JMH. I did not see her for a long time until early one sunny evening, I came across her walking in the lanes with a fine baby on her hip. Perambulators were not to be had, and this was the only way she could take her baby for an airing.

I got off my bike and congratulated her on her magnificent boy. It was unmistakably a boy, happy looking and well cared for. She herself looked unworried and serene, and told me that her grandfather had died, but that she continued to live in the house.

Soon after this, the Occupation came to an end and still she remained in her house, apparently happy and contented, with her baby. I often wondered what had happened to her lover.

That was the last time I saw her, but about a year later I heard that the young man, in mufti this time, had turned up suddenly after his period of internment, married her before a Catholic priest in Jersey, put up the house for sale, and whisked her off to Germany.

This was a nine-days' wonder in the vicinity, but naturally, as she had no relations and no real friends, nobody has had news of her since.

In a number of instances groups of girls, perhaps three or four, took over or were given by the Germans, evacuated houses, where they lived and kept open house for the military.

These girls often had jobs with the army, as cleaners, waitresses, etc, and the houses were not official brothels, in any sense of the term, but were usually maintained and patronised by particular units. One downstair room was a kind of bar where lemonade and coffee (both ersatz) were dispensed, and men requiring something stronger brought their own bottles.

At one of these houses, a girl called Louise graduated from

the universal to the particular, and reserved herself for a powerful-looking sergeant who became her especial protector. She was a pretty young thing with red hair, always neat and smart; he was about 45 or more, and was crazy about her.

When she became pregnant he gave her a sum of money to book a bed at the Millbrook nursing home, in case he received marching orders before her confinement. The sergeant was said to be heavily involved in the black market, trading with civilians in goods and petrol stolen from German stores. He was reputed to run the house out of his own pocket, and certainly money was no difficulty there. What he had feared was exactly what occurred. Not only he, but his whole unit, were whisked off without any notice to speak of, and the house left deserted except for the four girls, who must have had some funds for they continued to run the house as before, although not on the same lavish scale. One night some short time later, Louise awoke during the small hours with labour pains, but as the girls had not curfew passes and no one any more to escort or vouch for them, they decided to wait for daylight. But the pains became stronger very rapidly and, frightened out of their wits by now, two of the girls decided to walk with her to the home, which was not far away.

It was a fearful night, blustery and raining stair rods, and the girls were already soaked through. Stumbling up the drive, in the dark, Louise realised that she would never make it and, stopping in a squatting position, she gave birth to the baby, which fell in the road. One of the girls ran on to the Home, and after some delay attracted the notice of the night sister, who ran out, separated the baby, and wrapped it up; then the whole party walked up to the Home together.

As it happened, next morning I called at the home on my normal round, but rather earlier than usual, to find the baby better than one had any right to expect. At first it had been very blue and shocked, due both to its precipitate contact with the road, and exposure in the pouring rain. After a hot bath, however, it had begun to pick up, and in a few days showed little sign of its unceremonious entry into this world; except for some facial bruises.

The mother too made a quick and uninterrupted recovery,

but her traumatic experience had a very sobering effect upon her. Up to then she had been, to say the least, flighty, but, from the nursing home she contacted her parents, who took in her and the baby.

The baby was a beautiful blond boy, and Louise's sister, who was older by about fifteen years and childless, wanted to adopt him. This she did, with complete success, and the child, now a British Army sergeant currently serving in Germany, is married with two children of his own.

Louise herself caught the eye of a steady lad who came over with the liberating forces, married her, and took her to live in Worcestershire.

CHAPTER 7

With their famous efficiency but total lack of imagination, it was not until towards the end of 1941 that the High Command began to take notice of the needs of the troops; and decided to install an official brothel. Had they really done their homework properly, they would have realised that there was considerable enthusiastic competition from local amateur talent. But they quite overlooked this, with the result that the Hotel Victor Hugo was requisitioned and fitted up as a brothel, to take a considerable staff of French girls imported from Normandy. "Girls" was a euphemism, because of the forty or so who arrived, none were less than thirty and the majority were fifty or more.

Feelers were put out for a doctor to act as Medical Officer to the establishment, whose duty it would be to examine the girls weekly; one doctor who volunteered was so teased by his colleagues that he hastily withdrew his offer. The Germans then ordered us to select an MO by ballot, and we accordingly met one evening and, amidst a great many ribald jokes, folded blank papers were put in a hat. Only one paper, however, was inscribed and several obscene suggestions as to what should be written upon it, were put forward. I leave to the imagination what these might have been. One was "Der Herr Doktor", but mine of "Der Whore Doktor" was finally chosen. This was one of the least obscene.

Only one practitioner failed to turn up, and as we could not wait indefinitely, the draw took place. One by one the papers were taken out of the hat and we all unfolded them simultaneously, having left in the hat the paper of the missing member. Every single member attending had drawn a blank, and the inscribed paper fell to him. It was very difficult to persuade the missing member that the draw was bone fide. In fact he roundly accused us of cheating, and flatly refused to take up his duties. Finally, the President of the Jersey Medical Society wrote to the authorities explaining our point of view, and to everyone's surprise they nominated a young German military doctor to the post.

Every day, or at least when the weather allowed, the 'girls' were taken for a walk, two by two, like a schoolgirls' crocodile, except that they were not dewy fresh young things. They looked what they were, a dismal line of pathetic retreads, raddled and dyed, who had reached the bottom rung of their professional ladder—and knew it. They were always led by Madame, a grim lady, tightly corseted, with a powerful face, a large nose and a formidable bust. She strode along like a Sergeant Major, and obviously kept the girls under an iron discipline. Why they needed so much exercise I could never make out, but I had a shrewd suspicion that their intramural activities were not as strenuous as their sponsors had hoped, or perhaps they went out to exhibit their wares to troops they encountered on the road. Whatever it was, the project turned out to be a complete failure. There was no sign of any pawing and snorting on the part of the soldiers they encountered; rather, there were pitying or embarrassed looks, and some of the very young recruits seemed too scared even to glance their way.

The scheme hung on for more than a year, until even the authorities recognised that it was not fulfilling a need, and decided to return the girls to France. One foggy day, they were put, all together, on a small coaster commanded by a Dutch skipper. Somewhere near Corbière it hit a rock and went down in minutes, with the loss of almost all on board. Thereafter, those of us who travelled the Island within sight of the coast, would see the girls' bodies floating offshore, sometimes several together. What caught the eye was often their long peroxide hair floating behind them, and in a peculiar way it should have been funny, but actually it was infinitely pathetic and saddening.

In the early days of the Occupation, seasoned veterans from the various fronts, here on duty for limited periods as a kind of rest cure from the rigours of the fighting line, brought a number of diseases with them. Infective gingivitis—trench mouth—was the first and most common, followed by ascaris—the itch—an infection by tiny mites which burrowed into the skin between the fingers and also bends of elbows and knees. Predictably common, also, were the two venereal diseases—syphilis and gonorrhoea. All these spread rapidly amongst those civilians who had much to do with the troops, and became so prevalent that special clinics had to be set up and, at one stage, in-patient treatment resorted to.

I should here interpolate that all these infections were much worse than they would have been under ordinary conditions. Soap and hot water—a great help against ascaris—were in short supply, as well as all sorts of disinfectant. Also we had no access to modern sulphonamides, and later penicillin, which were then sovereign in the treatment of VD.

Local doctors were not encouraged to attend the troops for any kind of illness, but they were categorically forbidden to treat officer or man for venereal disease (although very many soldiers tried to get into our surgeries).

This, we found, was because those so infected, and reported by their own Medical Officers, were despatched at once to the Russian front, where a bullet would be more than likely to solve their messy problems.

One or two of our doctors, however, attended a number of them, whether for some important consideration or not, I cannot say, and were not detected. I treated two myself, I must confess. One was a young Austrian doctor who ought to have known better, but he had been extremely helpful during the mass deportation, and several of my patients, as well as myself, had reason to be very grateful to him.

I asked why he had not treated himself, as I presumed that the German Medical Service would have access to any quantity of sulphonamides, but he explained that although he saw and prescribed for VD cases, the tablets themselves were handed out directly to the patient by one of the top-ranking doctors, who kept them under lock and key.

As I have explained, the type of sulphonamides which we were able to get were old-fashioned and probably stale, and I pointed this out to him, but he was game to try and started the course. I suggested he should attempt to get a crew member from one of the French cargo ships to buy him some on the black market—at a price—and this he was eager to do, although he insisted on starting with the local drug at once. The infection began to respond, although very slowly, but he himself began to look awful. His colour became a dullish grey, his hair lost its gloss and texture and he shed weight alarmingly, because he always felt sick. However, he carried on manfully, and whenever he visited me he managed a sickly, rueful grin. Why his colleagues never asked the reason for the changes in his appearance, I cannot imagine, but he told me they never did.

At last his touching faith in the French black market was justified and the tablets arrived. I must confess that my own faith was not as strong, and even when I saw them I was enough of a cynic to think that they might turn out to be soda mints after all, or something of the sort. Inevitably, the black market is such an underhand business that once your money is paid, you have no redress if the goods are not up to specification.

However, they proved to be the real thing, and in less than two weeks my patient appeared to be completely cured, and was in seventh heaven. He was very anxious to give me all sorts of things, which in another context I would have been delighted to accept, but I thanked him for his help in my past difficulties and said I would be grateful for his assistance in any such future circumstances.

He brought me a box of a dozen tablets of French soap, which reeked of the Rue St Honore, and I felt that I could take these without prejudice.

Very soon after this, I saw him no more. He had probably been sent off to some active front, and I wondered whether his superiors had smelt a rat. I doubt if he was spotted visiting my surgery, for after the first time he always came after dark and after hours, but it may be that they had noticed his changed appearance, despite his belief to the contrary and put two and two together.

My second transgression was a young Italian, a mere boy, who turned up at my surgery late one evening suffering from gonorrhoea. I had just got up to show him out, with an abrupt refusal, when with tears in his eyes be begged me to treat him.

His English was so good, that I asked him where he had acquired it; he told me he had been born in the Rhondda Valley South Wales, and had lived there until he was fifteen. His father had made his pile from an ice cream or soft drinks parlour, and retired with the last few of a long family to Italy. The older ones were married and still living in Wales. I could scarcely refuse a fellow countryman.

He had been conscripted into the Italian army and ended up in Jersey somehow, but all his sympathy was with the British side, especially as he had never wanted to follow his parents to Italy in the first place. Also the Hitler-Mussolini pact was beginning to wear rather thin and the Germans treated all Italians like dirt. The upshot was that I put him on to the stuff we had available, and more by good luck than judgement he was very shortly cured.

Almost at the same time he received marching orders for France, and very soon after this Italy threw in the sponge. I never heard what happened to him, but before he departed he left a note asking me to be outside a house in a turning off Queen's Road at 6p.m. on a certain evening. I drove up, and had hardly put on the brake when a dark object shot out of the hedge and started rolling down the slope. No word, no sound.

I jumped out of the car, stopped what proved to be little barrel, and in one movement heaved it onto the front seat, without being seen by anyone. I found it to contain five gallons of Italian vermouth—of which I am not fond, but which

I kept nonetheless; a time came when I was not so choosy, and was glad to have it to enliven the home-made gin I was then producing.

Later in the year, thousands of foreign workers arrived, many from Middle Europe but also a large body of Spaniards. This was the first time we had seen such miserable wretched creatures at close quarters thin, hungry and poorly clad. Whenever they were not under the eye of their oppressors, they would beg pitifully for a crust of bread, and I learned that a very debilitating form of diarrhoea was rife among them.

The Spaniards were enclosed in a large area on what was then the Jersey Racecourse at Le Quennevais. This was in effect a pen surrounded by an eight-strand fence of barbed wire sketchily patrolled by guards. It contained no building at all, except a small hut which might have held ten men at the most. The remaining five hundred slept under the sky in all weathers.

So desperate were those men that many would try to break out each night and foraged the Island for food. Some begged, some stole and some found something to eat in the fields. On Sunday, their rest day, they could be seen combing the fields for rogue potatoes—those missed at harvest, which had started to sprout in the ground. The Germans seemed to pay them little heed, knowing I suppose that they would have to report back for work next day.

Some of them covered very big distances, and a friend of mine found three in a field at Grouville—at least ten miles from their camp.

Being a fluent Spanish speaker, my friend chatted for a while and finally took them home, where his wife gave them a square meal out of the family's meagre rations.

The three labourers proved to be a doctor, a dentist and a self-employed electrical engineer, who had unfortunately backed the wrong horse in the Spanish civil war. When the defeated side was in headlong retreat all over Spain, these men were part of a force of ten thousand soldiers in danger of being trapped by Franco's men near Andorra. Soon after crossing the frontier, they were met by French forces and, under escort, taken to a large expanse of barren moorland in the vicinity. Here they were given to understand that they would be interned, and a ridiculously inadequate number of tents were erected for them. An area of land about a mile square was enclosed with a strong barbed wire barricade, and patrolled by guards.

There was no water, no lavatory facilities and almost no shelter. Most of the men slept in the open, and at that time of year without too much complaining; but the enemy was boredom, with nothing whatever to do, day in, day out.

Some rough food was provided, water tankers were brought in, and various tools issued so they could dig latrines and ditches to take off the surplus water when it rained. In fact, they said: "We were like ducks in a pen, except that ducks had feathers, and we had only the very threadbare clothes we stood up in."

Then typhoid broke out and "dead" lorries became an everyday sight. The population of the camp began to dwindle rapidly, and at the end of eighteen months it stood at around two thousand. Those that were left were presumably now immune to every kind of infection and to every vagary of the weather.

With the connivance of the guards, sympathisers among the local population threw over the fence strips of old carpeting, sacks, bundles of old clothes and food, but even so the condition of the prisoners was a parlous one. They were skeleton-thin, dressed like scarecrows, and those who survived were men between twenty-five and forty-five. The youngsters and the older groups were almost all dead.

Then, with the fall of France came the Germans, and before the winter of 1940 descended upon them with all its severity, they were "liberated". The two thousand were split up into four equal groups and each group driven away in buses requisitioned from the French. None knew where the others had gone, and they did not meet up again.

At first they were comparatively well treated and well fed. This was not an entirely altruistic policy for, after all, the

Germans could get no sort of useful work out of a gang of skeletons. As they improved in health, they were put on to jobs of a labouring type—repairing bombed roads, bridges etc—and these occupied them for about two years.

Towards the end of this time, presumably because the supply of food throughout occupied territory was beginning to run low, their conditions again worsened considerably, and they were no longer capable of the very heavy work required of them. As a result, sometime during the summer of 1942, what remained of the group was shipped to Jersey.

There were now only about five hundred prisoners. When they first arrived the weather was mild and dry, but Le Quennevais is the bleakest part of the Island at all times and, although not as cold as the moorland at the foot of the Pyrenees, wet and very windy.

Scattered over the area was a quantity of old corrugated iron sheets—remnants of some derelict sheds—and those lucky enough to obtain one could sleep fairly dry in a shallow ditch scooped out of the sandy soil, with the iron pulled over them like a lid.

Water came from a standpipe at one end of the compound, but as there was very little pressure behind it only a very small stream flowed from the tap.

Their work in Jersey was the unloading of boats in the harbour, chiefly those carrying cement. Every morning, they were marched the five miles into St Helier, and after the days work marched back. On the homeward journey, they were covered from head to foot with cement dust—hair, eyebrows, eyelashes, lips and limbs.

The prisoners included several doctors, who were most insistent that the dust should be washed off each night as a precaution against cement dermatitis.

This was a major undertaking, with one small trickle of water from the standpipe, and men had to queue up until as late as 3am for their turn to wash off. Heavy rain was a blessing, and men stood in it, stark naked, rubbing themselves down with their hands.

In spite of this, many of them developed dermatitis which, for want of adequate treatment, turned into an unsightly and distressing wet eczema but were expected to continue working nevertheless.

Deaths among the group were fairly frequent, most commonly from chest complaints, and probably tuberculosis, but the vast majority survived the occupation, although in poor shape.

The three I had met continued to visit and be fed by my friends, until the latter went to Germany in the compulsory deportation of British subjects. After the War, the three got in touch with their benefactors and with each other. Two are still alive: one a highly successful dentist in Paris, the second a thriving general practitioner married to a French wife and living in Toulouse. The third, after somehow or other getting a pardon, joined his wife and family in Murcia where he died some years ago.

Nineteen forty-three started with heavy snow. Under the impact of heavy tanks and lorries, the roads were in a shocking condition, and there were deep potholes which filled with water during the thaw. Whether on foot or bicycle, our clothes were drenched with muddy slush thrown up by vehicles which refused to reduce speed.

Things like this, although they would be unimportant in ordinary conditions, made everyone edgy, and increasingly fed up with the Germans. They too were losing patience and perspective.

For instance, during a house-search some Germans found a revolver—but so rusted up by years of neglect that it could not possibly fire the aged ammunition found with it. Nevertheless it led to the arrest of its owner. He had never seen it before, and thought it might have belonged to his deceased father, who owned the house previously. Anyway, he received a sentence of five years in a German-run prison in France.

Because troops were somehow hearing too much adverse news from civilian sources, a last desperate attempt was made to call in all radio sets not already declared. Complete immunity was promised and no questions asked of those who did so, by a certain date. A few nervous ones complied, but most of us did not, and merely redoubled our precautions against leaks. The comparative nonsuccess of the bribe brought them over on another tack, and a series of blood-curdling threats were made against anyone caught with a radio in the future.

The last order produced a spate of anonymous telephone calls to German Headquarters and, for the first time, leaflets protesting against the order were printed and distributed Island-wide.

As a counter-measure, the Germans imprisoned ten leading citizens as hostages, whom they threatened to keep in custody until the perpetrator confessed.

The ten remained incarcerated for one week, when the man responsible, a Mr Gallichan, gave himself up. He received a five-year sentence, and his brother, who had assisted, one year.

The Germans were having problems of a different sort. Petrol was getting tight, and many officers of the middle grade could be seen riding bicycles—an unprecedented event.

A number of soldiers were arrested for stealing petrol from Army dumps and selling it to farmers, or exchanging it for produce. The farmers all received heavy sentences, but nothing was heard about the soldiers—they were just not seen again.

A further group of Russians arrived about this time. If possible, these were in a more pitiable state than the last lot. Several were found dead on the boat, when she docked, and many more died within days of arrival. Typhus was suspected and the bodies were all buried in quicklime.

As a result, a delousing station was installed and this did a brisk trade among the foreign nationals. In spite of this, the German Medical Forces were uneasily aware of the possibility of a mass Island infection, and showed a good deal more interest in their sick labourers than formerly.

The Russians had borne a great deal of hardship and ill-treatment, but were now in a desperate and truculent mood. Several instances occurred where they turned on their guards and one, who struck a soldier, was killed by him with a spade.

On the five mile road, an altercation with members of the Todt organisation supervising the work, resulted in the

Germans turning a machine gun on the Russians, and killing about thirty of them.

During this time, when relations between the foreign workers and their tormentors were more than usually acrimonious, I had a telephone call, one Sunday afternoon, from a great friend, a dental surgeon named Edward Ross.

He lived about six doors away from me in the town, and asked if I would like to take tea that afternoon with him and his wife. They were expecting a couple of Russians who had broken out from the camp on the Route d'Orange, and run into Ross at St Brelades.

They proved to be two foreign workers who were in the habit of crawling out of camp by night and on Sundays, but who were back in time to report for duty each morning.

When I arrived I saw two husky young men of middle height, spare, alert, blue-eyed and with ordinary fair hair. In other words, neither with any sort of distinguishing feature by which he would be recognised. I thought at the time that, if there were going to be any survivors, these two would be among them. One was á Pole and the other some sort of middle European, but for the purposes of forced labour, all were labelled Russian.

They were smiling, intelligent and very anxious to talk, but not until with deprecatory gestures they had applied themselves to the all too scanty food provided. This they did with a wolfish concentration that was almost terrifying.

As we had no language in common, we had to do the best we could with dumb show, pencil and paper, an atlas and the odd word in English, French or German.

Though both Ross and I had our radios, there were other snippets of information brought over by small bodies of workers, who were constantly being imported to Jersey from all over Europe. This was circulated by the prisoner grapevine and, although some of it was necessarily hearsay, most of it bore the ring of truth and all of it was encouraging.

But what was electrifying was the cold hate the two young men showed in response to the studied brutality of the Germans. (Possibly the fact that things were not going too happily on the Russian front, and annoyance with interference by the Red Cross, intensified the German's cruelty.)

There were tales of prisoners hung by their thumbs, or by their necks, with their toes just touching the ground. Others carrying heavy packs on their shoulders were forced at bayonet point to run till they dropped. Less imaginative, though equally brutal, was bludgeoning with heavy bone-breaking sticks.

Another torture, more refined, but equally fiendish in its way, occurred at mealtimes. One of the several Russian camps contained a round ornamental goldfish pond, which had been built on what was intended to be a garden. It now contained about two feet of water and, at the bottom, a thick black layer of partially rotted fallen leaves. At mealtimes the guards would come from the cookhouse staggering under the weight of an enormous cauldron of boiled potatoes, the staple diet of the prisoners, who would come running up, frantic for any food. But, instead of leaving it in the cauldron, or even tipping it on the concrete surround, the guards emptied it into the pond, and the prisoners were forced to scrabble about in the dirty water for what they could get.

Many, though not all, Germans thought this very amusing, and there was always a good congregation to see the Russians fed.

The two men we were talking to hated them more for this last indignity than for any of their more cruel practices, and the way their faces turned white with pent-up anger as they related this story made me sorry for any German who fell into their hands after the War.

After a long talk, during which Mrs Ross brought along every oddment of food she could lay her hands on, which was cleared up with the speed and precision of a pair of Hoovers, the guests slipped out of the house by the garden door. The Rosses decided to go for a bicycle ride, taking Mac, their black labrador, with them. Unknown to us the two workers had been followed to the house, and observed leaving. Presumably the Rosses were also tailed, because at St Brelades, on the Route d'Orange, they were challenged at the point where the perimeter of the camp impinges on the road.

I only heard the facts later: apparently Ross'was grabbed by a guard who, for his pains, was clouted over the head with a heavy bag and kicked on the shins by Mrs Ross. He then released Ross and grabbed his wife; Ross was now free to go into the attack and somewhere along the line Mac bit the guard. With the arrival of reinforcements, the Rosses and their bicycles were bundled into a car and taken off to the prison. Mac escaped.

Not knowing any of this, I had gone to bed unsuspecting and got up as usual to do my chores and see what was going on at the JMH.

I had arranged to give a dental anesthetic for Ross, and arrived just before 9am to be met by an ecstatic Mac and a bewildered receptionist, who had not been able to gain admittance, despite frequent attacks on the bell. I went round to the garden entrance in Apsley Road, found the usually locked door open, and saw that the two bicycles were missing from the shed.

We then realised what had almost certainly happened, and I telephoned the prison, where our fears were confirmed. The charge against them was "consorting with and assisting prisoners of war." I thought at once that if they were on to Ross, they would also be on to me, and all that day I was expecting each minute to be taken away; but nothing occurred and I went to bed as usual. Having had the whole day to get used to the idea of probable arrest, and concluding that there was nothing to be done about it anyway, I went off to sleep at once, as is my usual habit.

At about 4am I was awakened by a furious hammering at the front door and came out of my bedroom just in time to grab Mrs Ozouf who was already halfway down the second flight of stairs, on her way to answer the bell. Soundlessly I pushed her back to her own room, and whispered that I would explain later.

The window of the small room overlooking the front door, but two storeys up, was half open and, cautiously poking my head over the sill, I made out three soldiers below, two on the pavement and the other again addressing the door with the butt of his rifle.

Mrs Ozouf and I stood there palpitating, for there is

something very frightening about being awakened suddenly, in such a fashion, at that time of the night, but I was determined not to open up or show myself, unless they battered down the door.

As there was still no response, or sound of life within the house, the three held a muttered consultation, and while doing so there was a shout of alarm from somewhere at the Snow Hill end of Bath Street, or its vicinity. In the still of the night the shout was carried very clearly and we, in the house, heard it quite plainly. The three hurried off, and we were left at peace for the time being at any rate.

Mrs Ozouf already knew what had happened to the Rosses, and was very upset about it, but I finally persuaded her to go to bed and I did the same. I read for a short time, then put out the light and settled down to thinking what I should do next morning.

I decided that if they did not come back for me before I finished my breakfast, I would go off on my round as usual, and, having made that decision, dropped off to sleep.

Mrs Ozouf, long-faced and suspiciously red-eyed, brought my breakfast, telling me as she poured out my disgusting sugar-beet tea, that she had not had another wink of sleep. She certainly looked like it.

On leaving I gave her my list of calls as usual, telling her not to recall me if the Germans came, but to say that I would be at the surgery at 2.30pm.

On my return not a thing had happened, but every time the doorbell rang to announce another patient, I thought the Germans had come. However, nothing transpired and I went off on my evening round, during which I called on Mama-in-law and told her about the night's happenings.

She was very upset, but I cheered her up by explaining that the prisons were so full that people sentenced weeks before were still waiting for the summons to serve their term. This I genuinely believed to be the explanation of what had occurred, and subsequent events proved me to be right. With so many on the waiting list, they were obviously not going to come round again for someone not available at the first time of asking. Naturally, I kept my fingers tightly crossed for some days, but I never heard any more about the incident.

In the autumn of 1943, German discipline showed increasing laxity. The new replacements coming into the Island were either very young, or quite old, and none of them appeared properly trained.

Robberies, both by the forces and the Islanders, were rife, and the contents of unoccupied houses were looted wholesale. Not only unoccupied houses either, and householders attempting to protect their property were met with extreme violence by the looters.

An elderly man, a Mr Le Gresly of St Peter, was stabbed to death when he disturbed two intruders, and his sister was badly injured.

On the other hand, the amount of paperwork increased more than ever. The authorities fussed about the German language being compulsorily taught in the schools, and demanded from the Constables lists of people able to work but unemployed, and also lists of various kinds of undesirables.

A further and third, if not fourth, last chance of surrendering wireless sets was announced. This time a threat of long-term imprisonment, or even death, was made, but as those who had retained their sets thus far were *ex officio*, hard-liners, the response was minimal.

One bright spot was provided by a French plane, damaged on a flight over Guernsey, and having to make a forced landing near Dielament in Trinity parish. The very young pilot had three quarters of an hour before the arrival of any Germans, during which he was able to burn all his papers and to destroy any mechanism that was important. He laughed and chatted with the locals and told them that things were going very well for England. As he was driven away under arrest, he gave the V sign, without any protest from his captors.

This item of news flashed around the Island like wildfire and gave everyone's morale a lift at a rather depressing finish to the year.

CHAPTER 8

Having dealt with some of the facets of medical practice as they impinge on particular aspects of the Occupation, I will now turn to the effect of the Occupation on practice of a more general type.

One of my sad duties during the first few days was to attend three funerals, on three successive days. They were all elderly men who had retired to Jersey and, except for daily help, lived alone.

One aged nearly eighty had, the winter before, given me a worrying time pulling him through a bad bout of pneumonia, complicated by congestive heart failure, and in those pre-penicillin days I felt rather proud when I had him on his feet again. He had been cared for devotedly by his daughter-in-law, herself a first-class teaching hospital sister; but she had been forced to leave the Island because she had a serving husband and two children on the mainland.

By this time he had made a complete recovery, and was able to do shopping, and get about quite well, but I think he knew in his heart that he was unlikely to outlast the Occupation with all its discomforts, and that the gas oven was an easy way out.

He was a fine old man, but of a generation when men were not very good about the house and, although I was shocked, I could very easily see his point of view.

The second was a Jew, a charming man whose wife I had looked after until her death less than a month before. They had been a devoted couple, childless but very happy in their beautiful home, surrounded by all the things that money and culture could provide. After her death he had lost his grip, and although he could easily have joined the evacuation, did not seem to want to leave the place where he had been so happy.

He now had obviously come to the conclusion that he could no longer tolerate a life of waiting for that dreaded knock on the door, the order of deportation, and the indignity, when stripped even of all his clothes, of being herded into the gas ovens in distant Germany.

There were bottles and bottles of pain-killers and sleeping tablets, left behind by his wife. He took enough to make certain that he would never wake again.

The third had been a high-ranking officer in the Indian Army, and was sufficiently in touch with affairs to realise that the Empire of the British Raj was already showing signs of tottering. The taking of even such a small piece of British soil as Jersey was the last straw, and the sight of German officers swaggering through its streets was too much for his proud old spirit. It was completely in character that he should end his life with a bullet in the brain.

At each of the funerals there were, pathetically, only two mourners—myself and a lawyer—but at the funeral of the soldier an elderly man who was just about to leave the churchyard, turned back and followed the cortege into the church for the short service.

When it was over, I shook him by the hand and asked if by any chance he was a friend.

"No," he replied. "I know him only by name, but on the spur of the moment I thought I would join you. Only two mourners seemed such a shabby send-off, and it occurred to me that I might perhaps represent a number of people who were prevented from coming."

I gave him a lift back to Beaumont. He had walked out on his weekly pilgrimage to the grave of his wife, at St Brelade's churchyard.

The next problem was a sharp outbreak of diphtheria, imported with the German troops, which rapidly used up all our small store of anti-toxin, and then left us defenceless. All hospitals were closed to visitors, and notices put up urging the public to avoid any kind of gathering and places of entertainment.

One evening, just as I was about to leave the surgery, came a call for Beaumont, to a small boy who had had a sore throat for several days. In my bones I knew what I was going to find, and went at once. One look at the child's face was enough to tell me that there was no point in wasting our last tiny bit of anti-toxin. That we had to keep for cases which might be saved.

The mother had thought it was "just a sore throat" and was hovering in the background.

I knew that there was absolutely nothing to be done, for death was already in the child's face, and his pulse was almost undetectable. But for the mother's sake an examination had to be seen to be made, and as I looked down the child's throat and opened my own mouth wide to say "ah", he coughed straight into it.

I gargled immediately with water and spat it out, advised the other to send at once for her husband, and did my best to tell her how desperate matters were. She seemed unable, or more possibly, did not want to believe me, but the child a lovely boy of seven died two hours later.

When I got home I rang up Dr McKinstry to ask how we stood for anti-toxin, and he just said briefly: "Used it all up this afternoon. You're on your own now, baby." Fortunately I did not tell him why I had rung.

Next day I called my lawyer, and made a will. Never having been inoculated, it was very unlikely that I would fail to catch such a virulent form of the disease.

But as day followed day, and I still continued to enjoy my usual excellent health, I finally came to the conclusion that my guardian angel was watching over me. More likely I was healthy, and most important of all, I had acquired a passive immunity over years of doctoring.

Small quantities of inferior drugs came from France and a

species of M & B fell to my lot. I had never heard even of the make, and was very doubtful about using it, but the patient it was intended for was so gravely ill with a virulent type of pneumonia that I had to take a chance.

The patient was at the Limes nursing home, and on the third day of its use I received an urgent message that she had taken a turn for the worse.

When I arrived, I had a nasty shock, for she was a strong mauve colour and her lips very dark grey. She said she felt ghastly, but on examination her chest seemed a little better, and her heart holding its own. I concluded that the colour was due to the new drug and ordered that it be continued, but I forbade anyone to tell her how terrible she looked, or to give her a mirror. After four more days her chest was much clearer, and I decided to discontinue the M & B and leave the rest to nature, as since it seemed hardly possible that anything which behaved so peculiarly could fail eventually to have a generalised toxic effect.

The colour took about a fortnight to disappear, and she had quite a stormy convalescence, but with no other complication finally made a complete recovery, to live to be more than eighty.

The Limes was run by a Catholic sisterhood headed by Mêre Marie Madeleine, the Mother Superior. She was a stocky little woman of great dignity, with a stern face and a most endearing twinkle in her eye. One of her infrequent smiles was worth twenty from anyone else, and her laugh was young and carefree.

She kept a wireless set, well hidden—she and her God only knew where—and throughout the Occupation listened to the French news regularly. Very wisely only a very small circle was privileged to hear the news from her lips, and I was lucky to be one of them.

I saw her on one occasion confront a German officer, who had brought in his Jerry bag, from a bungled abortion, really very ill. She was infected up to the eyes, and I had refused to take her into JMH on the realistic grounds that she was a frightful risk to all the other mothers in the hospital.

To give the poor lad his due—he couldn't have been more

than twenty-one or two—he was thoroughly frightened, and therefore apt to throw his weight about.

He stamped into the hall and then into the Mother Superior's office, where she was calmly writing at her desk.

Before she had time to open her mouth, he started shouting orders and threats, in his atrocious French, but she just got to her feet, and without a word walked forward and confronted him face to face—hers very stern. She uttered not a word, but stood looking at him as he towered over her.

Gradually his abuse died down, and he too was silent. Then holding him firmly with her eye, she spoke: "I will take this girl in, not because of your abuse or threats, for which God will doubtless forgive you, but because she is ill and in pain, and to succour such a one, this establishment was founded."

She rang a bell and he metaphorically tiptoed out of her presence.

On one occasion an old lady patient was dying. She said to me: "I would go happily if I could only have one cup of strong real tea. This sugar-beet stuff has helped to kill me."

I went to the Mother Superior and made my request. Instantly she glided off, and came back with two screws of paper—one had a generous amount of tea, the other she put into my hand unopened. "You didn't think to ask her if she took sugar, I suppose," She said with a twinkle. Then she added: "Next time don't wait till they are dying. A little tea may even enable them to live, so come and ask me before it is too late."

Tea was not the only thing she dispensed. Most of the boats bringing supplies for the troops had a few Frenchmen in the crew, and these, by some means or other, found their way to the Limes, bringing little delicacies to the Reverend Mother.

Whenever I had a really ill patient whose stomach heaved at the coarse, boring food, an appeal from me brought half a stick of good French bread or a slice of tender veal, and on one occasion a delicious pink slice of Jambon de Yorke.

The Limes boasted quite a good operating theatre, where a

great deal of surgery was done, largely by the late Mr Claude Avarne, FRCS.

When an operation was over, the unconscious patient was manhandled off the table by resident staff, on a canvas carrying sheet (which had been put *in situ* before the operation commenced). This was rather rough and ready and also quite dangerous, so it was the great ambition of the Reverend Mother to install a lift. And so, after the Occupation when, at a grand party attended by everyone who loved her she was invested with the Legion d'Honneur, a subscription list was started.

Generous gifts poured in from all nationality and creed, and in a very short time a spacious lift was installed, which the Mother said was the best sort of memorial to her term of office that she could think of.

A few months after this, completely out of the blue, a tall thin nun appeared in the hall of the Limes, having walked up from the French boat. She asked to see the Mother Superior and without a word proferred a letter. The Reverend Mother opened it and read it with complete disbelief. It was from the Mother Directrice of the order, short and businesslike to the point of brutality.

In effect it said that as she had now reached a certain age, and was doubtless finding that her duties were getting beyond her (she who had every little detail of the place completely at her competent fingertips) was to hand over her papers and keys to the bearer of the letter, remain at her post for one week to train the latter in the routine of the institution, and then retire to a room (designated) on the third floor at the back.

Julienne, the concierge, gabbling with fury, informed me over the telephone about what had happened. I knew that there was nothing I could do, but I went down straightaway all the same.

The Reverend Mother was still in her office. Her white face seemed to have shrunk, and in fact her whole body seemed to have got smaller. She presented me to the new woman, who did not offer to shake hands, but bowed slightly and very stiffly. A wintry smile, which was so slight that it would not have registered on the Richter scale, flickered over her coffin-shaped face. We disliked each other on sight.

Thereafter I visited, once or twice a week, the little room where my old friend sat meditating with her hands in her lap. Often she was in tears and, when I asked her why, she said: "I ceaselessly pray God to give me grace to forgive, but somehow I can never let it into my heart. I dread meeting my maker with that sin still upon me."

On the very first of these visits, I had just entered the hall when the new woman came quickly out of the office.

"Have you come to see a patient?" she inquired tartly.

"No," I said, "I have come to see the Mother Superior."

Tight-lipped, she replied: "I am the Mother Superior." As I started for the stairs I said: "For me, and as long as she lives, Mêre Marie Madeleine is the Mother Superior of the Limes."

From then, the battle lines were drawn, and we never exchanged a word again, but her reign lasted a very short time, for she was never accepted, and she departed whence she came.

But by this time the Reverend Mother was dead—I verily believe of a broken heart. The Limes was never the same for me, and I practically ceased to send my work there.

CHAPTER 9

Although there were plenty of signs that a German occupation was imminent, it was nonetheless a shock when it actually occurred, and for some days the Islanders remained in a bemused state.

The shops were well stocked, as they always had been in normal times, but there was not an instant rush to buy. However, once people woke up to their situation there was a run on all sorts of commodities, and many people laid in stocks to the full extent of their purses and bank accounts. Like the rest, I bought as much as I could afford, but not having a wife to help me my money was not laid out as advantageously as it might have been. My godmother, long since dead, who loved an epigram (while still not actually believing it), used to say: "Anyone can have the necessities of life if only they will leave me the luxuries." I am afraid that in my purchases I was rather apt to follow this advice.

Nevertheless, I fully realised, right at the start, that the Occupation was likely to be a very long one, and that one's prospects of coming out of it in good shape, both mentally and physically, would depend on one's own efforts. My first move in this direction was entirely fortuitous and not planned in any way.

I had occasion to visit the housekeeper of a baker who had premises where the Eagle Tavern now stands. After seeing her I went into the bakehouse to report, and found her employer shovelling vast quantities of bread and rolls into the furnace. There were heaps of them lying all over the floor and, when I asked what it was all about, he replied that people were so upset and anxious about the situation that they had gone off their food and were eating less than half his usual output of bread. This had started piling up in the bakehouse and eventually left him very little room to work. "I couldn't think of any other way to get rid of it," he said, rather helplessly.

Asking him to stop burning it at once, I promised to clear the bakehouse before evening, and dashed off to my corn merchant, who supplied me with fifty strong paper sacks. The baker helped me fill them, and in a short time we had several rows of neatly tied sacks ranged along the wall.

I returned each day for further supplies, until the baker had adjusted himself to his customers' requirements, and by then I had nearly fifty full sacks.

In the meantime, Mrs Ozouf and I had got down to cutting the loaves into thick slices and stacking them on baking tins, with which we filled the gas oven. At that time we still had ample gas, and as soon as the slices were baked into bone-dry rusks they were returned to the sacks. These were securely tied and put aside in the shed, while we repeated the process over and over again. We did the same with the rolls, but these were left uncut.

The next problem was storage. This was not easy in the new, small house because absolute dryness, ventilation and protection from mice were of prime consideration. The only feasible place was the roof-space and there I drove stout nails, at intervals of two feet, on both sides of the roof tree. Here the sacks hung in two rows, side by side, to be used as required.

Most of the bread, soaked, and then mixed with any scraps available, was used to feed my four hens, but when ration bread stopped altogether, we ate the rolls, momentarily dipped in water and heated up ourselves. Even at the end of five years we could still do this. There was no fustiness or mould, and we found them surprisingly palatable. I do not suppose there was much vitamin in them but at least they were pleasant to eat and filled a gnawing void.

During the last few months of the Occupation, when many of us suffered from an intractable diarrhoea, I gave several bags away in the hope that their total lack of roughage content might stem the flow. They improved matters somewhat, but did not cure it, and we had to conclude that it was something other than the ration bread which caused the condition.

I next turned my attention to the question of fuel. At that time, we still had all the gas and electricity we could use, but it was obvious that with a lengthy occupation ahead of us such a situation could not last.

In my original house, 100 Bath Street, were about ten tons of oak trunks, cut into four-foot lengths, which I had bought from a felling project in the Vallée des Vaux about two years before. I had then paid ten shillings a ton, delivered, and little realised at the time that eventually they could be sold on the open market at twenty pounds a ton.

My very good friend, Dr Graeme Bentlif, who lived at 7 David Place, only a few doors away, was kind enough to put at my disposal a large double garage with stout doors which could be securely padlocked at night. By fixing wire netting on the inner side of the frame I made it a spacious hen house.

The communicating harness room was where I split and stored my wood, having carried it across the road, a few baulks at a time. I carried the wood each evening, just as it was getting dusk, and it took me the best part of a fortnight. Any spare time I had in daylight hours was spent digging and planting the adjoining garden with French beans, carrots, beet and salads which, in an ordinary year, would probably have done nothing at all but, as the autumn was unusually mild and open, gave a surprisingly good crop and helped me through the first winter.

During that long winter it became a routine for me to saw wood during the twilight hour or so, when it was too dark to read, and far too early to go to bed. Much later in the War, by sitting practically on the hearth I was able to read quite fairly well by firelight, which was at least as satisfactory as a candle (these rapidly became almost unprocurable anyway) or the makeshift lamps which we also tried to use.

I also took a weekly bag of logs to my mother-in-law at Beaumont, where it not only supplemented her own meagre wood ration but, being crisp and dry, enabled the ration logs, which were usually green and wet, to burn properly.

In 1941, I bought Beaupré—the house my family and I were to occupy after the War. After taking it over in 1942 I installed Albert Payne, my gardener/handyman, with his family, in the half of the house that had been restored. He and I established our own log depot. First we combed the property for dead trees and branches, which we dragged into the old press house and sawed up. Then we went around selecting trees in inconspicuous spots, which we marked for felling. We had to be extremely careful, for property owners, by strict German regulation, were forbidden to fell more than two trees a year, and then only on a written permit. But by this time I had found so many old patients who were entirely dependent on the wood ration for heating and cooking that I had to take the risk and break the law.

Much of the wood supplied on ration was quite unburnable—even having leaves on it—and a little dry wood was essential even if only one wanted to boil a kettle, much less do more complicated cooking.

I started my log round then, and kept it up throughout the Occupation, felling and splitting trees which were left to dry, as far as possible, before distribution. Fortunately Beaupré was well wooded when I took it over, and included an orchard of cider apple trees, of which nearly a half were dead, although still sound and standing.

Payne and I carried out our illegal task after dark, and always on wet, stormy nights, when patrols were less likely to be abroad and the noise of the saw drowned by the wind. The trees, cut into manageable lengths, were dragged into the press house before daylight and dealt with by Payne at his leisure behind closed doors. During the next five years we cut down and distributed nearly sixty trees, and to hide our traces dug out all the stumps by hand.

One couple who were the recipients of a regular wood supply were an elderly pair who had come to the Island from Western Australia, only a few months before the Occupation. They had lived there for forty years, but panicked at the possibility of a Japanese invasion. He was Jersey-born, and so he had fled with his wife across the world, from the frying pan into the fire. All his connections here were either dead or very old, and the couple had no one to turn to in any sort of emergency. They brought with them a very large pet monkey which they had had for a long time, and which, being childless themselves, they adored.

Realising that such things would shortly be unprocurable the wife laid in quantities of nuts and dried fruit to supplement the kind of monkey food that could be bought locally. What the creature really liked were bananas, but these very soon gave out and, getting bored with the increasing lack of variety, the monkey first became fractious and eventually downright savage. One day, quite without warning, it attacked her furiously, and I arrived to find her left hand mangled to a pulp. I am not very well up on monkeys and, although I have had to deal with many peculiar situations in my time, I was very relieved to find that the husband had enticed the monkey into a little study and locked it in.

As the husband, though reasonably fit, was over eighty, the wife refused point blank to leave him and go into hospital, so I was forced to treat her at home. In the absence of antibiotics, the hand almost inevitably became badly infected and she had a very stormy passage; but eventually it healed, leaving her with an almost useless claw.

It took a great deal of persuasion to induce her to consent to the destruction of the monkey but, after holding out for a couple of days, she was forced to admit that she herself could no longer look after it, while her husband stoutly refused even to go near it. While she was havering, the monkey had reduced the little study to shreds but, eventually, to my personal relief at any rate, it was put down.

As far as day-to-day supplies were concerned this couple were as badly placed as anyone could be. They were moderately well off, but did not have the kind of money to enter the black market, and lacked access to information which would lead them to the occasional small extra pickings available. I was able to get them a regular supply of potatoes and some vegetables at a fair price from a farmer patient, and I included them in my log round, but they spent a desperately dreary Occupation. She, I suspected, had a dash of Oriental blood in her, and as a result felt the cold terribly. They both lost weight to an alarming degree and in the final few months the husband suffered from famine oedema. She must have worn every single garment she possessed, and on her head a kind of quilted tea-cosy. At first sight one was confronted by an enormous barrel of a woman, but on closer inspection one found that her face was little bigger than your hand, and her wrists were pencil-thin.

Astonishingly enough, they both survived the Occupation and afterwards built a very small but comfortable bungalow at St Brelade. I persuaded them to name it "Samara", in view of their story.

My next move was to regularise the poultry situation. Before the Occupation I had always kept about two dozen hens, and these were still at 100 Bath Street, which remained empty. It was at once evident that I could not hope to go on feeding my hens, especially as just then my corn merchant notified me that he could guarantee supplies only for a further week. Reluctantly I had to reduce them to four only, which was as many as I could be sure of feeding and, with money having little value and likely to have less, I decided to kill them rather than sell.

So I started in on them in batches of five at a time, plucking them in an outhouse at 100 Bath Street. I brought them to my own house for dressing, and then they were steamed, with herbs and condiments, in an enormous casserole. When cooked and cool enough to handle, each one was carefully boned, leaving the skin with all the meat attached. This was rolled up into a sausage and dropped into a two-pound Kilner jar. The stock was reduced and then poured in sufficiently to cover the contents. The jars, with loose lids, were left in a cool oven overnight, when the lids were screwed down tightly and the jars left to become cold. These twenty jars kept perfectly and became my iron rations throughout the Occupation. Naturally they were used only on special occasions when, for instance, we heard something particularly exciting on the news to justify a celebration. I still have one, now forty years old, and it appears to be as good as ever.

Sugar was the next problem. I had a stock of thirty pounds of loaf sugar and, as I immediately cut out sugar on porridge, in tea and in coffee, most of this was still intact against a more pressing need later on.

Sugar-beet syrup and its byproducts, sugar-beet tea and sugar-beet coffee, were beginning to be made, but its characteristic flavour was so all-pervading that I longed for something else that did not taste of sugar beet.

The problem was solved for me in May 1941, when I was paying a professional visit to a middle-aged lady, a Miss Ahier, who lived in a solid granite house, halfway up Marais du Val, a small glen opening from the bottom of La Marquanderie Hill, St Brelades Bay.

I had often noticed the row of beehives in her garden, which she managed entirely herself, and on this occasion, panting and blowing though she was with the bronchitis for which I had been called out, she was hiving a large swarm of intimidating looking bees. Throwing back the black veil from her streaming face, she said: "Here's a lovely big swarm, the first of the season and early at that, but I've nothing to put them in except an old skep. You don't know of anyone who would like to buy them, I suppose?"

At once I made my decision, and before I had had time to consider all the implications of the transaction I was the owner of the swarm for two pounds.

I left them there in the skep, for the time being, and went off, taking with me a book on Bee Management which Miss Ahier loaned me. The same afternoon I paid a visit to G. D. Laurens, the universal hardware shop in Queen Street (alas no longer with us) and asked about hives. Yes, they had a hive—the last one—with all necessary equipment. And so, for fourteen pounds, which seemed an awful lot of money then, I drove off with everything in my car.

All my life I had been terrified of bees, having as a very

small boy put my foot into a wasps' nest while bird nesting on a hedgerow. On that occasion I must have received at least thirty stings, chiefly on my face and neck, and remember to this day not being able to open my eyes for about three days, and the beastly sensation of my head being twice its normal size.

Anyway, I had gone too far to draw back, and the next day I presented myself at Miss Ahier's house with the new hive and a brood box filled with sheets of wax foundation on frames. She had offered to transfer the bees for me and advised me to leave everything with her until they settled down.

Accordingly, a week later I called to fetch the bees in my Austin Seven, with the passenger seat removed. It was dusk, so the bee entrance could be firmly closed, and with the utmost care I lifted the hive and fitted it into the car. I had very little room for myself, and drove with the greatest circumspection to Dr Bentlif's country home at the head of the Vallée des Vaux, where I put the hive on a level site in the garden behind the house. With all the moving around, and a trip in the car, the occupants were making an awe-inspiring roar, but I quickly opened the entrance door and ran.

That summer was a very good one, warm and sunny, and the bees worked hard from morning till night. Super after super was filled with honey, until all three were full, and these were the only ones I was able to buy. Luckily, an old friend who had at one time kept bees, unearthed two more supers from a garden shed, and as Laurens still had some wax foundation I was able to add them to the hive.

In the autumn I took off four bulging supers, leaving one full of honey for use by the bees during the winter and early spring, since of course we had no sugar for making syrup, the more usual substitute for winter bee food.

I extracted in all nearly 120 pounds of honey and was forced to go around all my friends, begging for jam jars. That Christmas, jars of honey were my presents to my friends and were, as the American phrase has it, "more welcome than a powder puff at a fat man's ball".

The following spring I became more ambitious and took

my bees to the flowers. First they went to Stonewall Orchards for the apple and pear blossom and when that was over I extracted the honey immediately—twelve pounds, as smooth as face cream, with a bland, delicate flavour. Then followed a move to Summerland, Rouge Boullion, where there were hundreds of lime trees. This time I took only eight pounds, pale green in colour with the characteristic flavour of Tilleul.

Back then to Vallée des Vaux for mixed flowers—elder, hawthorn, clover, etc.—32 pounds. Finally, in early September, to Bonne Nuit for the heather—eighteen pounds. This did not approach the yield of the previous year but the summer was cold and wet, and possibly the frequent moves upset the bees. Anyway, all considered, I did extremely well and, having now acquired Beaupré, I moved them there, and there they remained.

In the later years of the Occupation, there were several cases of hives being robbed, either by German troops or possibly foreign workers. Most of this was done by lighting smudge fires of wet twigs around the hives and thus stupefying or killing the bees; the supers full of honey could then be lifted out and carried off. I am glad to say that this never happened to me.

During the winter of 1942 I made myself two new hives and, having bought up all the wax foundation left at Laurens, ended the Occupation with three flourishing stocks, to which I added a fourth after the cessation of hostilities.

But by this time I had lost all fear of bees and, especially at swarming times when they were always good-tempered, I handled them only in a hat (no veil) and without gloves.

The fourth hive proved my undoing. I had intended it for any swarm which might come out of one of my own three hives in spring 1946, and the hive was on its stand waiting for tenants. But one day in early May, while inspecting my hives (as I did each day), I found that bees were flying strongly from my new hive, and concluded that a swarm from elsewhere had taken possession. I noticed that the new bees were much darker than my own—almost black—and they shot out of the hive with the furious intensity of dive bombers.

I thought myself very lucky in my new bees since, as well as being "for free", they were nailers for work. When my own stumbled yawning out of the hive entrance, they had already been foraging for half an hour, and they kept on for a further half an hour when mine had knocked off for the day.

It was when I went to make my regular inspection of the inside of the hive that the shock came. Providentially I had donned my hat, veil and gloves, but all this helped very little. I had my smoker, which normally controls bees, working strongly, but the minute I lifted off the hive roof the strangers attacked in force, with unexampled ferocity. I puffed smoke furiously in every direction but, far from quieting them, it made them madder than ever. Wherever the veil touched my skin, whether it be nose or ear, there, ready to deal with it was a bee, and my legs from hip to ankle were stung countless times through a pair of thick flannel trousers. In the end I had to give them best, clap the roof on the hive and run for it.

When all the stings had been picked out with tweezers, and it is no consolation to think that each one meant a dead bee (bees, unlike wasps, die after stinging), I rang up an old friend, an apiarist of great experience. He nearly died of laughter at my tale of woe, and made me so wild that he was lucky to be at the end of a telephone and not within reach.

"Ah," he said, when he could stop his infuriating chuckles, "You have got hold of some Carpathians, or rather they have got hold of you. (He-he-he.) Nothing to do, old boy, except destroy them."

Next day I obtained a sulphur candle after a long search, and that night closed the bee entrance, opened the lid, put in the lighted candle, and covered the whole with a wet sack.

Cautiously next morning, hatted and veiled, for I still didn't trust those bees, I opened the hive, half expecting them to have eaten the candle and thrived on it, but they were all dead. In the short time I had had them the queen had filled the brood chamber with eggs, and they had made quite a lot of honey. It was very obvious that if they could have been controlled, they would have been my most productive hive.

But the most annoying sequel of all, was that from so much

bee venom injected into my system I became strongly allergic to the stings of my nice, gentle, Italian bees, and even a single sting made my hand swell up like a boxing glove. This was no fun for a doctor, especially for an obstetrician, and sadly I had to hand over the management of my hives to a paid apiarist.

Rabbits were my next venture. For fifteen shillings (75p) I bought a doe in kindle and kept her in a hutch which I made from a large packing case. I fed her on sow thistle, Besnard leaves and elm twigs, which I gathered every day. Previously I had only kept a rabbit, as a small boy, when all the surplus vegetables from a large kitchen garden were available in profusion. None of this was to be had, and I think if I had realised how much a pregnant rabbit could eat in one day, I doubt whether I would have entertained the project.

However, there she was, and had to be fed properly, so every other day saw me plucking a sack full of greenstuff to keep pace with her insatiable demands.

Quite soon she presented me with seven babies—more hutches to be made and seven more mouths to feed. They were rather smelly, too, so close to the house, but I could not keep them elsewhere because hutches too far from the house were invariably found empty, sooner or later. Some people who were at special risk were even reduced to keeping their hutches in a scullery, and not infrequently even these were raided.

A farmer patient gave me two sacks of swedes to eke out the other things I collected, and I struggled through the winter with this and my dried bread rusks.

During November to March I hand-dug the large unused vegetable garden at Vallée des Vaux, and as early as possible almost filled it with cabbage plants. These, as well as other things I grew, made things considerably easier, and after I took possession of Beaupré, I planted a large area with the Jersey Giant cabbage, whose stems used to be made into powerful walking sticks. This meant that feeding merely involved walking out daily to the field and collecting as much as was required, but the problem of theft was much greater than when they were kept in a town backyard.

Although it was not as bad as it became later, keeping possession of your own property became more difficult from day to day. Imported foreign workers—Russians, Spaniards and Irish—did the round of the farms almost nightly, and practically nothing was safe. Over a period of two years after this, they actually attacked isolated or poorly defended farmhouses and took what they wanted, but at this stage they merely lifted anything that was not cleverly concealed or strongly locked up.

I moved my hutches into a loft with one well barred window, and a door, reached by a ladder. By putting a stout padlock on the door and removing the ladder to the inside of the house at night, I managed to keep them safe.

The first eight or nine months of occupation were not too uncomfortable, although things rapidly disappeared from the shops and we were on fairly strict rations. Nobody, in his hearts of hearts, really believed that we would be isolated from the outside world for five years, although our brains should have told us to the contrary. Most people drew on their small stocks with a lighthearted faith that something or other would turn up. For instance, if one dropped in to see a friend, or he on you, it was normal, and only humane, to offer him a drink, though only one. This was accepted practice by all, but even such meagre hospitality eroded one's small supply and soon, very soon in some cases, the horrid fact had to be faced that the cupboard, if not actually bare, was looking pretty sick.

Personally, I had a good stock of wines which I brought out when people came for a meal. It helped down some usually indifferent food, but wine, with the exception of sherry, is not the same as a short drink at 6pm. It was obvious that something had to be done about it.

At first the Germans imported a good, sound, red table wine, which was on ration at one-and-sixpence (7½p) a bottle, per head per week. This was excellent but the quality of the wine, gradually deteriorated till finally most people ceased to buy their ration.

The one characteristic of the wine was that it was very

potent, and this gave me the idea of distilling it and turning the alcohol into something resembling gin.

Canvassing a circle of my friends I asked them to continue taking the wine, which I bought back from them at cost. I then went to see a friend who was a very clever metal worker and, in a few days, he made me a small copper still, connected by a long copper worm to a heavy glass bottle. Through the stopper of the still, as well as the end of the worm, was a thermometer and, by fixing the apparatus on the draining board, with a rubber pipe from the cold tap, elevated enough to flush cold water over the worm, alcoholic vapour condensed in the bottle.

I had to keep an eye on the thermometer and remove the source of heat (a Bunsen burner at that time) when the mash reached 34 degrees (I may be wrong about this figure but I knew it exactly then). The reason for this is that after 34 degrees Methylalcohol comes off (instead of Ethylalcohol), and this is very toxic to the nervous system, causing a polyneuritis of the extremities and, worse still, irreversible blindness. This part of the process needed great care, and naturally I erred on the side of caution, but the whole contraption worked like a charm and I produced nearly a bottle of white spirit from six bottles of wine.

I then went to see my chemist and wheedled out of him a few ounces of juniper berries, and a small bottle of Tincture of Cardamoms. A few berries were crushed finely in a pestle and mortar, added to the spirit, as well as an eggspoonful of Cardamoms, and hey presto!—a very passable, rather powerful gin. I therefore increased my buying of the neglected ration wine.

My next problem was to find a substitute for dry Martini. I already had a small barrel of sweet Martini which had been given me by an Italian, but none of us fancied it at the time and I was confident that I could make something with more customer appeal. Before the end most of them had to take the sweet Martini and like it, but this was still fairly early on, and my friends more choosy than they became later.

I got hold of a demijohn of really dry Jersey cider and divided it up into bottles. In the first I put a teaspoonful each of Tincture of Quinine and Tincture of Gentian, with half a bay leaf, and left it for three days. This proved to be too dry and too redolent of bay, so the dose of quinine and of bay were both halved and marinated as before.

After straining it through an old piece of fine linen, I had a very good imitation of dry Martini which met with universal approval, although some of my friends took a dash of the despised sweet Martini in addition.

I was able to carry on this illegal practice for some months until the wine ration dried up, and I had to think again.

The obvious choice was of course sugar beet, and I grated a large bowl of this which I put aside in a crock, covered with a cloth, to ferment. This bubbled and frothed merrily for about two weeks, when I strained off the pulp and started to distill the liquid. Everything went smoothly, and I got off a most satisfactory quantity of almost clear spirit. It tasted strongly of sugar beet, however, but I was not particularly worried as I had one or two antidotes up my sleeve.

I let it stand for three days over carbonate of lime, ran off the excess fluid and distilled again. This time a clearer spirit but still, though less, the unmistakable tang of sugar beet.

I next repeated the process with charcoal and left it to soak for a whole week before distilling, but all to no purpose. The spirit still would not do, and after filtering it through charcoal as a last resort I was forced to give it best.

Potatoes were the next choice and all was well except for a slight brackish taste in the spirit, which was easily disguised by the vermouth, but at least it had not the flavour of sugar beet, which seemed impervious to everything.

This solution seemed ideal, but in the summer of 1943 the ration had been reduced drastically and all potatoes (fifty per cent of them were bad anyway) were wanted for eating.

That year, all my own potatoes at Beaupré had been dug up and taken away for food, the night following the day on which they were planted, so I was dependent on the ration. (The culprits were undoubtedly foreign workers, and of course there was nothing one could do about it.)

After racking my brains, I remembered a tale told me by my old nannie, who had been my father's nannie before me.

In the 1880s, farm workers were paid so badly that their families were permanently on the poverty line, and reduced to every kind of ruse for living off the countryside. Roasted acorns, beech mast, corms of the wood anemone, salads of the young leaves of whitethorn, wild sorrel, Good King Henry, and flour from the roots of the wild arum. How they discovered this use for the arum passes my comprehension, but mothers of large families must have been at their wits' end, and hunger is a great spur to inventiveness.

The root itself is white and bulbous, though with a tapering tap root, not unlike a parsnip, and is very poisonous. What I cannot understand is how completely uneducated people worked out a way of getting over this problem. From what my nannie told me, parties of older children went out with sacks and dug up the Lords and Ladies, as they are called in Wales. This was best done in late autumn or early winter. The roots were well washed, finely grated and steeped in water for twenty-four hours. The water was carefully poured off, the process repeated twice more, then the whole thing poured through a sieve or coarse sacking. The milky fluid resulting was allowed to settle, leaving a white flour at the bottom of the bowl. This could be dried and was rather like potato flour, being used for milk puddings, custards or thickening in soups etc., and old Sarah said she often remembered eating it.

I had noticed quantities of wild arum growing on the banks in various parts of the Island, and one evening, with a garden fork and a sack, I mounted my bike and set off. The roots went down a depressingly long way, and very soon I persuaded myself that most of the starch would be in the thick upper end and ceased to bother with the tapering part.

I carried out all the instructions as far as I remembered them, and in the end had about two pints of white flour which tasted of nothing at all. I didn't bother to dry it off but just added water, stirred in some honey and put it aside in my crock to ferment. This it seemed reluctant to do, but a pinch of yeast, then in short supply, started it off and I ended up with an opalescent liquid which went into my still and produced a crystalline clear, quite tasteless alcohol. This made an extremely satisfactory gin, but the whole process involved an awful lot of work at a period when I had increasing calls on my time, so I made the stuff only on one further occasion, as I had several bottles of potato spirit left in my store cupboard.

A further inducement to give it up was that the trees in Beaupré orchard, which were very old and decrepit, appeared for the first time to promise a crop of cider apples. This turned out to be so, and I had my apples turned into sixty gallons of cider by a local farmer who had all the necessary apparatus.

From some of this I distilled about twenty bottles of Calvados and this lasted till the Occupation was over. It was pretty fiery stuff, and tasted much too strongly of its origin, but at that stage of events we were not over-fussy and a little glass not only warmed us up, but helped to offset the deadly monotony of our, by then, very inadequate diet. I still have a couple of the bottles which I have kept for old times' sake.

The next little luxury to be tackled was tobacco. The shops were cleared out of this in the first few months, and thereafter we had only a sporadic ration, usually of cigarettes but occasionally of pipe tobacco. Most of this, like a good many items that the French sold us, was rank and badly cured. It made a hot, unsatisfactory smoke, and in any case there were often many weeks between allocations. If one was a regular smoker one had to suffer extended periods of abstinence when one longed for a smoke, if only to allay the pangs of hunger.

Like everyone else I experimented with dried blackberry or cherry leaves, but all that came out of the pipe was smoke which tasted only of itself, and left a black, bad-tasting tongue. This vogue soon died and was replaced by the leaves of a weed known locally as Pied d'Ane, or sometimes Coltsfoot (which it most certainly was not). These were a rounded heart-shape, with a slightly furry surface, and after trying them once I decided that they were no improvement on the other substitutes, although very popular for a short time, even with the troops. Smoking them left one rather dizzy, and after the first attempt nothing would induce me to try again, especially after I had had two urgent calls to young men who had been found semiconscious in their chairs.

The first patient was a puzzle to me, as there was nothing pointing to the cause of the attack except a slow pulse, but with the second there was a pouch of dried Pied d'Ane on the low table and a pipe on the floor, where a hole had burned in the carpet. Obviously he had passed out while smoking the weed, and he too had a slow pulse.

Both men vomited as they came round, and afterwards recovered fairly quickly, but the news of these effects soon spread, and there was a rapid and dramatic slump in Pied d'Ane shares.

Most of the tobacconists opened only for a few hours, two or three times a week, in order to distribute any allocations of tobacco there might be, but going into my usual supplier to collect mine, I saw a wooden chest marked "Snuff. Best Rappee". I asked the proprietor if there was anything in it and he said: "Oh yes. The demand has been slight for many years, and since the Occupation started I haven't sold any."

Whether the box really contained Old Rappee, which I understood was top quality snuff, I have no idea but, on the spur of the moment, I bought two pounds, which was all the box contained; the proprietor seemed glad to get rid of it at the pre-war price.

I reasoned that snuff, after all, was nothing more or less than finely ground tobacco, and that I might satisfy my craving by becoming a snuffer. I could not have been more wrong. The stuff went right up my nose and down the back into my throat, and made me cough, splutter and sneeze until I nearly cracked a rib. I felt that it had even penetrated my skull, and so I gave it up instantly. Besides, it made my handkerchiefs filthy, which was a consideration when there was no soap for washing them.

I then looked around for a means with which to make the snuff smokable and decided upon tea leaves. A few people still had tea, and eked it out by drying the leaves, used after the first infusion, in a very hot oven. This made a second brew, nothing like as good or as strong as the first but infinitely better than the prevalent sugar beet tea or any other substitute. An attempt at a third infusion was a failure and the leaves were therefore thrown away after being used twice.

These I begged from everyone I knew and also from the kitchens at the Maternity Hospital, so that very soon I had several large biscuit tins full of carefully dried tea leaves. Taking out only about a quarter of a pound at a time, I sprinkled it with a little diluted black treacle which had been in the house for years. I left it to get tacky, then dusted it freely with snuff, mixing it thoroughly till no more adhered. This was spread fairly thinly on a tray to dry off some of the stickiness, when it was ready to smoke.

I will not go so far as to say that this was the best smoke I ever had, and again it left me with a black tongue, but it was immeasurably better than any other substitute I had tried, and I became suddenly very popular with my pipe-smoking friends.

In the spring of 1943, a very small quantity of tobacco seed was procured from France and I was lucky enough to get a small pinch. From this I grew four potato boxes of plants which I set out in what is now the lawn at Beaupré. When fully developed these were cut and hung upside down in the barn until completely dry. For a small charge they were processed at the old tobacco factory, and returned cut up and looking like rubbed plug.

This was not a resounding success, for the first few puffs gave a sensation of being tightly gripped by the throat, and at the end of a single pipe one felt unmistakably sick. But again, it removed all desire for food which, circumstances being what they were, was probably all to the good.

Tea was a problem that I could never solve. There was a tea bush in a garden at St Brelade's Bay, but a moment's thought told me that the amount to be got from a single, small bush would be infinitesimal, so I gave it up and drank water—I could never get on with sugar beet tea.

I could just about stomach sugar beet coffee, which I drank at the houses of friends, but I felt I could do something better than that, and set about experimenting.

Peasants all over the continent swear by their own particular blend, but here we had to be ruled by what was available. Even a tablespoonful of real coffee to a pound of ersatz would have made all the difference, but it was simply not to be had. Occasionally we received a small ration of what was labelled "coffee" but none of it had ever come within smelling distance of a genuine bean, and I decided that what I could produce myself would be quite as good, if not better. Materials available were barley (from gleanings), acorns and, in the absence of chicory, dandelion root.

The first two were tossed in a hot frying pan to a strong brown colour, and the last either baked almost black in a hot oven or, again, tossed in the pan. These were ground separately in a hand grinder and mixed in varying proportions to suit individual taste. This produced a pleasant, nutty, slightly bitter drink, which was quite palatable drunk black, but much improved with milk, when we had some.

Once, and once only, we had some dried figs on the ration and these, baked crisp and ground, improved the coffee enormously, but fig was not an ingredient we could rely on regularly. For a change I used to stir in a teaspoonful of black treacle, which at least varied the taste and gave an illusion of extra nourishment.

Soap very soon became a problem. I began with a fair stock but, be as careful as I might, it gradually dwindled, and had to be eked out with the ration soap from France. This came very sporadically, and was more than half composed of some sort of china clay, which made the tablet unnaturally heavy and, in addition, gave scarcely any lather. As we ceased to have hot running water at a very early stage, it can be imagined how difficult and unsatisfactory it was to have a good wash. A proper all-over bath in cold water, with French soap, was torture, until Mr and Mrs Hamon, good patients of mine, who were then in charge of the Milk Marketing premises in Don Street, came to the rescue. There was always plenty of hot water there for sterilising the milk bottles, and thither I made my way, with a towel and clean clothes, for my weekly bath. In the winter, certainly, it was the one time that I felt really warm, and I looked forward to it every week, like a child to a party. It also helped to protect me, I feel sure, from catching all sorts of nasty skin infections which were prevalent during the Occupation.

Some further assistance was provided by another patient, the housekeeper to a very rich couple, who had left in charge of their manor when they evacuated. The husband was a well-known hypochondriac with some sort of skin disease, and he always kept a considerable stock of a particular medicated soap, from which she gave me a dozen tablets. This soap was coal black, due to a high content of sphagnum moss, but it gave a good lather and, being very big, lasted a long time. But even so, they were all used up before the Occupation was half over, and I was reduced again to using the horrible French soap.

Then a piece of luck came my way. I was visiting a farm, where a large sow had just died of some kind of milk fever, after a recent farrowing, and the farmer was waiting for a German official to certify the body as having died a natural death, before giving a permit for burial. After these formalities were over I asked if I might have some fat before the body was disposed of, and after a rather messy interlude, came away with about twenty pounds of good abdominal lard which I melted down.

I borrowed a book from my chemist which gave clear directions on how to make soap, and although I cannot now remember the exact quantities and instructions, it turned out to be comparatively easy. It involved making a solution of caustic soda in hot water, of a precise strength, and adding a stated quantity of this to a precise amount of hot fat. This was stirred thoroughly, and then poured into a shallow dripping tin to set. It was then cut up into squares and put on a wire rack to dry. I put in a small amount of perfume which I found among my wife's things, and when the whole thing was properly dried I found myself with enough good soap to last till the end of the War. I doubt whether I would like to use it now, in view of its origin, but it was a thousand per cent better than the French soap, and those of my friends to whom I gave a few tablets said it was excellent.

The same lady who gave me the medicated soap also, at the same time, produced half a dozen toothbrushes of the finest quality, but with very soft bristles, because her employer had had pyorrhoea and his gums bled easily. But at least they were very much better than no brushes at all, and vigorous application offset their softness.

But my toothpaste very soon ran out and, although there was a small distribution of this late in the Occupation, I had by that time made my own, and had no need of it.

I collected from the beach, where we were still allowed to go at times, a large bag of cuttlefish bone, such as one gives to cagebirds. This was dried in the oven, when something else was being cooked, and then ground down to a very fine powder in a pestle and mortar.

After putting this through an ordinary kitchen sieve I weighed out one pound, added two ounces of fine salt (which was still procurable then), and one ounce of soap powder, again bought from a chemist. This was stored in a jar in which had been put a handful of verbena scented geranium leaves, and with strict economy I had enough tooth powder for the Occupation.

I still use an expensive proprietary powder of much the same constitution—though not so delicately scented—and attribute the good health of my gums exclusively to it.

While on the subject of salt, this was another commodity which gave out well before we reached the halfway mark. Tanker carts appeared on the streets, selling buckets of sea water at one or two pence each. This was supposed to be boiled to evaporation point, and the resulting salt used in food. But this was not possible.

In the first place, very few people had the fuel to boil away a whole bucket of water, and even when they had, as I did at Beaupré, the residue amounted to little more than a teaspoonful; and that was largely sand.

I tried every kind of way to eliminate this, and even went to the length of straining the water through a good felt hat, left behind by my wife. It was a beautiful hat, pink, with a large floppy brim, from Scotts of Piccadilly, and she was a bit boot-faced about it on her return, but even that let through most of the sand, and so we used the sea water straight, for boiling vegetables or making soup.

I kept the residue which I had boiled down, but in humid weather it turned into a pale brown paste which was quite unusable, and looked revolting.

As a result of this episode, one of the minor legacies of that time, for me, is a sense of fury when I see people putting a full spoonful of snow-white salt on the side of their plates and at the end of the meal, passing it up completely unused. Not only salt. I still hate seeing any kind of good food thrown into the dustbin, or indeed any wilful waste.

During the first few days of the Occupation I bought from my seedsman a good supply of all the vegetable seeds he had in his shop. As it was the end of the growing season this would ordinarily have been destroyed to make way for the new stock but, nonetheless, I laid in as much as I thought I might need for the next two years. This estimate proved to be correct, because by the end of that time we were able to get some seeds from France.

Kept cool and dry in airtight tins, all these seeds germinated. In the second year, germination was very patchy, but I got an adequate crop even so, and then, as I say, I got fresh seeds for the third and subsequent years. The one exception was the parsnip, which I have learned since it is pointless to keep for the following year.

At that time in Jersey, seeds were kept in little drawers, marked with their names, and sold loose in packets. In one packet of peas I found three large flat seeds, which I took to be those of marrow and, having plenty of land, sowed them just for luck. They were not marrows, although of the same family, and gave me several of the largest pumpkins I have ever seen. Some I was able to give to friends (in portions, of course), but few were very enthusiastic, for pumpkin is a tasteless thing, except with spices, sugar, butter and egg yolks—none of which we had. However, it seemed a waste not to do something with it. Mrs Ozouf and I cut up a large quantity into chunks and filled a jam boiler, to which we added about a gallon of the sickly sweet Greek wine, which I had in store. I also put in two or three leaves of Spanish laurel,* which I remembered as a child being put into rice pudding to give it an almond flavour.

This mixture we boiled down, stirring constantly as with Jersey black butter, until we were left with a thick paste which we spooned into glass jars, filling them to within about two inches of the top. It was quite pleasant eaten with a kind of porridge made from coarse ground wheat or barley, or even on bread. But I was sure that there was not enough sugar in it to ensure its keeping indefinitely, so I made a small quantity of genuine pumpkin and apple jam—a pound of sugar to a pound of fruit—and poured it boiling on top of the mixture in each jar. This layer was about one and a half inches thick and acted as a sealer to keep out fermenting agents in the air. Hot suet would have done as well but we had none.

This method acted like a charm and we made a second large batch, which in the winter I took to my lame ducks on the log round. My mother-in-law also liked it very much and I was able to keep her well supplied.

I was unfortunate in that most of my town house was fuelled by gas, and well before mid-occupation we were on ration, which became stricter very rapidly. Most days we were cut off for three or four hours at least, twice a day, and there was a total shutdown from 11pm till 7am. These times were not always exact, and it was maddening to miss a meal because the gas had gone off half an hour before expected, leaving whatever it was still uncooked. So I made two hay-boxes, one for a small casserole and the other for a much larger one. These proved a boon, and were in constant use. Various dishes, such as soups, stews, boiled potatoes and porridge were brought to the boil and then tucked up in the haybox to finish. Perhaps the contents were sometimes over- or under-cooked, but when the gas eventually came down to a mere whiff twice a day, they helped enormously.

Similarly, I persuaded my metalworker friend to make me a small oven out of heavy zinc plating. This was a metal cube, about one foot each way, with a door, and a baffle let into the base. It also had two shelves, one just above the baffle and the other halfway up. This oven was stood over a gas ring, which of course could be adjusted to the heat required, and was invaluable for baking a single dish, or sometimes two, where the heating of a large oven was unnecessarily wasteful of gas. I gave it away soon after the Occupation, under the entirely erroneous idea that we should never have to economise on fuel again. How wrong can one be?!!

I have already talked about soap, but shaving soap had never crossed my mind—neither had razor blades as I had always used an electric razor; run on a battery. When these were no longer procurable I had to take other measures.

There was a safety razor in the bathroom cupboard, which some pre-war guest had left behind, and there were occasional issues of continental razor blades, but these, like most French imports then, were of decidedly inferior quality and their working life extended to four days at most—usually three.

My sphagnum soap gave a sort of lather but it was certainly not shaving soap, and as, in addition, the water was always cold, I got to dread the morning chore of scraping my face.

The house was fitted with an extremely efficient gas central heating and hot water system, but after the first month our ration was barely enough to ignite the pilot light, and it was discontinued, never to be restarted. Having all this equipment to hand, but entirely useless, used to gall me quite beyond reason when I went through my morning torture.

My mother-in-law eventually came to the rescue with two wooden shaving bowls filled with the best pre-war shaving soap, a brush, and a case holding seven cut-throat razors, each inscribed with a different day of the week. These were sharpened for me weekly by my regular barber, and I used them till the end of the Occupation.

A cut-throat razor takes some getting used to and I soon learned not to be in a hurry or to allow my attention to wander. By not observing these rules I gave myself a nasty gash, three or four times, but on the whole the razors and I got on very well and I soon learned to get a good clean shave. When my children started to arrive, and were forever in and out of the bathroom, I thought it wiser to give them up while I still had a nose and two ears intact.

Clothes, naturally, began to worry me after a couple of years. At the beginning I had four suits, all in good condition, and decided right at the start to put two away in reserve. But the two in wear gradually got shabbier and shabbier, even by Occupation standards. It was not exactly that they wore out, but they got shiny, and somehow rather drab.

I took one to a very good local tailor, and for an outlay of thirty shillings he turned it completely, and made it look as good as new, which pleased me so much that I had the other turned also.

These two suits carried me along for some time, but with a decrease in the petrol ration, I had to abandon the car, except for emergencies and night calls, and do all my work on a bicycle. This was all very well in fine weather, but in spite of a suit of oilskins, and especially when it was windy as well as wet, I very often returned in the evening soaked down the back of my neck, sometimes to the waist, and always up to my knees.

In the absence of facilities for drying I had to use the second suit next day, and on occasions, when it rained every day for a month or more, as it did several times, all four suits were called into service and used in rotation. Often when I returned to the first one it was still horribly damp and sticky, but in spite of all this, and uncomfortable as it was, I never caught a cold.

To make matters worse, constantly being in the saddle, I soon wore through the seats of both older pairs of trousers, and was forced to sacrifice the waistcoats to have a matching patch put in. Mr Briard was a tailor who had really learned his craft, and the patches were grafted in so skilfully that they were scarcely noticeable.

But in spite of all these stratagems, trousers were my main problem, especially as I had left behind in Wales two good pairs of flannel bags, which would have been a godsend, and had with me only one old pair which soon disintegrated. So in a very short time I was reduced to my last two suits, which were already going the way of the others, and saw myself, if the Occupation lasted much longer, doing my visits in a kilt made from a travelling rug.

Again my mother-in-law stepped in. Early in the Occupation she had offered me two scarcely worn suits of my late father-in-law; I was forced reluctantly to refuse them, as at the time I was a brawny thirteen stone, whereas he, of the same height, weighed only eleven. But by now I was only ten and a half stone and, trying them on, found they fitted perfectly if a trifle loosely, so that suddenly I stood out like a tailor's model amongst my shabby fellow practitioners.

By the end of the Occupation I was a couple of pounds short of nine stone and my lovely suits hung on me like bags, which was at least a fault on the good side.

My bicycle was given to me by Mrs Thompstone of Deloraine St Saviour. It had belonged to her husband, also a doctor, who had died some years before, and as he was a very tall man, the bicycle was a perfect fit. It was very old and rather heavy, but built at a time when things were made to last, and it had two good tyres. Though the bicycle never once needed any kind of repair, the big daily mileage I had to do soon wore down the tyres, but a resourceful garage owner covered them with a tucked-in strip of inner tubing from a motor wheel. This and its successors kept me going for some years, when even inner tubing became unprocurable, and I ended my time with lengths of garden hose, wired to the rims. This was bumpy and hard going, but there was no alternative. I found my days took more out of me than formerly and, in fact, I lost more than one stone in weight during the time I rode on the hose.

My daily routine was as follows. I aimed to leave the house before 8am and always went first to the Maternity Hospital to find out if I was likely to be needed that morning, and to leave a plan, with telephone numbers (if any) of my itinerary. An identical list had been left with Mrs Ozouf.

On Monday, Wednesday and Friday I then went via First Tower, Millbrook and Beaumont to St Peter and St Ouen, then through St Mary and via St Lawrence to St John's

Village. I then turned south via Zion and Queen's Road to my 2.30pm surgery. This went on till about 5.30pm.

On Tuesday, Thursday and Saturday I started the morning by going along one or other of the east coast roads to Gorey, up to St Martin, then with sorties into St Saviour and Trinity again down to town for my 2.30 surgery. When this was over I visited in the town and contiguous parishes—getting home about 8pm.

After town surgery on the days of my west round, I took surgeries at St Aubin at 6.30pm and St Peter at 7.30pm or as soon after as I could manage, and usually arrived home at 9pm—sometimes later. I always carried a packed lunch with me, which I ate sitting on a hedge, or in a shed in wet weather, and carried all my equipment on the carrier behind me, in a rucksack on my back, and in the basket on the handlebars.

Ideally I was supposed to have Tuesday afternoons off, but as I always held an antenatal clinic at the Maternity Hospital from 9.30 till whenever it ended—always more than two hours—I could never fit in all my visits before lunch (which was the only time I always had it at home) and had to clear up whatever work was outstanding, in the afternoon and evening.

Sundays I tried to keep clear, but working single-handed I could never take a complete day off, though patients had to put up a really good case before I turned out on a Sunday. On my bicycle I averaged between thirty and forty miles a day.

In addition, being in sole charge of the Maternity Hospital, I was on call day and night for emergencies, surgical repairs, and difficult and instrumental deliveries. These got me up on average five nights a week, and an urgent call by day, saw me breaking off whatever I was doing and pedalling furiously back to town, wherever I was on the Island. The princely salary I received for this was fifty pounds a year.

In addition to all this, I made a point of calling to see my mother-in-law every single day, if only for a few minutes en passant, and I missed only once in five years.

I usually had supper with her every Sunday evening, and she had lunch with me every Tuesday and sometimes one other day. These were the occasions when I could ensure that she had a really square meal, but in spite of my efforts, and little extras that I was able to take her, she finished the Occupation weighing less than six stone.

For a woman who had been waited on and pampered all her life, she adapted herself, with a toughness that no one would have given her credit for, to harsh conditions which broke many seemingly hardier people. She never grumbled or bemoaned her lot, and lived to be 93.

Her great dread was of being arrested and tortured by the Gestapo, for she was very vulnerable to pain in any form, and it was at her pleading that I eventually supplied her with a lethal dose of morphia, which she always kept in her bag and which we subsequently found among her effects after her death. She was not afraid of death itself and, once she had the morphia, settled down happily and ceased to worry.

Naturally, the farming community did not suffer to the same degree as the townsfolk. Although by German decree all pigs, calves and cattle had to be brought to the public abattoir and offered for sale, the farmers were allowed to retain a small proportion for their own use. This proportion got considerably smaller as time went on, and the farmers would have been little better off than the townsfolk, except that they developed all sorts of little tricks to get over the problem. Some divided a building into two halves and fed a pig or pigs in the back portion, while keeping hens or machinery in the front half. Others had a pig in a small pen and built a complete haystack over it, camouflaging the entrance with hay bales. Others still fattened pigs in a bedroom—but only in a wing or dower cottage, I hope.

Not all of them got away with these infractions, and those caught were heavily fined and sometimes imprisoned, but although the Germans issued countless orders and regulations, the farmers always eventually found and took advantage of a loophole.

For instance, every litter of pigs had to be notified and an inspector would arrive to count the number of new piglets, of which they kept close track right up to slaughtering age. If one died, the corpse had to be seen by an official who certified it as dead, and one unit was deleted from the records when slaughtering time came.

The wily farmers turned this to their advantage as follows. Suppose a pig died a natural death, was examined and a certificate given; the corpse was then rushed off to another farm, often a long way off, and a message sent to the inspector, ensuring a second certificate. In this way four or five certificates were obtained, and each farmer holding one of these, was able to keep one pig from a litter for his absolute use.

When, as happened in the beginning, the inspector had been in private life as a clerk or an actor, certificates were easily obtained. To such a man a pig was a pig, and some of them were still issuing certificates when the poor little corpse began to get distinctly high.

But the pace was too hot to last and someone in authority smelled, not a pig, but a rat. Inspectors who had been farmers in private life were substituted. They recognised the corpses on the second viewing, and put an end to the racket by cutting off one ear.

Soon after this all cows, horses and pigs were tattooed (the piglets at birth) and entered in a register, which for a time made things much more difficult for the farmer. He bypassed this block, by sending one pig in a comfortable basket, so that it would not squeal, to a neighbour, who kept it till after the inspector had paid his visit and tattooed the rest of the family, when it was returned to its mother.

Ultimately, the Germans must have guessed that something was going on, for they instituted a series of spot checks, and anyone caught with a pig that had no tattoo, was severely punished.

The killing of an illegal pig presented considerable difficulty, for unless the premises where this took place were fairly isolated, the squeals of the unfortunate animal were bound to give the show away. And many farms, even if they *were* remote, were likely as not to have a German strong point within hearing distance, and therefore had to be ruled out.

One farmer thought he had hit on a solution and consulted a friend, a local surgeon, who offered to anesthetise the pig and to slaughter it silently in the best surgical tradition. This was done, using chloroform, and everything went completely according to plan.

Unfortunately, however, when the meat was in the oven the whole kitchen smelt like an operating theatre, and eating the pork was quite out of the question. The victim was regretfully and secretly interred, and the whole episode rather shamefacedly forgotten as soon as possible.

But there was a solution, very simple, very natural and very traditional. His name was Emil Ferey, a man of many talents—farmer, marksman, builder, fisherman and pig slaughterer. Emil's technique was as follows.

On his instructions the pig did not receive his breakfast that morning, and on Emil's arrival came up to ask what the devil was happening. A hungry pig is usually concerned solely with his food and nothing else. Emil had no equipment, no ropes, no bench, no nothing, except a way with pigs, his consummate skill and a knowledge of porcine anatomy. He rubbed the pig along its back, scratched it around the ears, and then reaching into an inside pocket, produced a keenly pointed steel blade, honed to razor sharpness on both sides. Leaning over the pig, he slid the knife deep into the throat, just at the base of the neck. There was no avoiding action, no panic, no squeal, in fact no sign that the pig felt anything. It looked with some surprise at the stream of blood gushing out, then, as lack of blood to the brain began almost at once to take effect, grunted once or twice, and subsided quietly on the floor. That was all. No animal in an abattoir, despatched with all the benefits of modern science and hygiene, ever had an easier or more peaceful end. The pig had no slightest idea or apprehension of what was coming, and there was nothing that the most avid animal lover, or vegetarian, could cavil at.

More than once, Emil is known to have carried out an assignment in a farmyard where a German unit occupied the press house at the other end; in consequence his services were in great demand.

The unit, however, must have realised that something of the sort had probably happened, for the next time an illegal pig had been fattened, and was about ready for slaughter, the farmer one morning found its shed empty. To add insult to injury, the intestines had been left on the floor for the farmer to clear out, and the pig's tail nailed to the shed door. There was nothing the farmer could do. The pig was illegal and therefore had no legal existence. What was worst of all was the daily smell of frying pork which emanated from the press house.

The unit did not make use of the head. This was found a day later in a ditch behind the farmhouse, with a neat bullet hole in the centre of the forehead. No one had heard the shot, though it must have been fired no more than twenty yards from the house, and on a still night.

In the latter part of the Occupation this sort of pig rustling became fairly common and resulted in pigs being fattened in bedrooms, as I mentioned earlier on.

Eventually it became evident to the Germans, from the amount of pork on the black market, that there was a big traffic in illegal pigs, and two units, each of three men, were detailed to descend without warning on several farms in a selected district and search them from end to end.

A farmer in Trinity Parish had just killed a pig, which was dressed and hanging to set, from a stretcher in the barn. Suddenly a breathless boy arrived from the next-door farm, owned by the farmer's brother, with the news that the Germans had just started a search there.

The pig was hurriedly taken down, while people distractedly dashed from building to building, looking for a suitable place to hide it. But a pig is a large item to hide successfully in a hurry, and it fell to the farmer's wife to think up a solution. Putting her husband to cutting off the forelegs, which were sticking forwards and would give the show away, she hastily prepared the best bedroom and had the pig laid on a white sheet on the bed. All the bedclothes were cleared away, the blinds drawn, a little Eau de Cologne sprinkled about, and another large white sheet draped over the pig.

A small table was brought up to the foot of the bed, with two candlesticks holding precious candles and lighted for the occasion. The family Bible placed between them completed the picture.

All was ready just in time, and the arriving Germans were met by the grim-faced farmer and his wife in tears. These, she told me afterwards, were not just castor oil or induced by onion, but genuine tears of sheer fright.

Nobody said a word, since no one spoke German, but the farmer knew why they were there and so did the soldiers, who at once set about their task.

A minute search of the buildings yielded no result and they started on the house—which was a large one. Everything was gone through minutely, every cupboard examined and moved away from the wall, even settees tipped over and thumped, but no luck. Then came the turn of the bedroom floor, and this was where mother took over.

They went through the first four bedrooms with the same thoroughness, and finally came to the best bedroom. She opened the door and burst into sobs as the leading soldier pushed past her, and suddenly halted in his tracks. He had just caught sight of the dim interior, the still figure on the bed covered by a white sheet, the candles on the table at the foot, and the Bible.

With a muttered apology he backed out in shamed embarrassment, before the other two had a chance to see inside, and at a muttered order from him they all clattered down the stairs.

At this point mother fainted (genuine this time) and hit the floor with a thud. Her husband rushed up to see what had happened, and by the time he came down again the soldiers had gone.

When they told me the story, I had an uncomfortable feeling that a basic sense of human decency had been exploited, and perhaps rather tactlessly said so, but I did not pursue the subject because I quickly realised that I was in a minority of one.

As the Occupation proceeded, robberies became more and more frequent, not so much from private premises as from stores and warehouses.

The proceeds of these thefts usually filtered through into the black market, where things like sugar, butter, tea and tinned foods fetched ten or twenty times their pre-war price.

The black marketeers had become so specialised and crafty that, although the Germans organised spot searches, they very seldom found anything. On one search, the result I imagine of a tip-off, they found in the house of a very well respected member of the community, a really massive store of every kind of food and drink which the average Islander had not seen for nearly five years.

There was no suggestion that this had necessarily been obtained on the black market or was loot of any kind, but the opportunity was too good for the Germans not to make propaganda out of it. They took over a large shop window in King Street and filled it with their capture, very tastefully displayed. There were cases of best wine, spirits, packets of tea, a great deal of tinned stuff—enough to fill the whole window. It might have been a display put on by an old-fashioned high-class grocer, except for a large notice, the wording of which I forget but the sense of which was:

"See how, in spite of requests and orders from the occupying authorities, some of the local bourgeoisie indulge themselves, while most of their fellow citizens are on the verge of starvation."

The exhibition went on for about two weeks and everyone went to see it. Most of us felt sorry for the culprits, and the general opinion was that if they were fortunate enough to have all that stuff—the best of British luck to them!

Another racket was the sale, for Reichmarks, of English silver and paper money. This was usually sold to the French crews who came on cargo boats from the Britanny and Normandy ports.

In 1942 a one pound note fetched £1.6.0d, but by 1944 as much as £2.10.0d could be got for it. One could ask, and usually get, almost anything for a gold sovereign, and I heard of a three-bedroom, solidly built granite house, in the older part of the town, which in early 1944 changed hands for ten sovereigns.

We reached the nadir of our privations around Christmas 1944, when we were without bread for three weeks, and the vast majority of families had not even a chicken or some pork, much less a turkey for Christmas.

The Germans requisitioned two thousand head of poultry for their own Christmas dinners and paid for them the handsome sum of six-and-sixpence a head (32½p). The troops complained bitterly that while officers had half a bird each, they had to divide one chicken between seven.

A Dutchman, skipper of a boat in the harbour, bought two large cats for his dinner, and it was at this time that the soldiers took to bringing cats and dogs into the abattoir to be killed and dressed for their own consumption.

As had been their custom throughout the last four years, the Bailiff and Mrs Contanche came to Christmas dinner, with mother-in-law, but all we could offer them on this occasion was one of my bottled chickens with vegetables. I had, however, something that I had stored up for four and a half years and hoped to cherish till Ann came back.

At our marriage, as was then the custom (and may well still be) the top tier of our wedding cake was hermetically sealed in a tin box, and set aside for christening the first child of the union. I had destined this as the *pièce de résistance* of our first celebration, but the fare set before my Mama-in-law and our guests looked so pathetic that on the spur of the moment I opened the box. The cake inside looked to be in prime condition, except that the icing had become slightly powdery. The almond paste looked and tasted as if made yesterday and the cake itself delicious. So we had an adequate Christmas dinner after all, and Ann, when she arrived, wondered why we had not eaten it years before.

The *Vega* arrived soon after Christmas bringing food parcels, which added an almost forgotten variety to our diet, as well as a number of other commodities which we had always hitherto regarded as essential to comfort, but had learned to live without.

CHAPTER 10

As the drug situation became more and more serious, Dr McKinstry decided that the items we were getting in penny numbers from France were very unsatisfactory, and he approached the Germans with a comprehensive list and asked that it be forwarded to the Red Cross. This had been done previously, with absolutely no response, and we came to the conclusion that that list had either never been forwarded or possibly lost in transit.

The worry uppermost in our minds was the plight of the diabetics, for the insulin supply was becoming frighteningly low.

When the evacuation first became a certainty, I had gone the round of all my diabetic patients and urged them to leave for the mainland. All except one, took my advice and went, but a surprising number of diabetics who were not my patients (I never knew exactly how many, but I believe about thirty) sat tight and refused to be budged.

As soon as it became obvious that his second request was not going to bear fruit, Dr McKinstry took all the serious diabetics into one of the side wards of the hospital, so that they could be given strict bed rest and also have their diet rigidly controlled. This measure caused them to need less insulin, and it was hoped that what we still had left would last until a new supply arrived.

But as day followed day, without a sign of anything, morale on the ward dropped steadily, especially as patients saw some of their fellows getting drowsy as a prelude to diabetic coma and death.

Then suddenly the news flashed through the ward that a Red Cross crate was waiting on the quay. A horse-drawn vehicle was despatched at once, and the crate was brought back to the hospital and opened. Sure enough, among all the sawdust inside was the box labelled Insulin. All the diabetics—even those in pre-coma—hearing the news on the bush telegraph, roused themselves and waited eagerly for the life-giving injection.

But when the box was opened it was found to be absolutely empty. It had been rifled somewhere on the journey, for in France itself insulin was very short and fetching fabulous prices, and the thieves undoubtedly had sold it on the black market.

One after another the patients sank into coma and died, until finally the ward was quite empty. One patient who had discharged himself early on, inexplicably survived and is still living.

Supreme irony of all, a few days after the last death, another crate arrived and in it was a large supply of insulin.

Among other things procured for us in France by a buying commission of Islanders, sponsored by the Germans, was an almost unlimited supply of brandy. This was only issued on medical prescription, at the rate of one bottle a month, and it was an eye-opener how many irreproachable maiden ladies found that they had always been subject to sudden fainting fits, which could be cured by nothing else than—you've guessed it—brandy.

"Of course I don't like it, doctor, but my sister (or my aunt, or the baker's boy) has advised me that it is the only thing for my condition."

To the doctors was allocated responsibility for release to suitable cases (strictly medical of course) and there was an ugly rush at the surgeries, as people I had never suspected claimed heart pains, windypops and almost everything else down to flat feet.

As the supply seemed, at the beginning anyhow, practically limitless, we did not ask too many questions, but with increasing danger and difficulty of transport, things became much tighter, and eventually the brandy reached only those who seriously needed it.

One morning I received a polite little note on expensive thick paper, in a spidery old-fashioned hand, asking if I would visit (only at my own convenience) an address in the hinterland of St Clement's parish. It was signed Adela de la Poer (not her real name, incidentally). I did not know her, but I knew and had admired her house many times, though not having any idea till then to whom it belonged.

Curiosity has always been my besetting sin, and strangely enough I found it convenient to call upon her that very morning. Ringing the bell I was admitted by a respectable middle-aged woman in a black silk dress, which was nearly, but not quite, a uniform.

She showed me into a charming room full of beautiful old things, and almost immediately the lady of the house appeared. She was very tall, straight as a ramrod, with wavy white hair, simply dressed, and wearing a black frock with a jabot of cream lace. Giving me a small cool hand, she asked me to be seated.

She explained that her family doctor ("whom I seldom trouble, by the way") had evacuated and that she had got my name from a very dear friend.

"I have very little wrong with me," she explained, "but I have always been accustomed to take a little brandy from time to time, and seeing that it is available on prescription, I would be much in your debt if you could let me have an appropriate form."

I looked again at her cameo profile, clear pale complexion and, for her age (I judged her to be seventy or so), admirably preserved figure. Somehow she did not look the sort of woman who would take brandy, even a noggin at night, but I said that I would be delighted to give her a prescription and wrote one out, on the spot. Taking out a lorgnette and picking up the paper, she read it and her face fell.

"Do I understand," she said, "that this allows me one

bottle per month only?" I said that those were the rules.

"Such a pittance," she said, "is not of the slightest use to me. I have taken a bottle of brandy a day for the last twenty-five years at least, and I cannot exist without it."

As the saying goes, "you could have knocked me down with a feather", but I rallied sufficiently to say: "Well, then, perhaps you have a stock sufficient to last you till we see happier times."

She admitted that she had a fair stock, but was taking steps against a time when it should be exhausted. She said "I really cannot cut it out; I cannot even cut it down. What other measures do you suggest I take to ensure a supply?"

I mentioned the black market, but that the cost there was almost prohibitive—five pounds a bottle.

"Oh, that is quite immaterial," she said airily with a note of relief in her voice. "Could you put me in touch with a discreet individual who could keep me regularly supplied?"

I said that I could name no one offhand, but promised to make enquiries, which I did. The black marketeer I found, a highly respectable, bible-punching, mortgage-foreclosing pillar of the Methodist church, kept her supplied until we were freed, but he managed to push the price up to ten pounds a bottle before the end.

I saw her obituary notice early in the fifties and her age was given as 92. She must have been 82 when I first saw her.

Whatever she did die of, it was certainly not cirrhosis of the liver. She was one of those "nip-all-through-the-day" drinkers, and I am prepared to wager that she was never tight, or even fuddled, in her life. Once she could get her regular brandy, her only problem would have been the disposing of the bottles without her neighbours finding out.

As the Occupation progressed our transport became more and more difficult. At the outset, each doctor was allowed four gallons of petrol per week, and in an Austin Seven, such as I had, one could with careful planning cover most of the countryside, while keeping the bicycle for short daytime visits in the town.

Gradually however the ration was reduced, at first to three gallons, then to two and then to one. Finally, with typical

German precision, our allocation was fixed at six gallons a week between ten able-bodied doctors. This involved all sorts of vulgar fractions, and we had a meeting on the subject.

I knew for a fact that two of our number never paid a visit either by car or bicycle, and consulted only from their own surgeries. I also knew for a fact (and could prove it) that one of these two sold his allocation on the black market.

In the meeting at which both these members were present, I moved that they should be removed from the list of able-bodied doctors, which would leave eight applicable. This meant three quarters of a gallon each, per week—not exactly a munificent amount, but much easier to administer.

All hell broke loose, and the black marketeer was by far the most vociferous. Shaking his fist at me, he shouted "You young whipper-snapper, coming here and proposing such things. I fought in the last War!"

This should have flattened me, but instead I said quietly: "Really, on which side?"

He sat down as if shot, and we had no further word from him for the rest of the meeting. We got our three quarters of a gallon.

This meant that doctors too elderly to cycle far, could make only one or two short trips by car per week, and were otherwise limited to cycle or foot visits in the town and its environs. It also meant that most country and distant visits fell to the lot of the young and strong.

My own plan was to keep my miniscule amount of petrol purely for night calls, and to cycle all over the Island by day. But nevertheless, before the end of each week, one almost always reached a stage when the petrol gauge registered nil, and one thought that perhaps one might get there, but certainly would not get back.

The farmers, who had an extra allocation for ploughing etc, desperate for a doctor, would say: "If you can get here, doctor, I'll make sure you can get back."

No more was said, because the telephones were often tapped.

But the Germans began to suspect there was a discrepancy somewhere, and each Monday, when we collected our petrol, a reading of our speedometer was taken; if the mileage was significantly above what might be expected from the ration, awkward questions were asked.

I then took to disconnecting the speedometer, as soon as I got out into the countryside, and of reconnecting it as I approached town.

The disconnecting was easy, but reconnecting was a fiddling job, done by feel under the dash-board, and although I got used to it, and could usually manage it in a few minutes, this was not invariably so and in an emergency I sweated blood.

But again after a time the Germans began to suspect that there was a loophole somewhere, and posted soldiers along the roads to look for disconnected speedometers. All this trouble for six gallons a week, when their own troops were stealing enormous quantities of petrol, and selling it on the black market.

One beautiful morning, speedometer adrift, I was driving along a straight road in St Mary's parish, when suddenly I saw ahead of me a soldier sitting on a low wall. When he caught sight of me he got to his feet and moved into the road, preparing to carry out an inspection.

At first I thought I was trapped, but there was a farm entrance with gate open on my left, and without decreasing speed, I turned into it just as if I were paying visit there. Out of the corner of my eye I saw the soldier move towards the gateway, where he was obviously going to wait until I emerged.

Instead I drove across the farmyard, through an opening on the other side and just escaping being bogged down in a pile of manure, found myself in a field which was luckily down to grass. Even so, it had plainly been down to potatoes fairly recently, and as I bumped across its corrugated surface, I wondered if my back axle would hold.

An open gateway led me into another field, and at its far end was a heavy oak gate, chained and padlocked which gave on to a narrow little-used lane. Desperation gave me strength, and with one mighty heave I lifted the gate off both its hinges, dragged it aside and drove into the lane, and finally away.

The speedometer inspection cannot have proved very successful, for the Germans soon abandoned it and tried another scheme.

The petrol ration for doctors and a few others essentially employed was dyed pink, whereas that for farmers was green.

So pickets were posted on the outskirts of the town, on all the principal roads leading in. Usually if one had a really good knowledge of the lay out of St Helier, one could avoid these by getting into a residential area in the outskirts and crossing a main road at right angles, to get into the town.

One afternoon I had to leave a surgery full of people to go on a very urgent call at St Lawrence. My tank was almost dry, but as was customary the farmer put a few pints in my tank, while I was attending his little boy.

As I was in such hurry to get back, I decided to chance coming through First Tower, on the inner road. Just opposite the People's Park, two soldiers stepped into the road and flagged me down.

I was travelling fairly fast, and had to think quickly. I braked hard and purposely mounted the pavement with the two near-side wheels apparently in a great fluster. The petrol tank of the Austin was a narrow cylindrical affair, horizontally attached at the back, and almost the width of the car. The screw cap for the petrol was on the same side as the wheels that were on the pavement, and the small quantity of petrol I had, had gravitated to the other end of the sloping tank.

The soldiers came up, one unscrewed the cap and inserted a glass rod, with a rubber bulb at the end, like a gigantic fountain pen filler. He squeezed the bulb and nothing happened. Twice more and still nothing. By the Grace of God they failed to figure out why, and with a grin and slap on the back one said in German something which I took to mean "You won't get far on that lot" and waved me off. After that I used the car strictly at night, when the squeegee service did not operate, and when by day I had the wrong colour petrol I observed the circuitous routes into the town.

Cycling in fine weather was rather fun but I recollect several occasions when we had almost continuous rain for a month and, during one autumn rain and wind for six solid weeks.

Every day, in spite of a waterproof coat, I was soaked right down to my shirt when I came in to the afternoon surgery; I never bothered to change, because I knew that with my evening round ahead of me I would be just as wet again.

With the shortage of any kind of fuel, there was no possibility of drying my clothes between peeling them off at 8.30—9pm and setting off again at 8am next morning. After three such days every garment I possessed was either damp or downright wet. When we had the occasional dry day, they could be hung outside on the line, but they were never less than damp, and in a month of wet weather, fighting one's way into wet clothes on dark mornings, was depressing to say the least, and not an encouraging start to the day's work.

My unpleasant dressing ordeal, which was preceded by a shave with cold water, often ersatz soap and cut-throat razor, was followed by breakfast.

This consisted of one ounce of often fusty oatmeal made into porridge with water and eaten with part of one's daily ration of half a pint of skim milk. No sugar of course.

Lunch was almost always a heap of parboiled potatoes, scorched in a dry pan—no fat—and eaten cold with a slice of Occupation bread, scraped with butter.

Supper was an egg (if available), usually with more scorched potatoes, or sometimes a gruel of minced wheat with sugar beet syrup.

This was my basic daily diet. Occasionally when I had someone to lunch, Mrs Ozouf put on a special show as far as supplies allowed, but at least we always had a bottle of good wine. Once my car hit a wood pigeon which was a second too late taking off from the roadside. Another time, a German officer shooting moorhens on St Ouens pond failed to kill one outright and I scooped it up as it came scuttering alongside my bicycle. Then sometimes we had a rabbit, or a morsel of meat donated by a kind farmer, with no questions asked. And, exceptionally, a tin from the small stock I had bought at the outset.

Many times we were reduced to a deplorably over-ripe

Camembert with bread and a glass of wine—a cheese which was known as Tramp's Foot.

These cheeses which had long passed the point where even the French could not stomach them, were shipped over to us, and bought by those who had the hardiness to eat them. They were stored in a Lock-up garage and most people crossed to the other side of the road when they walked past, for the stench was beyond belief. But in very small doses they added a little interest to the bread, as well as perhaps a little nourishment, and I was an unashamedly willing buyer.

The bread was half coarse-ground wheat, oats and peas and half mashed potato. Probably it was very good for something, and no doubt it would be readily stocked by a health shop, but it sat very heavy on the stomach, and was quite deplorably flatulent. The condition it produced was known by the unattractive name of "The Jersey Rattles".

Some housewives were remarkably ingenious in their attempts to make the food more interesting. Cooking-fat was a great problem, so someone, spotting a bottle of linseed oil in her husband's paint shop, cooked a meal of chips, which although golden and irresistibly appetising in appearance, proved to be quite uneatable. But when the first lot had been thrown away, and she was returning the oil to the bottle, she fancied that it no longer smelt so horrible, and cooked a second batch. These were at least eatable, and each subsequent lot was better than the last.

While eating them they were delicious, but if you were unfortunate enough to belch a little later there was a revolting taste of paint in your mouth.

Still you cannot have it every way, and as the news got around there was a run on linseed oil, at all hardware stores, while supplies lasted.

Very early, all sorts of baking powder and raising agents were snapped up, and while we had any flour left women sought around for every possible substitute. Eno's fruit salt was at a premium, and soon gave out, but one clever woman whose husband suffered from a kidney complaint noticed that the tablets he took regularly, effervesced when dropped into a glass of water.

Two of these tablets caused a cake to rise perfectly, and until I learnt the reason for it, I wondered why there was such a sudden rush on prescriptions for this particular product.

There was no question but that it was the women who bore the brunt of the Occupation. A great many men refused to work for the enemy, especially in handling war materials, but some acted as furnacemen, gardeners or general handymen in the officers' billets, and got well paid as well as drawing a somewhat higher ration than other civilian workers. Some of them even got fed in the mess as well.

To obviate unemployed men being forcibly enrolled for German war work, the Island Powers instigated the building of what is now the New North Road, and so gave work to many. But there were still large numbers of unemployed, and a few of these were just plain lazy.

I happened to visit a family at First Tower during the lunch hour, and the mother was just serving lunch to a husband and six children, all sitting around a table. The children all showed signs of under-nourishment, and the mother was gaunt and tired as she ladled out squares of plain turnip boiled in water. The husband, sitting with his back to the window said "Did you ever think, doctor, that we should come to this pass? It looks as if God has forgotten us."

I looked beyond him, through the window into a very large garden which was carrying about three years growth of weeds, and which could, if well cared for, have provided his family with a great deal of food. I merely said "God helps those who help themselves Mr le Sorre," and left the house.

Other men explored every way to help their families. Until the beaches were declared out of bounds to civilians, some fished with lines or a drag net, or collected limpets. Others worked, usually for their food only, on the farms, and they brought back potatoes, etc, with them, but it was the women who suffered, coping with hungry children, trying to keep one room at least reasonably warm, and cleaning the house with hardly any materials.

Those who were handy with their needles cut up and made coats and dresses for themselves and their children, from spare curtains, bedspreads and the most improbable materials. They showed a great deal of flair and imagination, too, and in these days when garments seem to be made up of three, four or five different materials, upon which young women spend hundreds of pounds in an attempt to look like Indian gypsies, some of clothes made then would be the height of fashion.

Then there was the constant fight for food to eke out the meagre rations. They stood for hours in queues every day, sometimes in appalling weather, or took long treks on foot, out into the country, to fetch a bag of vegetables from more affluent farming relations or friends.

Those of my readers who have coped with young babies, can sympathise with a mother who had to get up at night, in freezing conditions, without any light and no means of heating feeds. Every thermos flask on the Island had been bought or borrowed, and yet there were not enough to go round.

It is bad enough when one had plenty of heating and lighting, to pace the bedroom, hour after hour, trying to pacify a crying baby, but to do so in total darkness, at a freezing temperature is a real test, not only of fortitude but of parental love.

However, parents with small children belong to the younger age group and were more able to stand the hardship, but an elderly couple, often both of them sick and having to look after each other, were a really pathetic case.

One of the saddest cases of my professional life concerned an elderly couple and their middle-aged daughter. They were not Jersey-born, and had come here to retire many years before the War.

I had treated the wife for various trivial things, almost from my own arrival here, and had become very fond of her. She was lively, with a high intelligence, a multitude of interests and a great sense of humour.

In the first year of the Occupation, she came to my surgery with a number of indefinite symptoms, and after examining her, I came to the conclusion that she was in the early stages of Parkinson's Disease.

This is a malady which varies greatly, in its speed of onset and progress, and as at that time drugs which are so helpful now had not been introduced, I thought it better not to tell her outright the true nature of her disease.

It seemed kinder to give her a year or two of happiness, before she had to face up to the bitter truth. But she forestalled me.

"I know you are trying to be kind, doctor," she said on her second visit, "but I want to know the facts. I shall tell no one else as yet, especially my husband; it would be too much of a shock for him, at his age." (The husband was seventy-five and she was about sixty.)

She went on "It's Parkinson's Disease, isn't it? I had an aunt with it, and I've already read up the whole subject."

That pulled the rug from under my feet, and I had to admit to her that she was right. But I tried to cheer her up by saying that by leading a quiet life and taking care to avoid infections, and over-tiredness, she could slow down its progress.

"Yes," she said, "naturally I will do all that, but what happens when I get to the point that I can do nothing for myself, and I'm only an animated vegetable?"

These are the occasions which every doctor hates, when he has his back to the wall, and vague optimistic encouragement falls flat.

She fixed me with a bright blue eye and said: "I want your promise to do something tremendous for me. When the time comes, that I can no longer suffer the discomfort, indignity and dependence on others, will you help me to slip quietly out of this life? It will give me more comfort that I can say, to face what is before me, knowing that I can rely on your help when the time comes."

What was I to do? She was not a strong woman, physically, and in the pious hope that perhaps some infection would intervene and carry her off in the meantime, I reluctantly, but I hope with some conviction and good grace, gave her my promise.

I could have kicked myself when she left. Life was full enough of problems for me, as it was. But looking back on it I do not see that I could do anything else. No one with any heart could leave that brave woman to face her tragic future without the certainty of help at the last.

During the following years I saw her regularly, and for some time she did not seem to be going too badly. She was still able to get about the house, if carefully and slowly, and she read widely. The ban on wireless sets was a great blow to her and, had she been able to make her own choice, she would have kept hers. But her husband was nervous about it, and Letty, her daughter, even worse.

A good neighbour dropped in a couple of times a week, to keep her abreast of current news, but she sorely missed the talks, the music and so many other interesting features.

Then, when electricity was cut off except from 7.30am to 9am, 11am to 1.30pm, and 7pm to 11pm, she was very badly hit, because she felt the cold terribly, and often needed a fire even in summer. In the dark evenings she no longer had the consolation of reading, and her morale sagged noticeably.

The coarse diet did not worry her unduly, for she had always eaten simply and sparingly, but it caused intestinal problems, and because of this she ate less than ever, and began steadily to lose weight. Her husband and Letty also tolerated the rations very poorly, and he especially became noticeably frail.

By this time she was confined to her bed for most of the day, sitting up in a chair for short periods, mainly to ease her position and take pressure off her back. Even in bed, wrapped up in woollies, she felt cold and although I included her in my log round, the amount of warmth produced from a small wood fire did little to help.

Then she started getting agonising cramp in her legs and feet, and without warning a foot would suddenly contract and the sole curve downwards almost into a half-circle, causing her to scream in agony. One or other of her attendants would have to jump to the rescue, and bend the foot back till the spasm passed.

This meant that someone had to be at her side all around the clock. By day her husband or Letty could sit by her and read or talk, but at night the leaping out of bed countless times became so wearing that they took turns at sleeping, two hours on and two off, remaining fully clothed and sitting in an armchair in the dark, wrapped in a rug.

Drugs which initially eased her pain, began to be less effective, and in any case the supply became so short that it was impossible to control it effectively.

Both her husband and Letty were marvellously patient, but he had aged ten years in as many months, and Letty began to babble, and seemed to be losing her memory.

I considered getting the mother into a nursing home, but her husband flatly refused to let her go for, as he rightly said, she could never get such individual service round the clock as they were able to give.

It had got to the point when I began to wonder which of the three would be the first to go, when one morning, as Letty was out of the room for some reason, she looked up at me, perfectly lucidly and said, in a whisper, but quite plainly, "The time has come."

I nodded dumbly, realising in my heart that she was quite right, but at the same time wondering how I was going to go about it. I had for several months given it some consideration, but my mind had shied away from the problem which I now had to face squarely.

I could not stomach the thought of giving her a terminal injection in cold blood, and equally unthinkable would have been offering her a lethal dose which I would have to assist her to take by mouth, while both of us knew what it meant.

Eventually I hit upon a scheme. I had in a safe drawer, four grains of hyoscine, which I had kept for my own use if I had to undergo torture of a sort that I could not endure. I hoped never to have to fall back on it, but one had heard of events of that kind overtaking the most unlikely people.

This I took to a chemist I could trust implicitly, and had him roll me seven indentical pills, only one of which contained the hyoscine. These I took out with me, and said that they were a new drug I had got hold of, and was trying out as a last resort. One pill had to be taken every night for a week. My patient looked at me rather doubtfully, but finally smiled and nodded. She was not an easy woman to deceive.

Six days went by and I began to wonder whether hyoscine

could lose its potency by keeping, when on the seventh day the telephone rang at 6am. It was Letty.

"Come at once," she said. "Something has happened to Mother, I cannot wake her."

I flung on my clothes, jumped on my bike and did the four miles in under fifteen minutes. Letty was in tears, and the husband sitting in a heap in his chair, as I examined my patient and said she had had a stroke. I assured them that she had not suffered, which was absolutely true, because she had just gone to sleep under a massive dose of hyoscine, not knowing what she had taken.

I warned them that she was not likely to recover, and that I would call later in the day. This I did immediately after my surgery, and she had just breathed her last as I walked into the house.

Neither had any suspicion of what had actually happened, but I sensed that under their very genuine sorrow was a feeling of relief that all was over.

My problems were not over however, for both father and daughter were in a perilously low condition, especially now that they had nothing to keep them up to concert pitch.

They needed skilled nursing attention and good food, but neither was available just then, until I suddenly thought of a retired nursing sister who lived a short walking distance away. She and I had worked together before, and when I outlined to her their predicament she at once volunteered to walk over twice a day to keep an eye upon them until they recovered their equilibrium, although she knew neither of them personally.

She herself, belonging to a large prosperous farming family, was able to take over each day various little titbits, which, with her kindly presence and easy chat, started them back on the road to normality. For the first week they did little more than sleep, night and day, but after that they began to take interest.

Each time I called in, they seemed a little better and showed that they were getting ready to face life once more. Then the

Vega came, with the Red Cross parcels, and Letty made a quick recovery; she was able to look after her father, who never really recovered his health.

Now both are dead, or I would never have been at liberty to narrate this tragic tale.

CHAPTER 11

One morning in the late summer or early autumn of 1943 I was making up my list of visits for Mrs. Ozouf, prior to starting my daily round, when the telephone rang. It was my friend, Bob Vaynor, who, as was our rule at the time, was as terse as possible on the telephone: would it be at all possible for me to call at High Barn that morning? It was not urgent but he would be much obliged if I could.

"Is it a matter of life and death in any sense?" I asked.

"Not at all," was the reply. "But Connie will be very relieved to see you."

Connie was his wife. A nod's as good as a wink to a blind horse, and without asking any further questions I was there within the hour, having manipulated my round somewhat to take in High Barn.

I confess that some of my promptitude was due to curiosity, for I had never known Bob or Connie to suffer from anything except the occasional hangover, and from the tone of Bob's voice I had a feeling that the call was nothing to do with an illness. But never in a month of Sundays would I have guessed as to why I was called that morning.

Bob himself opened the door to me, and took me into his study where, sitting bolt upright on a hard chair and looking ill at ease, but by no means nervous, was a chunky young man of 23 or 24. He was in baggy grey trousers, a shirt and a dressing gown, which I recognised as belonging to Bob, with stockinged feet but no shoes.

No one said anything at first and I waited for an introduction. Then Bob said:

"This is Serge, a Russian. I picked him up last night. We are going to keep him here if we can. From what I can gather he has done something for which the Germans were going to punish him, and he made up his mind to escape. He has had a bath, this morning Connie found his pillow crawling with lice, and wants to know if you can get rid of them."

Apparently Bob had gone to feed his few hens, at dusk the previous evening, and had heard some rustling between the shed and a high bank behind. Going to investigate he saw a man crouching there who, after some hesitation, came out with his hands raised. Bob at once recognised that he must be a Russian, and he looked so thin and ill that there was nothing for it but to take him into the house.

He was a sad object with filthy, matted brown hair and beard, dressed in layer upon layer of dirty rags, and feet encased in tattered shoes, bound on with rags also.

They stayed in the kitchen and boiled him three eggs which, with half a loaf and a pint of sweet sugar-beet coffee, he bolted in ten seconds flat. Beyond a few words in French, they had no language in common but, after the meal, he looked less woebegone and tried to express his gratitude.

Bob gave him a cigarette, which he lit up with every sign of rapture and, while he was smoking, Bob and Connie went into the living room to discuss what they were going to do next. It was decided to keep him for the night, and they then went back into the kitchen to explain as best they could what they intended to do.

While they had sat in the kitchen with the Russian, they had been aware of a certain amount of what is termed "body odour" but, returning from the fresh air, the stench was like that of a goat pit; Connie started to gulp and had to make a dash for the garden. Bob walked straight into the now unused staff bathroom, turned on both taps, threw in a handful of bath salts, gave Serge a cake of carbolic soap and a towel, and motioned him to undress.

When Bob returned, twenty minutes later, the Russian had washed his hair and beard, and was still luxuriating in a full bath of hot water, with a broad grin on his face.

Bob picked up the heap of disgusting clothes from the bathroom floor and, flicking his cigarette lighter, held it towards him with an enquiring look on his face. The Russian cottoned on at once, gave a deep, bellowing laugh and motioned Bob to go ahead. He took the things to the bonfire site, set them alight and watched them burn to ashes. He then returned to look out some of his own things for his guest.

They then gave him another large meal and packed him off to bed, which Connie had made up in the staff bedroom. It was while she was making up the bed the next morning that she saw lice on the pillow, and that was where I came into the picture.

Ordinarily this was the sort of case I left to the District Nurse. After several years of Occupation, with shortage of soap and hot water, infestation with lice was a fairly common occurrence, and the nurses were adept at dealing with them. But, of course, in the circumstances, it was not practical to let yet another person into the secret, and I had to go home and look up the treatment in a book.

This consisted of damping all the hair with a carbolic solution of a certain strength, tying up the head in a towel and leaving it for eight hours. It sounded easy and, to make things easier still, Bob and and I decided to cut short the beard and crop the hair as best we could. In a hilarious half-hour we clipped the beard closely and left Serge to do his best with a safety razor. Connie then set to work on his head and gave him a very neat short back and sides. I applied the carbolic, tied up his head and went on my round, while Connie put everything to soak in disinfectant.

That night he had another all-over bath and next morning I dropped in to look for survivors, but found none.

What I encountered was a thin young man with dark grey eyes, and mid-brown hair neatly parted on one side. He was dressed in a rather baggy, rather shabby suit with a shirt, collar and tie, all too big for him, but nothing remained that remotely resembled the Russian bear of the previous day.

He had eaten an enormous breakfast and, when I arrived, was poring, with some astonishment, over some very old numbers of *Esquire* provided by Bob. Both Bob and Connie were plainly delighted with their new plaything and, loath as I was to act as a wet blanket, I felt I had to point out some of the snags.

1. Feeding: Serge was obviously eating twice as much, at least, as an ordinary man and would undoubtedly continue to do so till the void in his body was filled up.

This was brushed aside. Connie said that she herself only ate half her rations (which was true) and that as Bob was overweight it would do him good to share some of his. They also had a cow which was rented out to a local smallholder in return for a gallon of milk per day (quite illegal of course). They had their own hens, a very productive kitchen garden, and could buy extra potatoes on the black market. In addition they could tap friends for seasonal surpluses. Anyway, he couldn't be worse off than he had been in the camp.

2. Clothes: I knew that by this time Bob was pretty well down to rock bottom for clothes, as I was myself, and anyway Serge was difficult to fit, being enormously broad in the shoulder, with a chest of about 46 inches and yet only about five feet six inches tall. Connie, with a wicked look at me, said: "Haven't you any big fat men in your practice who you could bump off? His coats and waistcoats would fit Serge and I could always shorten the trousers." I assured her that I would do almost anything in reason for her, except that, but promised to ask discreetly among my patients.

In the end, what she had suggested nearly happened, except that a very large patient died a natural death instead of having to be bumped off. The deceased's wife asked if I had any poor patients who would be glad of his clothes, and so I came away with two large cases of clothes in very good condition. As well as suits, there were shirts, socks, ties and shoes—the latter on the big side but useable. Serge was now completely fitted up.

3. Boredom: I pointed out that a young, active man could not possibly remain in a house week in, week out, without going off his rocker, but Bob argued that persons in solitary confinement did just that and, anyway, he could garden in unobserved corners, or sit reading in the sun, etc., etc.

"Besides," added Bob, who was a teacher *manqué*, "I shall teach him English. You can see he is very intelligent, and Russians are notorious for being good at languages." That sounded more hopeful and I offered to try and find an English-Russian grammar. Bob gave me an amused glance, as if to say, "Well, I'm a bit of a crazy optimist myself, but ....!"

As it happened I had a patient—a very old lady who for over thirty years had been governess to a succession of children in Russian aristocratic families. She was Jersey-born, and had many years before returned to end her days in her native Island. When I went to see her she was quite hopeful and said that she had a trunkful of books in her attic and that if I cared to come back in a few days she would see what she could find.

As asked, I went back and, sure enough, she produced two—one elementary and one more advanced. Both were yellow and fusty but they were unquestionably what we wanted.

Serge, as I predicted, was already getting bored, and fastened on to the books with such enthusiasm that Bob's sole function was to correct Serge's accent and pronunciation.

4. Exercise: Serge had already coped with that, and was doing physical exercises every day in his room, and walking round and round the garden each evening after dusk. He was already beginning to show the benefit of good, regular food and was losing his haggard appearance.

5. Discovery: Nobody but ourselves must know about Serge, and that was eventually bound to present a problem. As it was, Bob, Connie and myself were the only ones in the know, and of course Mrs Chalus. She was a middle-aged lady of

French origin, who was what is known as a "treasure". She had been with the Vaynors as a daily for five or six years, and they had the utmost confidence in her. She came in for mornings only and, even if they wanted to, there was no way in which the secret could be kept from her—anyway, there was no need, she could be trusted implicitly.

Window cleaners, postmen, the tradesmen could all be circumvented, but not Mrs Chalus! She knew that the Vaynors had kept two wireless sets, drank illegal milk, had a lot of wine stashed away, but never a word leaked out.

Everything seemed to be working out most satisfactorily until, after about three weeks Bob, looking for something in his desk, uncovered a snuff-box in which he kept a few golden sovereigns. There had been five, but some weeks before he had taken one to give as a christening present, and it struck him that perhaps it would be more sensible to keep them in the safe. However, on opening the box, he was astonished to find it empty, but he concluded that perhaps Connie had had the same idea as himself, and transferred them elsewhere. When he asked her, Connie was equally surprised and suggested that perhaps Mrs Chalus had put them somewhere safer. Bob asked her, and she replied, without batting an eyelid:

"Yes, I took them. I knew for some time where they were and, as a sovereign now fetches ten pounds I thought they would be worth having."

The overt threat was evident, and Bob and Connie looked at each other aghast—not only at the predicament which suddenly faced them, but also at the fact that Mrs Chalus could have betrayed them so cynically.

They walked out of the room speechless, Connie in tears, while Mrs Chalus went on with her polishing as if nothing had happened.

Then Bob acted. He was not the sort of man to allow himself to be blackmailed, no matter what the consequences. I remembered, at the time of Munich, his quoting Kipling:

"Once you start paying Danegeld
You'll never get rid of the Dane."

He shut himself in his study and got on the telephone to a mutual friend, asking him to come at once in his lorry. No explanation. Connie helped Serge pack every single thing that might be incriminating and, before the friend even arrived, Bob gave Mrs Chalus the sack. She, astonishingly enough, made out to be very hard done by and created quite a scene, but Bob managed to bundle her out of the house before the friend arrived.

A few words of explanation were all that were required and Serge, smartly dressed, with a pair of dark glasses, went off in the lorry to a farm at the other end of the Island.

Bob dumped the larger wireless set into the septic tank, while Connie put all Serge's bed linen into the washing machine, made up the spare-room bed afresh and obliterated every trace of Serge's stay in the house. His bathroom was meticulously cleaned and left looking as if it had not been used for months, and even the gully at the back of the hencoop, where Serge had originally been found, was raked to wipe out possible footmarks.

As Connie sewed the smaller wireless set into a feather pillow, Bob tried me several times on the telephone, and finally got me as I was finishing lunch. I could tell at once by his voice that I had better go immediately. He told me afterwards that what he really wanted was third person's eye on the scene of the crime. He had gone over the house himself with a small tooth comb but he was not at all sure that he might not have missed some little thing.

Whether he had or not was beside the point, for I arrived to find a German staff car beside the front door. Mrs Chalus had lost little time.

I could have driven off there and then, but I thought that perhaps I could help and, grabbing a medical bag and my stethescope, walked in through the open door. Bob appeared at once and said to the soldier in the hall, who came forward to find out what I wanted: "This is the doctor who has come to see my wife."

He looked at me with a certain fixity of expression, for he did not dare to say more, but I caught the message and, turning my back on the soldier, who was young and unsure of what to do next, started up the stairs.

Connie was in bed and there were three Gestapo men in the room. The officer was leaving all the searching to the two underlings while he stood still and kept his eyes riveted on Connie, watching to see if she showed any extra emotion at any particular point of the search. He was a tall thin, very blonde man of about forty with the pale, almost opalescent skin that one sometimes sees in the very fair. His hair was cropped almost to the skull and his very pale blue eyes, with hooded eyelids like organstops, looked out of thick-lensed glasses, set in flimsy gold frames.

He spoke quite good English and, with a slight bow, hoped that my patient was not too seriously ill.

I replied that was what I had come to find out and, to give Connie an idea of what she was supposed to have wrong with her. I explained that she was subject to recurrent lung infections.

At this point, Connie—who always had a smoker's cough anyway—gave vent to a very convincing hacking croak.

He looked at her with a little more sympathy after that, and indeed, no one could have doubted that she had every appearance of being extremely ill.

Connie was not one to scare easily and it was difficult to account for the tallow candle colour of her skin and the cold sweat on her forehead.

It flashed across my mind that perhaps she really was ill, although I had seen her in perfect health the night before. What I did not know was that she was sitting propped up in bed on three pillows, the middle one of which contained the wireless set. Furthermore, her feet were resting against a covered hot-water bottle into which had been stuffed a small, pearl-handled revolver. Not handing in a firearm was an offence, in certain cases involving death. I asked the officer to remove the soldiers from the room while I examined my patient, hoping that he too would take the hint, but he stood his ground, although he had the grace to turn his back and look out of the window, whistling tunelessly through his teeth. I went through all the drill: temperature, tongue, pulse, ausculation of the chest, and found nothing wrong, but I lingered over the chest for some time, and told the officer that she had some congestion of both lungs and must be kept warm and quiet.

Promising to get some medicine out to her somehow, I bowed to the officer, thanked him and went downstairs. The two soldiers were occupying their time by going through drawers in the hall furniture and taking up the carpet.

Not wishing them to realise how friendly I was with Bob, I shook his hand and wished him a formal goodbye, just restraining a wink as I saw one of the soldiers observing me in the hall mirror. I left, saying that I would call next morning. This I did and found Connie singing gaily as she brushed down the stairs with a hand-broom and dustpan. She was bubbling over with excitement and was anxious to tell me about the search and how the Germans had missed several incriminating things. But I cut it all off by asking "What would you do if the Germans walked in this minute and found you dancing around with a dustpan?" "Oh, they wouldn't do that", she said, "they've finished with us now. They didn't find anything remotely suspicious."

"Perhaps not," I said. "Mrs Chalus must have told them so much that they must wonder why they were able to find nothing. I'm sure they will be back to search some more, so up you go and get into bed."

She pouted and made to refuse, but Bob backed me up and she was barely settled in bed when, coming out of the study where we had been chatting for a few minutes, we found the officer standing quietly in the hall. No one had heard him enter.

This time they had approached from another direction, had entered by the garden gate, and were in the house via the French window before anyone would have had time to take avoiding action. They seemed disappointed as well as surprised to see Connie still in bed, and as she was less frightened this time she consequently looked much better. I was able to assure them with some satisfaction that her condition was much improved.

I formed the opinion that this was a catching-out visit, for they made no search on this occasion but walked off with Bob's list of personal telephone numbers which had been sitting on the hall table.

Thereafter every single name on that list was investigated and most of their houses searched, but by some special dispensation of providence, the farm to which Serge had gone was not on the telephone.

Meanwhile, the problem of Serge had to be gone into in depth. A band of helpers was formed and it was decided that, in the interests of security, Serge should never sleep for more than one night in any house. This was not entirely possible for the first couple of months, but as the organisation got under way not only did Serge not sleep more than one night in any house, he never slept in the same parish on two successive nights.

This entailed a good deal of planning and very often the host for the night would manage to get Serge to his next billet, but from time to time Arthur Halliwell and myself did the transport, when we had the necessary petrol. As we had a minute knowledge of the narrow lanes, the risk to both of us was not as great as it might seem, but as any soldier had the right to stop us and ask for our identity cards it was a risk that certainly could not be entirely discounted. We therefore had to get hold of an identity card for Serge.

It happened that at about this time a young man from one of the central parishes died of long-standing TB although I had nothing to do with his case, his married sister was one of my patients. While talking to her about him one day I tentatively asked whether his identity card had been handed in as by German order the relatives were compelled to do so. It had in fact been handed in, but by an astounding piece of good luck she still had one belonging to another brother who had escaped from the Island the previous autumn.

The photograph on this showed a young man with hair parted in the middle, and a rather large moustache. So Serge copied the hairstyle and started to cultivate a moustache. The escaped brother had also left behind a bicycle and, although these were fetching very high prices, the parents were glad to donate it to a good cause.

So, as soon as Serge's moustache had grown to the requisite size and he was mobile, he began moving about the Island in an unobtrusive way. He looked enough like the photograph to pass anything but a very minute examination and, as by this time he spoke more than average English, we had no fear that he would fail to get past the ordinary soldier.

The danger would be if he encountered an officer, several of whom spoke absolutely idiomatic English and had in fact been to school in England. Our hope was that as the name on the identity card was a Breton one they might put his rather strange accent down to that fact. As a point of interest, especially as he now mixed with many different people, Serge's English improved with every week that went by, and before the Occupation ended he could easily be mistaken for an Englishman.

At first he was fiercely Russian and was furious at any criticism of the regime, but after many long arguments with his various hosts about totalitarianism versus democracy, his attitude began to change, and doubts about the all-prevading benefits of Communism to appear. Eventually he announced that when the War was over he would not return to Russia, but would try to get to Canada and start a new life there.

We taught him Bridge and he rapidly became a very competent player, so that gradually the problem of boredom ceased to exist. In addition to this he very soon became a voracious reader of English books and we were hard put to it to keep up with his appetite.

We started him on *Swiss Family Robinson* and some of *Captain Marryat*, but after he had raced through Somerset Maugham with the utmost delight, there was no holding him. We threw Henty, Rider Haggard and Edgar Wallace at him, and almost every paperback we could find, and he devoured them all. Many of them I had never read myself. As his confidence grew he took to exploring the Island on his bike, and even went to the cinema. His friends contributed to making him a small allowance so that he could do that sort of thing, but as there was very little to spend it on I imagine he became a capitalist in a very, very small way.

By this time he had filled out considerably and had become a very powerfully built young man—not fat, but a close-knit chunk of muscle with magnificent shoulders.

We were now in early 1945 and he had already escaped two comprehensive searches for escaped Russians, by the German military police. He still slept in a different house every night, but now he moved himself from place to place on his own bike, and was accepted as an ordinary Islander, by people who had no knowledge of his origin. Occasionally he came to Beaupré, usually on Tuesday—my day off—and helped in the garden. He got through an enormous amount of work, taking great delight in doing jobs which I found too heavy for myself and which I purposely left for him. After nightfall we played Nap with Claude Avarne and sometimes went on so late that he had to stay the night, while I, with my curfew pass, was able to cycle home in the dark.

Sometimes, instead of playing cards we would talk and he would tell us about his life in Russia. He was very coherent and could describe events and things expressively. His father had been an officer in the Czar's army and fought as a very young man in the First World War. His mother was the daughter of a civil servant and when he was born to them, rather late in life, they moved to Leningrad where his father took some sort of clerical job. Life was rather drab and money was short, but as a family they were happy and made the most of simple pleasures. A couple of years before the war Serge managed to get into the University and then suddenly, one evening towards the end of his first year, while Serge was visiting a friend, the secret police called and took his father away. For a long time his mother did everything in her power to find out where his father was, or at least the charge against him, but invariably she met a blank wall and they never heard from him again.

With the German invasion of Russia, Serge was drafted, but after fighting for only about six months he was taken prisoner and was sent to work with a large group at Lorient.

Here he survived several British bombings in which many of his fellow prisoners were killed and, during the confusion following one of them, he escaped. He remained at liberty for almost two months, wandering about France and living on stolen food, but eventually he was re-captured and shipped off with a mixed bag of nationalities to Jersey.

Their guards were a sub-human, sadistic lot and one evening when Serge witnessed a prisoner's arm almost amputated with the edge of a spade, he laid out the guard with his fist. He thinks he broke his neck. Knowing the inevitable consequences, and realising he had nothing to lose, Serge ran for it, and when he was too tired to go further he hid behind the hen-house where he was discovered by Bob.

Then Serge fell in love. It was almost inevitable in a husky young man of his age, but the girl of his choice happened to be a well-known Jerry bag. At least she was not one of the strident ones, but she had been seen for some time going about with a particular German soldier. I did not know her name, but I remembered her from the time she was a teenager going to a small private school in the town. One could not help noticing her for she was an amber colour all over: amber hair, amber eyes and a warm honey coloured skin. She had a pleasant expression and a very sweet face, and I felt that she could not have been as bad as she was made out to be, but Bob was absolutely furious, had Serge up to High Barn and gave him a monumental dressing down. But Serge was completely besotted, and was constantly seen escorting her around the town. From their first meeting, so far as I know, she was never seen with a German again and although I pointed this out to Bob, it cut no ice at all. Serge, in his turn, would not be budged and, to make matters worse, he gave up going to all his old haunts and moved in with the girl and her widowed mother.

Some of us encountered him from time to time, always in the town and he was invariably pleasant and glad to see us, but the special relationship was broken and we felt that he no longer required our help and advice.

Had this happened six months before, the state of affairs might have been much more dangerous, but by the time of which I am writing, the Germans realised that the tide was now running against them, and they made only a few half-hearted attempts to capture escaped foreign workers.

The sad thing was that, had we all been in contact and on the same footing, we would almost certainly have advised Serge not to give himself up to the Russian authorities when they came to collect their nationals from Jersey. However, he did give himself up, and in fact had left Jersey before any of us even realised that such a thing was happening, and the only one of us ever to see him again was Bob Vaynor.

What happened was that very soon after the Liberation, a posse of Russian Military Police arrived to take off all the private soldiers who were at large on the Island. There were about a dozen and what their fate was is wrapped in mystery. There were horrific tales as to their end but they were only tales.

About a week after, the escaped officers were taken off separately. There were four from Jersey, including Serge, and three from Guernsey.

Serge managed to get out to High Barn to try and see Bob, and to effect a reconciliation. Connie was at home but Bob had gone out and Serge could not wait indefinitely. On his return Bob at once tried to find him, but he had already left for the mainland.

About two months after the Liberation, Bob and Connie managed to get over to England and went to stay with Bob's sister at a large house in semi-rural Surrey. One of the first things they wanted to see was a good play, and the night after their arrival were driven up to a London theatre in the sister's car. On their return, well after midnight, as they came up the shrub-lined drive, they saw a man in some sort of uniform, with a peaked cap, who dived into the rhododendrons and disappeared. A little further on another man similarly dodged out of sight. Over a short nightcap Bob mentioned this to his sister and she said, "Yes, very close to us here is a big enclosed area, a sort of camp, I suppose, containing a number of large buildings which no one ever seems to enter or is encouraged to approach. There are always guards patrolling the boundaries and I have been told that it is an extraterritorial bit of Russia; apparently what takes place there is entirely their own concern, and our local authorities have no jurisdiction over it. From time to time people seem to escape, and this is not the first time guards have been beating my shrubbery in an effort to find them. I do hope they don't catch this one."

The Vaynors then went off to bed in a first-floor room with a French window opening on to a balcony which ran along the whole front of the house. As they were undressing there was a scratching at the closed window and, opening the curtains suddenly, Bob saw a man standing outside. He was just about to give the alarm when he saw the man put his finger to his lips and motion him to open the window. Something about the figure seemed familiar, and in stepped Serge.

He was bedraggled and dirty and obviously very distressed. He asked if he could stay there till the hue and cry had died down and also if he could possibly have something to eat. Bob went down, rummaged in the larder and brought up almost everything edible he could find, with memories of Serge's enormous appetite. Serge absorbed every last crumb and apologised, saying that he had not eaten for twenty-four hours.

He told Bob that after they came over from Jersey they were brought to the camp, where a decontamination course was put under way. In other words they had to be thoroughly brainwashed before they could safely be returned to Russia.

Four members were from Jersey, three from Guernsey and one, supposedly, from Alderney, and they were all housed in a separate unit of bedrooms opening on to a communal club-cum-dining room.

When they were not receiving instruction they sat and read or chatted in the clubroom, and the officer from Alderney was very charming and friendly to them all. None of them was allowed outside.

Soon Serge found himself extolling the democratic way of life, and even told his new friend about his plan to settle in Canada.

That was enough. The man from Alderney was a stool-pigeon, for no officers had been taken from Alderney, although it was impossible for the Jersey and Guernsey officers to know that.

Serge was arrested and put in a cell to await further interrogation, but the same night he managed to escape by breaking through the roof. While on the run and concealed in *Lady Radcliffe's* grounds he was astounded to see the Vaynors leaving the house in a car. Fearful of being captured while awaiting their return, he had hidden in a rainwater butt, which he first emptied by turning on the tap. While inside he heard the guards calling constantly to each other, while they moved about in the gardens.

The minute he saw a light go on upstairs he swarmed up a pillar of the verandah and scratched on the window, praying hard that he would not be spotted from the garden before he gained admittance.

While Connie went to bed, Serge and Bob sat in the latter's dressing room waiting for the hue and cry to die down. Serge described to Bob all that he could of the enclave from the inside. The windows were all of frosted glass and, as none of them were allowed outside, he had no idea of the extent or layout of the area.

He and his fellows were virtually prisoners, guarded night and day inside their own block. Their treatment was very good otherwise. There was plenty of good plain food, books and games were at their disposal but no papers or radio. No one talked to them at all, except their allotted brain-washers.

This, Serge said, made him more than ever determined to seek the freedom of a democratic society.

After a couple of hours without seeing anything or hearing a sound outside, Serge decided that the guards had called it off for the night, and that now he might have a chance to get clear.

Bob went through his own pockets, as well as Connie's handbag, and came up with something short of fifteen pounds, which he handed over.

He advised Serge to make for the nearest railway, and follow it to a station from which he could get into central London; then to make for a minor seaport and either stow away or get a job on any boat going to the North American continent. He had enough confidence in Serge's powers of survival not to advise him further than that. Letting Serge out by the way he had come—the bedroom window—was too risky, and they chose the basement door opening into the yard at the back, through which coal, wines, etc. were carried into the cellar.

Opening it noiselessly, Serge shook hands without a word and had just put his foot upon the first of the three steps leading up to the yard, when Bob grabbed his arm and pointed soundlessly at the low fence at the far end. There, silhouetted against the night sky, were the head and shoulders of a man. He obviously neither heard nor saw them, for he did not move, so they quietly closed the door, crept up to Bob's room once more, where they spent the night drinking endless cups of tea, and talking.

In the morning Bob waited for his sister to come down and, as was only fair, put her in possession of all the facts about the situation.

Game old lady that she was, she took a grip of the situation at once. Sending for the local police immediately, she explained to the officer who arrived that her privacy was being disturbed by persons, Russian she believed, who were trespassing on her grounds.

Could the police search her property, and approach any that they found with the request that they leave immediately and did not repeat the offence? If they refused, they were to be threatened that contact would instantly be made with the Home Office.

The police could and did. A whistle from the first guard approached, brought in two others and, while they were arguing at some distance from the house, the chauffeur driving the family limousine appeared in the back drive. Serge was whisked into it, quite unseen by anyone and driven off to a destination decided upon by *Lady Radcliffe*.

Bob and Connie were quite in the dark about where this was until the chauffeur returned and reported that Serge had been safely delivered at a small port in Devon, where he had holed up at a modest boarding house under the eye of an old retired naval friend of *Lady Radcliffe*.

This all seemed highly satisfactory until, something more than a week later, an unknown voice on the telephone, asking to speak to *Lady Radcliffe*, announced that she would no longer be annoyed by agents on her property, because the fugitive in question had been captured and would give her no further trouble.

This was shattering news, especially as the plan had seemed so fool-proof. The overt threat that "the fugitive would give no further trouble" was very distressing, and they were also disturbed as to how the Russians had run Serge to earth. They discussed endlessly the various possibilities but no one ever came up with a viable solution.

About eight or nine weeks later, when they had returned to Jersey, a fat envelope—almost a parcel—bearing a Belgian postmark, arrived at High Barn addressed to Colonel Vaynor. It was from Serge and written from "a farmhouse in Belgium", nothing more specific.

After his nerve wracking experience of the far-reaching tentacles of the Soviet system, Serge obviously did not wish to implicate his protectors. It was evident from the amount of detail he wrote about his life since Bob had last seen him, that Serge had plenty of time on his hands.

His stay in Devon had not lasted very long. He was very careful never to venture outside during daylight, but on the third evening, longing for a breath of fresh air, he took a quiet stroll, after first dark, towards the harbour. He had not left the house ten minutes when, without any warning, he felt a crushing blow on the back of his head and woke up to find himself handcuffed and spancelled in the back seat of a fast car, with a man on either side, and a third man driving. None of his captors uttered a word, and when the car stopped he realised that he was back in the enclave in Surrey from which he had escaped only a week before.

This time he was shut into a far more secure cell than the previous one and, although his legs were freed, he remained handcuffed night and day except for feeding and other necessary functions, when a guard remained in the cell with him.

During the time he was there, about two weeks he thought, none of the guards exchanged a single word with him; and no attempt was made to put him under interrogation. But he had no illusions about his ultimate fate. Probably for diplomatic or similar reasons the Russians felt it unsafe to liquidate him in Surrey, and were waiting for an opportunity to turn up, when this could be done with greater security.

Finally, one morning he was led out to a car, still handcuffed, and he set out again with the same three men. Again, he ended up at a seaport—a fairly large one as far as he could judge—but his memory of this was very vague, because about ten minutes before reaching their destination, one of the men produced a ready-loaded syringe and jabbed it into his leg through the cloth of his trousers. At the same time the handcuffs were removed, but they were no longer necessary, for by now he was so hazy in his mind and unsteady on his feet that the two men had to clutch him firmly under the arms and half carry him aboard. They went straight down to the cabin where he fell asleep.

At the port of arrival, he had no idea where, he was roused and similarly carried ashore where a boat train was waiting and a carriage reserved. Once aboard the train his handcuffs were again put on and, after a long wait, the interminably slow journey across Europe commenced. He slept again, and when he awoke there was only one guard in the carriage, the other returned some time after smelling of beer, and saying in Russian that the food in the restaurant car was very good. The second guard then went off and similarly returned in about an hour. Serge, by this time, was very much more wide awake, but he gave no sign other than that he was completely drowsy.

The afternoon was beginning to be very hot, and both guards took off their coats and flung them on to the rack above. Serge pretended to rouse somewhat and in a thick voice asked for something to drink. One of the guards brought a plastic mug of coffee, which Serge—pretending to be half shot and very clumsy—managed to drink with his handcuffed hands. The coffee cleared his head completely, but he lay there still pretending to be in a drugged sleep, while he wondered what to do next.

By and by, what with the heat of the afternoon and all the

beer they had drunk, one of the guards began to snore and soon the other dropped off too. The track was in a very poor state and at times the train slowed to a crawl. Once it stopped altogether, and both guards woke up but, seeing their charge apparently sound asleep, dozed off again.

Soon after this, Serge looked out of the window and saw that the track was making a wide curve towards a fairly large river, spanned by a temporary bridge, obviously put up to replace one destroyed in the war.

It had no parapet and looked very flimsy, which it probably was, for the train slowed down to less than walking pace as it approached. Because of the heat of the day both windows were let down to their fullest extent and Serge made an instant decision. When the carriage was over the middle of the river he eased himself stealthily to his feet and, stretching his handcuffed hands in front of him, dived head first through the window. He broke a rib or two on the frame, which he did not feel at the time, but such was the power of his dive that he cleared the edge of the bridge and landed straight in the river.

He surfaced almost immediately, and luckily there was little current so he was able to keep afloat. By kicking his legs and thrashing with his handcuffed hands, he was able to make some headway and made for a flat bank downstream. What current there was was in his favour and quite soon he was climbing out and making for a sparse wood across a small field. Meanwhile, the train, which had not stopped on the bridge, halted some way off and he heard shouts from its direction, though he could not see what was happening. But this in itself acted as a spur, to set him running as fast as he could towards the far side of the wood and then across a large field of sugar beet. His broken ribs were now beginning to be very painful, but he kept on running and soon came to a road which he followed in a direction which took him away from the railway. Almost at once he was overtaken by a man driving a tractor and empty trailer, which he stopped at once. The farmer, astounded to see that the running man was handcuffed and that his clothes were soaked from head to foot, leaned over and said something. Serge, whose French was rudimentary and who had no time for long explanations, jumped into the trailer which only held some sacks. The farmer, though surprised by the liberty Serge was taking, plainly caught the sense of urgency and, without stopping the engine, drove off at a good round speed. All this time they were out of sight of the train and could hear nothing, but as a precaution, Serge lay down in the trailer and covered himself with sacks. They drove for the best part of an hour and at length the tractor entered the yard of a large, rather prosperous looking farmstead, where the farmer helped Serge, who by now was in agony from his ribs, to get down.

They were met at the door by a woman who was plainly the farmer's wife. But the farmer brushed past her into the kitchen and, setting Serge down on a chair, wanted to know that it was all about. Now that there was no urgency, Serge in his halting French managed to get across the story of what had happened, and the other, once satisfied that Serge was not a criminal, appeared to be on his side.

Not so the wife, however, and such a furious argument arose that Serge was almost preparing to start on his flight again when—what with the emotional upheaval and the pain in his chest—he passed out completely. He came to, lying on a couch with the woman forcing some cognac between his lips and the farmer covering him with a blanket. The quarrel seemed to be over, and the farmer left the kitchen while his wife started spooning some hot soup into Serge, who heard the tractor starting up and wondered what was going to happen next. In less than half an hour there were sounds of the tractor returning and the farmer entered, followed by another man carrying a bag of blackmith's tools. After quite a tussle, and a good deal of chafed skin, the handcuffs were off and Serge sat down with his benefactors to a much needed evening meal. They were quite chatty and communicative and he learned that they had two sons, one in America where he had been for some years, and the other a dentist practising in Liège. This meant that there were only three of them living in the house and soon they became on very good terms. Serge helped the woman as far as he was able, but could do nothing at all active on account of the pain in his chest, which was severe for some time. They dared not, for fear of discovery, send for a doctor but the pain eased, at first slowly, then rapidly, and eventually it went altogether. Serge then helped about the farm, but only very early in the mornings and late evenings, for the farm workers were about during the ordinary hours of employment.

He picked up French quite quickly so that soon they were able to chat quite easily and he became genuinely attached to his hosts, especially the wife, who was not in very good health and had to spend long hours alone on the farm.

As I mentioned earlier, the length of his letter meant that Serge had plenty of time on his hands, but we all marvelled at how good his English was, although his spelling was rather peculiar. He confided to his hosts his plans for getting to Canada, and Mr Baels, the farmer, had given his blessing to the project, even to the extent of making enquiries about a job on a cargo boat sailing out of Antwerp. Serge had it all worked out that once in Canada he would jump ship and seek political asylum there.

There were pages of what he planned to do when he was granted political asylum, and he promised to write again as soon as he knew more exactly what was happening. He repeated again all his feelings of gratitude to Bob for saving his life twice, and for opening up another wider world than he could ever have in Russia. He did not know how soon he would be able to leave Belgium, and thought he would almost certainly write once more from his present address. But if he did not, he would let us know where we could get in touch with him in Canada, on his arrival there.

In addition, he gave us Mr Baels' address, but warned us not to contact him for at least six months, when presumably he, Serge, would have safely reached Canada.

We never heard from Serge again. After letting one year go by just to be on the safe side, Bob wrote to Mr Baels asking him for any news he could give us, but there was never any reply.

In his letter, Serge had stated specifically that there had been no sign of the Russians and no suspicious circumstances to indicate that they were on his track, but somehow, somewhere—possibly in Antwerp, they had caught up with him and finished the hunt which they had followed with such gruesome tenacity.

Such was his devotion to Bob that had he been alive, no matter where—except possibly in Russia—he would have unquestionably got in touch.

We were forced to believe that he must now be dead.

CHAPTER 12

For me at least, the deprivation of light was much harder to bear than lack of fuel or food. We learned to wear three or four woollies indoors, wrap ourselves in rugs or blankets and even to resort to gloves, but light was a problem.

Up to about halfway through the Occupation, candles could be bought on the black market at a pound a-piece (and they went even higher before the end), and there was the occasional ration of paraffin, usually half a pint a head, but these things went nowhere in the winter when it was dark soon after 4.30pm, and there was no proper daylight till 7.30am at least. I had a small brass nursery night lamp of the kind that cannot be upset, with a white tulip-shaped globe and a flame about the size of a large pea. This, when placed actually on my book enabled me to read but, although its oil consumption was minimal, even that came to an end. A farmer's wife gave me a small bottle of a mixture of paraffin, petrol and diesel oil which she herself burned in a lamp. She warned me that when the lamp began to make a singing sound, it was about to explode, and I must put it out immediately and not relight it until it became quite cold.

This I tried, but what with the waiting for the singing noise to start, and then sitting in the dark until the lamp was cold—which was upwards of an hour—I decided it was not worth the risk and thereafter kept the lamp only for dressing and undressing.

I kept the pure paraffin from the ration strictly for my bicycle lamp, without which my journeys in the dark would have been even more hazardous than they were.

One night, having already been out once in the car and exhausted the petrol, my telephone rang just after I had dropped off to sleep. An agitated man's voice asked me to come out as quickly as possible to see his wife, who was bleeding badly from, as he rather inelegantly put it, "a cut in her backside". I knew that this time it would have to be the bicycle, and I warned him that he could not expect me for upwards of an hour, for he lived at the top of Grêve de Lecq hill, about six miles away, and most of it against the collar.

It was a dark night, with no moon, a lot of cloud and a threat of rain. I was sailing along, at a good speed past Le Catelet Farm, when suddenly, without any warning except a snarling growl, a large dog flew at me and fastened his teeth in my trouser leg. Fortunately I was wearing oilskin leggings over my trousers, so at least my skin escaped, but he refused to let go. Entangled in the back wheel, we both collapsed in a heap onto the road.

I scrambled quickly to my feet, and he came at me again, but there was just enough light for me to see his white ruff, and I kicked with all my force. With a yelp he made off, but remained in the hedge growling, while I gathered up my things. In the mix-up my bicycle-lamp had come off; it was impossible to find in the darkness, so I had to ride on without it. Besides, the dog was plainly trying to work up courage for another attack, and I did not want to be caught, literally, bending.

I was especially annoyed by the loss of my lamp because I often relied on it when I had some surgical procedure to do in a house that had no light.

Arriving there at last, I found that the husband had not exaggerated. By the light of a match, I could see an alarming amount of blood on the floor and on the bed, and as I had feared there was no light of any sort.

In the kitchen, where he had had the sense to boil a kettle, there was a handful of embers in the grate, but by no means enough to see what I was doing. I thought that I could manage if he had sufficient newspaper to light successive sheets in the bedroom fireplace, but he had none of that either. Finally he found a book of poetry, bought at a jumble sale long before, and preserved on account of its attractive binding.

We put the woman on her side, on the edge of the bed, and the husband stood at the grate lighting sheet after sheet of the book, one from another.

What had happened was that, prior to retiring, she had sat on a chamber pot, which had broken under her weight and inflicted a very deep jagged wound, low down in her buttock, An artery which had been severed was still pumping blood, and this I had to secure and tie off.

Having done this, in the ebb and flow of the light, I could now take my time, and though I say it as shouldn't, I performed a very natty piece of stitchery. I had to put in about a dozen sutures, and should really have put in more, but again stocks of silkworm gut were at a low ebb, and a not very sightly scar in just that position would not have been a major tragedy.

The wound healed by first intention, and I was able to take out the stitches on the eighth day with the wound firmly healed.

On my way back, by now in quite heavy rain, I ran into the back of a parked car, also without lights, under some overhanging trees. Two German soldiers tumbled out, more than a little drunk, and handling their rifles with complete unconcern for my safety. They asked to see my papers which they looked at upside-down, and which they handed back in rather a bad temper. I was no more cordial myself, and that was perhaps why, when I was about fifty yards away, one of them loosed off a shot at me. How wide of the mark it was, I don't know. It certainly didn't hit me.

At first light I went back to the site of my encounter with the dog, and fortunately found my lamp in the ditch. It would not have done to leave it until later in the day, for a bicycle-lamp, and indeed any lamp, was more precious than rubies.

One of the most traumatic experiences, from the point of view of a general practitioner, was the forced deportation to Germany of people of English birth, which took place in September 1942.

On 15 September, there appeared, without any kind of warning, the following announcement in the German-controlled Jersey press.

"By order of Higher Authority, the following British subjects will be evacuated and transported to Germany:

(a) People who have their permanent residence not in the Channel Islands, for instance those caught there by the outbreak of war.

(b) All those men not born in the Channel Islands and 16—70 years of age, who belong to the English people, together with their families.

der Field Commandant
Knackfuss. Oberst."

The Jersey *Evening Post* is always published in the late afternoon, and as the deportation was scheduled for the following day, the consternation can well be imagined.

Almost everyone in the Island was either related to, or close friends with, those directly affected, and the distress caused was far greater than that of the official evacuation to England in 1940.

No logical reason for this brutal move has ever been adduced, but it was learned that this was a direct order from Hitler himself and that it had to be carried out without delay. Most people thought that it was probably a spiteful reprisal for the bombing of German towns by the RAF, but this can only be conjecture.

The Island Heads of Government were summoned by the Germans, and the Constables of the Parishes were given the distasteful task of telling the people to their faces that they must prepare themselves for deportation to Germany. This they categorically refused to do. They said, in effect, that if the Germans wanted it, then the Germans must do their own dirty work. The regular soldiers liked the whole business no more than we did ourselves, and finally it devolved upon office staff, who still had to be accompanied by local officials since they were naturally the only ones who knew exactly where the designated people lived.

Most of these received their summons in tight-lipped silence, but Dr H. G. Oliver, a respected and outspoken general practitioner, opened his door to be confronted by a German and a Parish official who said; "Dr Oliver, you know who I am and what I have come for?"

The reply was: "Yes, I do know you, but I cannot remember your name offhand. I think it's something like Judas Iscariot, isn't it?"

The notice handed to each deportee said:

"In persuance of a Higher Command, British subjects are to be evacuated and brought to Germany.

You have to appear therefore, on 16/9/42 not later than 4pm at the Garage, Weighbridge, St Helier, with wife and minor children.

Bring with you, all papers proving identity.

It is necessary to outfit yourselves with warm clothing, stout boots, and provisions for two days, meal dishes, drinking bowl, and if possible a blanket.

Your luggage must not be heavier than you can carry, and must bear a label with your full address.

It is further left to you to place ready, for each person, a trunk packed with clothes, to be sent afterwards, labelled with full address.

It is also left to you to take with you an amount of money not exceeding Reichmarks 10 (approximately one pound) in German notes, for each person, in Reichs credit notes.

All valuables and jewels must be deposited with the banks.

Keys of all houses must be handed to the Constables of the Parish.

Should you fail to obey the order, sentence by Court Martial shall be effected.

Knackfuss"

Warning the three hundred or so people involved in the first evacuation meant that cars bearing the messengers were circulating the Island all night.

Some families in outlying districts, who either had not received the local paper, or in a cursory reading had missed the notice, received their first intimation, with that ominous knock at the door during the small hours.

Others, who had gone to spend the evening with friends and, as sometimes happened, stayed the night as a way of avoiding the early break-up of a congenial gathering by the curfew, did not receive their warning until the next day.

The preparations for the deportation caused utter confusion—fitting up the family, especially children, with warm clothes (if available), assembling what food could be scratched together for the journey, arranging for pets to be looked after, houses cared for, relatives informed by Red Cross messages and, above all, farewells to friends and loved ones.

There were various exemption clauses of which one or two took advantage, but the whole affair was so chaotic and sudden that very few really had time to think about an appeal, and many went who could on one ground or another have stayed behind.

I had a number of patients among those leaving, and where possible visited them at home to advise on simple measures for the preservation of health, in the camps, but of course I could not get around to them all, and so went down early to the weighbridge to catch some of these, and say goodbye to all.

German soldiers with rifles and machine-guns blocked entry to the weighbridge through Conway Street and Mulcaster Street, but hundreds of people lined the route, along which trudged the deportees carrying luggage and household articles, while their small children, delighted at all the excitement, clutched toys and pathetic little dolls donated by well-wishers.

People in the crowd, seeing friends among the deportees, broke ranks and rushed to embrace them in the road way, clinging together until they were moved on by soldiers. Most people among the crowd were weeping, and the first-aid men were busy tending women who had fainted.

The German private soldiers themselves were very unhappy about the whole thing, which they felt was quite unnecessary and cruel. Several even said so, although not when officers were in earshot.

Within the limits of their orders, they were as kind and considerate as could be, and many of them were uncomfortable and shamefaced when confronting the sorrowing, bitter Islanders.

All except one young officer (whose name I forget, except that it started with a P.), who buzzed about here and there like an angry hornet, chivvying the guards and urging them to greater strictness. He had always been noted for his arrogance and lack of co-operation with Island leaders, as well as for his elegance and immaculate grooming.

Armed with an expensive cine-camera, he dodged in and out among the deportees, taking a sadistic delight in getting shots of any kind of human misery that caught his fancy.

One such scene particularly appealed to his warped nature. An old lady, heartbroken at parting from her only daughter and a string of grandchildren was weeping helplessly, while the latter, weeping too, with her arms around her mother, was trying to comfort her. The guards, too upset to watch had turned their backs, and were looking over the heads of the crowd.

But P., in an effort to get yet another dramatic shot of their grief-twisted faces from an advantageous angle, was bent double and busy looking into his view finder, when out of the crowd darted a young man. He may well have been the striker for a local football team, for he certainly knew, with unnerving accuracy where to place his toe.

With the force of his rush behind him, he delivered a tremendous kick, just in the right position, well forward in the German's crutch. The force of the blow lifted the officer, and sent him forwards about six feet. Still holding the camera, he had no hands to protect himself, and his face ploughed along the tarmac with no benefit to his undoubted good looks.

There was a full-throated roar from as many of the crowd as witnessed the incident, and the soldier guarding that section, put his hand over his mouth to hide a grin; but the lad responsible did not wait to be recognised. With the same speed that he had darted out, he darted in again, and was lost in the crowd.

P. was helped, in fact almost carried off, for his legs could not support him. Gone was the arrogant swagger and the insolent stare. He was plainly in deep shock, and his battered, bleeding face was a fish-belly white. He had also vomited over his nice uniform, but I don't think it was the pain in his face which made him do that.

At the garage, hot milk and bread and jam helped to pass the long period of waiting, and at last buses arrived to carry the deportees down to the two boats tied up at the quay. These were quite clean, well-found little craft, with berths for everyone, and the Red Cross personnel aboard saw that everyone was all comfortable.

The heights of Mount Bingham and Pier Road were black with people watching them move out into the bay, and the singing of "There'll Always Be an England" followed by "There'll Be Bluebirds Over the White Cliffs of Dover" floated back to us across the water. The crowd took up the same songs and continued until the ships were out of sight.

The next deportation was fixed for 18 September, and these three days enabled people to make every effort to escape the draft.

Every doctor's surgery was besieged with frantic men and women, who had reason to think they were not fit to go. Women especially confessed that, though their passports described them as 65 or 67, they were in fact 71, 72 or 73. Many brought outdated passports, carrying their true date of birth, and these I took in a sheaf to the German Authorities, who were very humane, smiled tolerantly, and crossed their names off the list.

I had less success with a patient, admittedly only 67, but with a bad heart and severe kidney stone. The latter could not be removed operatively on account of his serious heart condition, and scarcely a month passed when I did not have to rush to his home where he would be writhing in his bed or even on the floor, in the hideous agony of renal colic. A shot of morphia was the only thing that relieved him, and I shuddered to think of what might happen on the long journey to Germany.

I went to the chief MO of the German forces, confident that my plea would receive sympathetic consideration. As it happened, I could not have chosen a more unfortunate day and, as I outlined my case for a certificate of exemption, I suddenly had the feeling that something was very wrong.

The poor man was haggard and grey with worry. He spoke excellent English, and was perfectly polite, but he said: "I have just had news that my home town has been practically obliterated by your RAF, and there is no word of my beloved wife and our four lovely children. The loss of life has been terrible, with thousands killed, so I am afraid I cannot find it within myself at the moment, to show concern for just one man, who, on your own showing, has not long to live anyway."

I pointed out that it was not death that I feared for him, but the intense agony that would lead up to it, but he was quite adamant, and I left hoping that in the final medical examination at the weighbridge before embarkation, he would fail to pass. However, pass he did, and left with 346 others on the boat of 18 September.

A second boat should have left the same evening but, at the last moment, the authorities decided that she was unfit to take the deportees (although why was not stated), and about two hundred were sent back and told to report the following week.

An elderly couple, having packed up their house at Beaumont and given away most of their things, could not face starting up everything for another week. Having screwed up the courage to face a deportation which was now put off, they thought it easier to put their heads in a gas oven. Others, more resilient, went to stay with friends or camped out in their already packed up houses.

These deportees showed the same indomitable spirit as the previous group and left the Germans gaping with amazement. All the people who came to see them off called encouragement, and sang patriotic songs with such fervour that the Germans had to clear the approach to the weighbridge. But the crowds merely took up positions on high ground overlooking the bay, and shouting and singing went on till well after dark.

Some months later, four deportees were returned to Jersey

from a transit camp, on account of crippling illness, and one told me the rest of the story of my kidney patient.

On the long slow journey to Paris, en route for Germany, he was seized with an attack of renal colic, with no one present to give any relief.

The train was crowded to the doors, five people seated on each side and five standing in the gang-way in each carriage, and the corridors as full of people as they could hold. People were glad to stand in twos and threes in the lavatories.

My patient had a seat in a carriage, but the agony was such that he slid to the floor where his body was straddled by the feet of standing passengers. He lay there screaming in agony, and throwing himself about until he died, either of shock or of heart failure. His body was dragged out, and left at the next station where they halted.

The third deportation was fixed for 25 September, and this time my own name was on the list. This was no surprise; in fact I wondered why I had not gone already. Later Dr McKinstry, without my knowledge, made representations that there was no one else to run the JMH, and the order was cancelled.

On 25 September a further three hundred arrived at the weighbridge, but were sent back home and told to report again on 29 September. This draft included single women, and elderly widows, and a number of men who were serving sentences for various crimes imposed by the Germans, were added.

As before, crowds turned up to bid goodbye, but this time the Germans had blocked off not only all the streets leading to the weighbridge, but also all points having a view of the harbour, so that relations and friends were cheated of their last farewells.

Assembly was at 2pm, but a small batch were instructed not to arrive until an hour later. They were lucky for, by the time they arrived, the ship had a full complement and they were told to go home. After the departure of this boatload, the Germans announced that there would be no more deportations for the time being.

Deprived of the excitement of a patriotic demonstration,

parties of teenagers marched through the streets, singing and giving the V sign. They were chased away by soldiers, but groups reformed at other points, and carried on baiting the enemy.

At last the soldiers, not entirely unreasonably, lost their tempers when a boy knocked off a German helmet and the others started kicking it around. A German officer began bully-ragging one of them, a well grown teenager of about fourteen, who suddenly hauled off and gave the officer a sock on the jaw which laid him out cold.

The soldiers then drew their bayonets, which had a very sobering effect; fourteen boys were carted off to prison, where they remained for a fortnight.

They were then tried by court martial. Those of sixteen and under were released, after having had a thorough fright. The older ones received varying, not very severe sentences, but a man alleged to have incited them was sentenced to three years in a German prison. After this drama, we settled down to our customary dull existence.

Diphtheria broke out sporadically, and therefore the hospitals were closed to visitors. Places of entertainment and public gatherings were also banned.

Whooping cough also took its toll and, in the absence of vaccines and medicines, it ran an unusually stormy course and spread everywhere.

Women—overworked, underfed and suffering many sleepless nights—looked haggard and worn, a state of affairs that was not helped by unbecoming clothes and complete lack of that great morale-booster—make-up. Practically the only females worth a glance were the Jerry bags, who looked radiant and smart, with all the gifts brought from Paris by their Nazi boy-friends. Small wonder that sorely tried housewives, scurrying around town from queue to queue in the rain, gritted their teeth and muttered, "Just wait!"

Gymnastics at school and many sporting events were forbidden because the authorities thought that any energy people had must be conserved for survival. Youngsters seemed cheerful and looked reasonably well, but Dr McKinstry, conducted a survey of the schools in the fourth year of the

Occupation, and reported that the growth rate for all the age groups was substantially under the norm.

It was among the middle-aged and elderly that changes were most evident and, if one had not seen someone for a year or so, one had great difficulty in recognising that person.

One man, who for years had weighed 24 stone, and had been to countless specialists in England and on the Continent, only to be told that the cause was glandular and nothing to do with his eating habits, ended the War weighing only fourteen stone.

Another, a patient of mine, quite a small-framed man who originally weighed eighteen stone, went down to nine in less than two years. After the first period of deprivation when he complained bitterly about bodily weakness, he said that he felt better than he had done for many years—although he looked awful to me. After the War he at once went back to his bad old ways of two large meals a day, washed down with various forms of high-priced alcohol. In less than two years he had put on every ounce of the nine stone he had lost, and one day at a groaning dinner table, while boasting to a guest of his feat, he suddenly collapsed and died.

As might have been expected, the TB germ took full advantage of the conditions, and cases began to multiply rapidly. New drugs like streptomycin had not reached us, and the special rations allocated for TB were not really sufficient to make much difference. Bone tubercle (which had been previously rare in the Island) made its appearance and had to be treated as best we could with the limited drugs available.

For most of the last year, I (like a good many others) suffered from a completely intractable form of chronic diarrhoea, which also helped to melt off any surplus fat that still remained.

And then came a massive outbreak of infective hepatitis which occurred sporadically—attacking both the just and the unjust. A whole household would be affected, with the exception of one person; in Trinity Parish, for instance, every farm in quite a large area had one or more cases, while a single farm right in the middle escaped entirely. Several deaths occurred, mostly among the young and strong. A young policeman, for instance, who considered himself completely cured, was pushing a handcart of firewood along the parade and dropped dead. There were several similar cases.

Elderly people began to have badly swollen legs, which was certainly not due to a cardiac condition and, for want of a better diagnosis, was put down to famine edema.

Others began to suffer from pulpy gums and loosening teeth and, although none of us had ever seen this condition before, we began to talk of scurvy. However, I was never completely convinced that this was right.

Things were at their very lowest ebb in December 1944 when we ran out of bread altogether, having already been on half rations (ie. one and three quarter pounds per week) for a fortnight. This total shortage lasted for three weeks, and people subsisted as best they could on boiled potatoes, swedes and turnips. In Guernsey it was even worse, and I have somewhere a cutting from a Guernsey newspaper, giving a recipe for nourishing and palatable dish made from potato peelings.

Morale had reached its very lowest ebb, when suddenly came news of a Red Cross ship, and rumours ran around the Island like wildfire. After several false alarms, the *Vega* arrived on 31 December 1944 and her cargo was unloaded and stored in a heavily guarded warehouse on the quay.

Distribution of parcels started on 2 January and a typical parcel contained six ounces of chocolate, twenty ounces of biscuits, four ounces of tea, twenty ounces of butter, six ounces of sugar, a two ounce tin of milk, fifteen ounces of marmalade, fourteen ounces of corned beef, thirteen ounces of ham or pork, ten ounces of salmon, five ounces of sardines, eight ounces of rasins, six ounces of prunes, four ounces of cheese, a three ounce tablet of soap, one ounce of pepper or salt.

In addition there was a consignment of special-diet and invalid parcels, plus a number of layettes for new-born babies, supplied from a fund set up by Lady Campbell, wife of the British Ambassador to Lisbon.

Everyone in the Islands received two parcels, and there was a surplus which was withheld and would only be distributed when it was known that the *Vega* had left Lisbon on her second journey.

In addition the *Vega* brought a good supply of white flour, and the bread ration was re-established for the time being.

As well as the parcels, the *Vega* also brought small quantities of cigarettes, tobacco, medicines and shoe leather, and we began to feel almost pampered.

She continued to visit about every five or six weeks and, in addition to her usual cargo, she brought things like paraffin, candles, seeds, nails, matches and clothing.

Thereafter, the diet was much more varied and interesting although by no means ample, and the other odds and ends filled many a long-felt want.

The spirits of the Islanders began to rise. They never stopped rising until our longed-for liberation on 9 May 1945.

CHAPTER 13

In Chapter Seven I described how the brothel opened by the authorities at the Hotel Victor Hugo was not a success, and how the ladies were killed when their boat foundered near Corbière. Undeterred by this fiasco, the Germans, who are nothing if not triers, opened a brothel for the Todt workers at the Abergeldie Hotel. The new inmates were if possible even less appetising than the previous bunch, but I was told, encountered considerably less sales resistance.

The men of Organisation Todt were a rather scruffy lot, a good many approaching middle age and getting thick around the middle. Although they had more money to spend than the soldiers, they did not appeal so much to the local Jerry bags, who to their credit were not in the game primarily for material reward.

The Todt were not, as far as I could make out, an Army Corps at all, though they wore uniforms. They were more a colossal construction organisation, attached to the Army, but not under Army regulations or discipline.

Generally they were much more involved in brawls. They drank heavily and treated with great brutality the foreign labourers who had been detailed to work for them.

A ship came in with fifty natives of Eire, who had been employed on the Island before the War and who, when supplies got tight, volunteered to work in Germany. In a short time they discovered that they had jumped from the frying pan into the fire, and at their own request were re-admitted into Jersey.

The boat which brought them returned to France with 250 Russian workers, all of them ill and some too weak to walk up the gang plank. I could not help speculating as to why they were being taken away, and as to their ultimate fate. I should have thought that 250 sick Russians would have been no more welcome in occupied France than were 50 hungry Irishmen in starving Jersey. Perhaps they could be more easily disposed of on the other side.

Letters arrived from deportees appealing for food parcels and warm clothes. None of the trunks we had forwarded had up to then reached their camp, and I believe they never did.

Hard on this came news from members of the last of the four deportations. There were 357 people aboard, the seas were mountainous, everybody was sick and, with only two lavatories for the whole consignment, the rest can be left to the imagination.

On arrival, people who were more dead than alive with no respite to wash or clean themselves up, were hustled for the long overland journey, into filthy unheated trains, with no sleepers, no corridors and practically no amenities.

I was given a description of this by some teenage children whose family had been patients of mine for a long time. Their mother had had to be carried off the train on arrival, and she died in the camp a few weeks afterwards.

Letters also came from members of the first deportation, complaining of rough food, damp, cheerless accommodation and atrocious weather. To make matters worse, the eagerly awaited trunks of warm clothing, which had been sent to follow them, never arrived, and the clothes they stood up in were wearing thin and, anyhow, were designed for summer wear. A letter which arrived several days later said that a few trunks, but only a very few, had in fact been delivered at last.

About this time there was an especially ugly and nauseating development on the Island. Certain people—who must have been mentally deranged—took to writing anonymous letters, or telephoning, the occupying authorities, denouncing neighbours for possessing wireless sets, black marketeering, having guns, or whatever. Many of these letters never reached their destinations, for sorters at the GPO learnt what was afoot, and opened and destroyed anything addressed to Military Headquarters. Furthermore, they went to the length of contacting those denounced, and warning them to get rid of any incriminating evidence.

Even the Germans must have been sickened by these filthy letters, for they issued an order that in future, any such information must be communicated in hand-written, grammatical German. Most of them then stopped.

This sort of decent behaviour made for a mutual respect between the Germans and the Islanders, and something else which happened about then increased it.

By official order from Paris, all bank managers were called to College House and told to open for inspection all the safe-deposit boxes in their keeping, on a certain day. Although, a couple of days before the Occupation, money and securities to the tune of many millions had been safely sent off to London, I am told that a surprising amount came to light. Among the loot was a quantity of gold bars, uncut diamonds, securities and valuable jewels but, although the Germans made a detailed list, none of it was taken away then or, as far as I know, at any time later.

Conversely, although the tide was now running against them, the military police and Gestapo seemed to go out of their way to chivvy us. People seen using a lighter in the street were stopped and asked to explain where they got the petrol.

Two people cycling abreast (if they had been convicted of the same offence before) were sent to prison in Germany. All civilian rations were drastically reduced on the pretext that this was a reprisal for a highly uncomplimentary speech about Hitler made by Mr Churchill.

A group of people who gathered regularly to listen to an illegal radio hidden in the tower of St Saviour's Church were discovered and sentenced for one to three years' incarceration. This had to be served in Germany and most of them never returned, including the Rector, Canon Cohu.

The corpses of two RAF officers were taken from the sea, and buried with military honours, including a firing party, and there was a large wreath from the German Air Force. Three German officers followed the hearse, and many Island officials were at the graveside. The Bailiff laid one wreath on behalf of the King, and another from the Island of Jersey.

The time of the funeral was not advertised beforehand, and the public were not permitted within the churchyard walls, but somehow the word got around, and thousands lined the roads solidly, from the hospital to the cemetery, and stood in silence outside the walls during the service.

After the burial, what might have been a very ugly incident was narrowly averted by the honorary police. A married woman, with a husband serving overseas, had become a Jerry bag and was observed watching the proceedings. A posse of wives, without a sound but with deadly menace, surrounded and grabbed her. What might have happened is anybody's guess. She had the sense not to struggle, but screamed at full pitch. The scrum was broken up before the German Military Police could intervene.

But the fracas had obviously been observed, and the implications of so much national feeling digested, for a few days afterwards, when the body of an American airman was found at Bonne Nuit Bay, the funeral was advertised for 12 noon the next day.

No time for wreaths or the staging of any big demonstration, but just in case of trouble, the body was taken in complete secrecy to the cemetery and buried, not at 12 noon, but at 4am, by the light of car headlights.

Someone, however, suspecting that advertising the hour so openly was some sort of trick, forestalled the Germans. As the coffin was about to be lowered, someone spotted an object lying on the floor of the grave. It was an enormous red, white and blue wreath, with a stars and stripes flag attached.

After this, unofficial wreaths were not allowed to be laid till the day after the funeral. For the two RAF sergeants there had been two waggon-loads of wreaths, and for the American one. All the cards of sympathy were removed and sent to the next of kin after the War.

As the conflict hotted up, we started to see more action off the Island, and began to feel more involved in the War.

Four German boats on their regular run to the French coast were attacked by our planes and three sunk. During a naval engagement in the Bay of St Malo, the British cruiser Charybdis and a destroyer were sunk and twenty nine British bodies buried in a mass grave at Mont à l'Abbe. There was a German guard of honour and a firing party, as well as high ranking officers of both Army and Navy, at the interment ceremony.

The Germans were now reduced to scraping the bottom of the barrel for troops. Large numbers of fit trained men were sent from here to France and replaced by elderly men with big corporations, and by beardless boys.

As late as July 1943, a final order for handing in radio sets was issued. This time non-compliance carried only one penalty—death—but as far as I know not a single one was handed in.

This, I think, was a last desperate attempt by the German authorities to keep the true state of affairs from their own troops, who were showing signs of realising the hopelessness of their situation. A number of ordinary soldiers committed suicide, and an officer at College House blew out his brains. Another poor man, after getting news that his wife and four children had been killed in an air raid, cut his throat, while a number of men, due to go on leave, asked to stay on the Island, because their homes were destroyed, their families missing, and they had nowhere to go.

News came that Advocate Ogier, who had been sent to a concentration camp in France had died. His son Dick had been convicted of being in possession of a marked ordnance map, and he himself was punished for harbouring his son—in other words for not betraying him to the Gestapo. They were sent to the same camp. Dick died in Jersey, very soon after the Liberation.

A kind of anarchy now set in. The troops became so heedless of discipline that where they found a door unlocked, they entered and started going through the cupboards for food, or valuables in the presence of the owners. When challenged they showed a gun, but there is no record of one being used.

One farmer, after midnight, heard a party of foreign workers breaking down his front door. Grabbing a heavy stick he rushed at them without any warning, and laid about him right and left. After a half-hearted resistance, they made off leaving two of their number on the floor. One was found to be dead, and the other died later. No charge was made.

A notice was inserted in the paper advising people under similar circumstances, not to open up, but to raise the noisiest alarm possible.

As an illustration of how desperate for food these poor wretches were, the late Dr Frazer of Augres Manor (now the Jersey Zoo) went to bed one night leaving an old tin of chicken food on the hob in the kitchen. As there were practically no scraps except perhaps a few potato peelings, he kept only two hens. The tin contained their feed: a few dregs from cups and a handful of damaged corn tailings largely chaff. In the morning there was a silver spoon in the tin, but the contents had been eaten to the last grain by a foreign worker who had forced the kitchen window.

The fine dry autumn and mild winter of that year had encouraged the rat population to breed much faster than usual. Some of this, no doubt, was due to people concealing foodstuffs under floorboards and in other places where they would not be found by human intruders. But the rats had no difficulty in finding them. And so a "rat week" was declared. In the absence of sufficient traps and a reliable rat poison, I could not see it being much of a success; it was not, so we had rather more than our share of rats and mice, until after the War.

The first of January, 1944 dawned with high hopes in all our hearts, and the day itself was marked by an incident which showed how far respect for German discipline had dropped.

Four French workers, who had celebrated the occasion rather too freely, started a ruckus and threw a bottle through a pub window. An honorary policeman was called, but they all drew knives and rushed at him. The policeman dashed off for reinforcements, and in the meantime the military police arrived and challenged the workers. They attempted to escape, whereupon the police opened fire; this was returned by the fugitives, who each had a gun.

They all escaped. No one was hit, no one was caught, and the military police made no attempt to follow up the matter.

February saw a heavy fall of snow, which added to our miseries and made getting about even more difficult. Children looked pathetically pinched, and some of their parents were really emaciated. The snow emphasised how very little reserve energy we had, and how near to rock-bottom we were.

A little gleam of hope showed itself early in February when Joe Krebs of Milwaukee, Wisconsin, flying a single-seater American fighter was forced to parachute, and landed at St Peter. Before being taken off to prison and subsequently to hospital, as he was slightly injured, he told onlookers: "Keep your pecker up, folks, the big show is just about to start." Somehow we felt that this was no empty encouragement.

One day, British ships could be seen with the naked eye, off St Ouen's Bay, and the big guns at Les Landes opened up, but nothing was hit.

Following the rape of a woman at St Mary by an Algerian, the Germans made another attempt to round up wandering foreign workers. Several had tried to get jobs on farms, so as to escape being sent to France, and one had shacked up with a young widow in the town. All this is defiance of direct German orders.

Whether as a result of this drive or not, a St Ouen's lady, Mrs Gould, was arrested for harbouring a Russian. It was said that this followed information lodged against her in an anonymous letter, and even that the name of the informant was known, but no solid proof of this was forthcoming.

Mrs Gould, a kind and charming woman in late middle age, was very much loved and respected in the parish; whoever had given her away must have been mentally sick.

The Russian, a mere boy, had sought shelter with her almost two years before, when in a deplorable condition and, out of her kind heart, she had clothed, housed and looked after him so well that eventually he could easily be mistaken for any ordinary young Islander rather than a pathetic scarecrow. In fact she treated him like a grandson, and he even went shopping with her in St Helier, quite undetected.

The search of her home came like a bombshell, and revealed also an illegal wireless set. The boy escaped, and was never recaptured, but Mrs Gould was sentenced to two years in a concentration camp—Ravensbruk in fact. Her brother Mr le Druillenecq, who was headmaster of St John's school, was also arrested and sent to Belsen.

Also sent with them were a father and his sixteen-year-old son, who had been arrested for having a gun and ammunition. The boy, who was keen on firearms, had had the gun for several years and had taken it to pieces long before the War, and, in the manner of boys, had never reassembled it! In fact he had completely forgotten its existence, but all explanations were ignored and he was sent off, with his father as an accessory.

On the long journey across Europe, in bitter weather and open trucks, the boy was taken ill; in spite of their efforts to save him, he died with his head in Mrs Gould's lap. His father died in a concentration camp not long after.

For the rest of her life there, Mrs Gould was a ministering angel to everybody, caring for the sick, cheering the depressed, and setting an example to everyone in her calm courage. But worn out by forced labour she was no longer of use to her captors and was executed in the gas chambers.

In fact, Mr le Druillenecq was the only survivor of those who went there from Jersey, and sometime after the War, in appreciation for what he had suffered in helping a Russian, he was officially invited to pay a visit to the Soviet Union. There he was presented with a gold medal, and a meeting was arranged with the boy he had helped to save.

But even this was typical of the peculiar humour and lack of sensitivity of the Russians. Mr le Druillenecq was put up at one of the best hotels in Moscow, and taken to see all the sights, but he was not told that he was to meet his protégé.

The Russian, on the other hand, who was now married

with several children and lived more than six hundred miles away, returned one evening from work and found two soldiers awaiting his return. They were sitting in his house, had given his wife no explanation of their errand, and she was beside herself with anxiety.

On his return they ordered him to change his clothes immediately and when this was done, still with no kind of explanation to either of them, they took him off.

They drove to the airport and accompanied him in the plane bound for Moscow. During the trip he sat there between them, eaten up with anxiety, and wondering what he had, or had not done, and what charge was going to be brought against him. He tried questioning the soldiers, but they gave nothing away.

In Moscow, he was driven to the smartest hotel he had ever seen, still accompanied by the soldiers, and marched into the foyer.

There, he saw a man seated in a chair, also guarded by two soldiers, and he was brought up to the man. For several seconds nothing happened. One man was puzzled, the other terrified, but suddenly recognition came, and they embraced each other. At the dénouement, the soldiers were all smiles, clapping everyone on the back and shouting with laughter. The genius who thought the whole thing up must have been completely satisfied, but the terror of the poor man, during that nightmare journey, must have put years on his life.

Curfew passes were now almost totally withdrawn, and there were signs of panic among the foreign workers, who were anxious to get out of the Island if it was at all possible.

Some fields of growing wheat had to be cut by the German soldiers themselves, to prevent British parachutists hiding themselves there. The foreign labourers refused to do it.

The fall of Rome was received with much jubilation and the whole Island was prevaded by an air of expectancy.

On the evening of 5 June, I went to bed early, as I expected a confinement call later in the night. But it came earlier than I expected, and I was cycling home in the small hours when I became aware of an enormous number of planes passing over—but very high up. The Germans opened up with a terrific anti-aircraft barrage, but there was no sign of anything having been hit.

I was too excited to go back to bed, and instead carried a couple of rugs and some pillows out into the garden and lay there staring skywards, while luxuriating in the almost continuous roar, as wave after wave of aircraft went over. Although I could see nothing, the sheer number and power of their engines was one of the most thrilling things that had ever happened to me, and of course on top of it was the excitement of the thought that at last liberation was in sight.

They were still passing when I rushed indoors to turn on the seven o'clock news, but imagine my complete disbelief, when the announcer just gave the news as usual—nothing whatever about the exciting events which I had been listening to all night. I was so unhappy that I could scarcely choke down my breakfast. Mrs Ozouf, who had slept through it all, was sympathetic, but slightly incredulous, almost as if I had dreamt it all, and in spite of wave after wave still going over (and they continued to do so for most of the morning) she adopted the attitude that it was just a rather larger raid than usual.

Half-heartedly I switched on the eight o'clock news, and there it was in all its glorious detail. I was far too excited to go off on my round and, while waiting for the nine o'clock news, took a stroll around the town.

There was no doubt about it. Although the Germans had at once taken over the telephone system, the news had travelled like lightning over the Island grapevine, and broadly smiling faces were the order of the day. Conditioned as we were to fear the Gestapo, no one stopped to chat about the news, but the extreme cordiality with which people in the street greeted each other and slapped each other's backs, told its own tale. The nine o'clock news brought further details of what was happening, but after I heard it, I had to pull myself together and go off on the round. Here of course there was only one topic of conversation, and all except the very sick were more interested in discussing the events of the day than their own ailments.

The Germans were like a disturbed ants nest. Ambulances

were stationed at all sorts of seemingly unlikely places, guards were doubled everywhere, large Red Crosses appeared at every hospital and in several locations where they had no right to be, and guards in steel helmets, carrying rifles, sported Red Cross armbands.

A proclamation announced:

To the population of the Island of Jersey. Germany's enemy is on the point of attacking French soil.

I expect the population of Jersey, to keep its head, remain calm, to refrain from any acts of sabotage and from hostile acts against the German forces, even should the fighting spread to Jersey.

At the first sign of unrest, or trouble, I will close the streets to all traffic, and will secure hostages.

Attacks against the German forces will be punishable by death.

Der Kommandant der Festung Jersey.

(Signed) Heine Oberst.

Electricity works, gas works, water supply and harbour, all had strong guards posted, and very few soldiers were seen on the streets. On the night following the proclamation, a number of small boats carrying German nurses, female canteen and office workers, stole out of the harbour and made for the French coast. The boats returned in the small hours of the following day, bringing supplies, obviously intended for an expected siege.

As an illustration of the iron discipline still obtaining in some sections of the army, a horrifying incident occurred at this time.

In the early hours of one morning, four Germans on guard at La Rocque were seen standing on a rock which was being rapidly overtaken by the tide.

Local people who saw what was happening shouted a warning, but the soldiers seemed quite unconcerned and remained at their post. They could easily have been rescued by a La Rocque fisherman, but the soldiers would not allow themselves to be rescued. By the time a boat, manned by inexperienced soldiers, had put out from Gorey all four were drowned, and at low tide their bodies, in full uniform, still clutching their rifles were found in the gulley at the base of the rock.

Bombing of targets on the Island by British planes now became much more frequent. Gun emplacements, and boats in the harbour or offshore, were attacked and there were numerous casualties. Planes bombed guns at St Ouen, and one plane came down in flames, completely demolishing a house at Grantez. The pilot was burned to death.

There was a great deal of activity in moving stores to underground shelters, which were subsequently mined, so that they could be blown up at once, in the event of a British invasion.

Almost any convoy attempting to cross the channel, in either direction, was attacked and a number of seriously damaged vessels were either pulled up on the hard, or beached nearby.

There was a constant flow of seriously injured casualties being rushed to the hospitals, but what happened to the dead was a mystery, for no more graves were being dug in the cemetery at St Brelades. The only explanation was that they were sent over to France by boat. By daylight the harbour was virtually empty, but there was great activity after dark. Boats came in, were loaded or unloaded at top speed so as to complete the journey across the channel before day broke.

An attack on a gun emplacement at La Rocque, where two heavy bombs were dropped, resulted in more than a dozen houses being almost completely wrecked. No one was killed and the dispossessed owners, together with what they could rescue from the debris, were taken in by neighbours.

As the channel crossing became more hazardous the Germans began making more use of the airport, but not with conspicuous success. One night a low-flying German bomber was hit by fire from German anti-aircraft guns situated in the harbour. It crashed in a field at St Clements and all five crew were killed.

About this time the Germans decided to evacuate Alderney

and, taking a chance, six smallish vessels arrived one morning with 1,500 men, a completely mixed bag. Most were foreign workers, a few evacuees from Cherbourg, some foreign workers from Guernsey, Jerseymen who had been forced to work in Alderney, and the contents of a concentration pen, also on the Island. These especially were in a pitiable state, Jews, Russians, Poles and even German political prisoners, most of them wearing the blue and white striped pyjamas associated with the death camps. There were also a number of Frenchmen and a few women. Some were taken for the night to Fort Regent, some to West Park Pavilion and the rest to local hotels. During the day they were free to roam about the town, and the whole place was swarming with them. However, any cafes or eating places were denied them by guards posted at the doors.

In the evening they were shepherded down to the harbour, where they waited for some time; but the authorities decided that the sea was too rough, and dejectedly they returned to their billets. Local spectators who watched these wretched people being very roughly treated by their guards, threw cigarettes to them and were rewarded by the V sign.

Two days after, a much larger vessel arrived and the evacuees were all shipped off to France. A considerable crowd of Islanders gathered to cheer them off, but were driven away by troops and the military police.

We thought then that we had seen the last of them, but in the early hours they returned, having sighted units of the Royal Navy off St Malo. The human cargo was allowed to roam the town again that day, and a few Italian cafes were open to them. They gorged themselves on ersatz coffee and synthetic lemonade!

The next night they left once again, this time in two boats, which took different routes, and we heard that they had arrived safely. As their ultimate destination was a large German concentration camp, it all seemed hardly worth it.

The D-Day invasion was now about a month old, and although there was every evidence of intense activity from the coast of France, we ourselves seemed no nearer liberation. In a sense we were worse off for, with the curtailment of shipping between us and France, supplies of food were correspondingly reduced. The occasional small boat or barge managed to get through under cover of darkness, but the relatively small amount of provisions carried seemed to be almost exclusively absorbed by the Germans.

One barge brought a number of fine cattle from Normandy, which were put out to pasture at St Peters, under the charge of a French cowman. Some of these, at least twice as large as our own cows, and coloured black and white or red and white, were a constant attraction for local sightseers, some of whom had never seen anything except a Jersey cow.

While looking at them myself, I heard a woman (obviously accustomed to our own fawn satin hides) say: "Cor, don't they look funny, they're covered with fur!"

These animals were intended to supplement the increasing levy of cattle for the troops, but I cannot say what happened to a delightful little black-and-white spotted calf, which was, I am sure, born unexpectedly, and which ran with its mother for some weeks, to the great interest of the locals.

At this time the Germans issued a statement which said that on account of the military situation a State of Emergency might have to be declared. In such a case:

a) The civil population would be confined strictly to their homes.
b) The distribution of food would be entirely suspended.

In these circumstances it was decided that a supply of emergency rations should be distributed to every member of the community against such a contingency. These foodstuffs, issued free, must not be consumed unless the emergency arose, and anything perishable must be replaced from the normal ration.

The parcel contained three pounds of bread, five pounds of potatoes, three ounces of sugar, two ounces of butter, one tin of sardines and eight ounces of macaroni. For all children of two years or under, there were twelve tins of condensed milk.

Less than one week after the issue of this ration, the bread was found to be covered with mildew, and after the crust was cut off had to be consumed immediately, and thereafter replaced weekly by the normal bread ration.

To add to our worries (which no one openly voiced), the Allied sweep through France seemed to have passed us by. The garrison at St Malo, in spite of almost continuous bombing, still held out and was kept supplied with bread and water by a barge which left the Island every night.

Very little in the way of supplies was coming for the civilian community, and the local Medical Officer of Health sent a memorandum to the occupying authority pointing out that further prolongation of the siege might well result in a serious and permanent effect upon the health of the Island as a whole.

We were devastated by the reply that the High Command considered that the siege could be maintained till 31 January 1945 at the earliest.

This was the end of August, and not only were we all looking thin and worn, but the troops themselves were hungry and sick of the whole thing.

At this point I had the surprise of my life to hear that two pleasant and apparently inoffensive patients of mine had been arrested by the Germans and were in prison. As one of them was extremely delicate, I made a request to visit them there, but was peremptorily refused.

Their names were Lucille Schwob and Suzanne Malherbe, French nationals and step-sisters, but with no blood tie for each was the child of a couple who had married for the second time. They had left France, and settled in Jersey some years before, and lived at La Rocquaise, St Brelades Bay, which after the War they sold to the present Duke of Bedford. They appeared to be very comfortably off, and both spoke excellent English.

Lucille was thin, elegant, highly intellectual, widely read and a first-rate hypochondriac. She wore rather peculiar clothes, surrounded herself with every sort of avant-garde objet d'art and was in the habit of sitting in rooms during the day with the curtains half drawn, and the light on.

Suzanne, on the other hand, was the practical down-to-earth one, who ran the house, saw to all the business affairs, spent as much time as she could in the garden, and looked after Lucille with a breezy but tender solicitude. She was thick set with an out-of-doors complexion, and short-cropped black hair, whose favourite garb was slacks and a bulky sweater, and who took an early morning bathe for at least eight months of the year.

The couple had a maid who worked for about eight hours daily, but lived out in a small cottage of her own. She had been with them for some years, and was not in her first youth. She was an independent, stand-and-deliver sort of woman whose name was Hilda.

It seemed a very satisfactory arrangement. A well-balanced household and a comfortable easy billet for Hilda, for the step-sisters lived very simply and never entertained.

For some months past, and at a time when the High Command was trying to keep from their rank and file the true state of affairs, both in Germany and in Europe, some soldiers managed to get news on the radio from various sources. The edict went forth that such soldiers caught either listening to, or disseminating, such information would be summarily shot. This immediately stopped the spread of unpalatable news among the troops.

Then, suddenly, soldiers would find in their pockets a small roll of fine paper, about the size of a cigarette, on which was typewritten, in good German, a resumé of the last four days' news. This, of course, was circulated with avidity from hand to hand, and the occupying troops soon came to rely upon it as the only source of absolutely reliable information about the progress of the War.

These little pieces of paper originated on a typewriter in Lucille's bedroom, where the sisters had kept a radio ever since the beginning. They never talked about the news, or divulged it to a soul, so that to all intents and purposes they were completely safe.

The set was kept in an ottoman with a hinged lid, upholstered and covered with multi-coloured cushions, on which Lucille took her frequent rests. Most of the time she could switch on and, lying on the ottoman, listen to the news which was quiet enough not to be heard outside, or even at the other end of the room. When she was making a typewritten précis of the news, the set was sitting on a cushion beside the typewriter, ready to be whisked into the ottoman at the slightest sign of danger.

About twenty copies were made of each newsletter and, after they had rolled them, the sisters cycled into town where they mingled with groups outside shops or other places where troops and civilians congregated. There, very skilfully and unostentatiously, they popped their little rolls into knapsacks and unsuspecting pockets.

The sisters varied their appearance and clothes to an astonishing degree, and although the Germans must have been on the look out for them, they were never caught. I suspect that some of the recipients had a notion that one was being planted on him, but he would be the last one to inform higher authority. The task of detecting them should have been fairly easy, but the Military Police and even the Gestapo were getting slack, and, except for the really rabid Nazis, everyone was heartily sick of the war, so that they made no superhuman effort to effect a capture.

Who informed on the couple was never discovered for they were very cautious. Suzanne was positive that they were never spotted while carrying out their activities in the town, and when returning they covered their tracks very skilfully. As in every community there are one or two lunatics, and we were not immune from this sort of thing. Some prying neighbour must have put two and two together, informed the Feldgendarmerie and of course they had to act.

Quite unsuspecting, the sisters were just sitting down to their evening meal when there was a sharp rap at the door. Opening it, Suzanne was confronted by a German officer and two soldiers. Lucille made a dash for the stairs, but before she reached even the bottom step was seized and thrown into a chair.

One soldier stayed watching the couple in the sitting room, while the other started searching upstairs. He was not long about it, and soon came down with the radio and the typewriter. Lucille was in a state of shock, ashen and trembling, but Suzanne her usual competent self.

The officer said, in excellent English: "I am afraid you must consider yourselves under arrest, and accompany me to Headquarters." At this Lucille fainted, and while the officer (who was not a bad sort of chap) was helping a soldier to give her some water, Suzanne said: "My sister has a heart condition and, if we are going to prison, I must ask your permission to get her tablets from her room."

Actually, Lucille had, or thought she had, almost everything except a bad heart, but she genuinely suffered from chronic insomnia for which she took two tablets of gardenal, and Suzanne knew exactly where to put her hand on them.

She realised that the offence they had committed would mean a stiff sentence—probably to be served in one of the horror camps—and that certainly Lucille and possibly she herself would never survive it. So she reasoned that an overdose of gardenal would probably save a lot of bother and suffering in the long run.

The officer gave permission, and Suzanne flew upstairs, grabbed the full bottle of gardenal which she hid in her pocket, and another bottle—any bottle (and there were plenty to choose from)—to show to the Germans. Lucille, almost carried by Suzanne and one soldier, was helped into the military car outside—the two women with a soldier in the back, and the other soldier driving.

On their way into St Helier, Suzanne surreptitously unscrewed the gardenal bottle and poured a half, as nearly as she could judge, into Lucille's hand. The rest she put into her own mouth. Both chewed and chewed as silently as possible, although the taste was horrible, but they managed to get most of it down with the aid of their own saliva.

At the prison, it was decided that on account of the lateness of the hour the two women should be put in a cell for the night, and interrogated in the morning. Already they were feeling drowsy, and as soon as the key was turned on them they collapsed on the two pallets, and almost at once slid into unconsciousness.

Had no one gone to see them till the morning, they would

unquestionably have been found dead, but a guard, after about an hour, suspicious of the complete silence and lack of any movement, decided to investigate and entered the cell. Shaking each woman and getting no sort of response, he raised the alarm.

The sisters were rushed to hospital and their stomachs pumped out, but they had already absorbed a large quantity of the drug and their chances of survival looked rather poor. Drips were put in their veins and the faint flicker of life maintained.

After two days Suzanne started to show some sign of recovery, and Lucille the following day, but neither woman was able to think properly or answer any questions for over a week. They were then put through a course of rigorous interrogation, but no kind of torture. The War was already too far advanced in our favour for the enemy to add any further to their list of indictable crimes. Finally the sisters were condemned to life imprisonment.

This sentence was generally regarded more as a joke than anything else, although had they been arrested and sentenced only a month before, when communications were still open, they would have been sent to serve their term in a concentration camp.

As it was, they were kept in Jersey Prison, which was bad enough, but they knew, and their guards knew, that any kind of inhumane treatment would have to be answered for, sooner or later—and probably sooner. Every German then on the Island recognised that he was there till the end of the War, and would have to account for his actions when that time arrived.

Nonetheless, the sisters had to endure another winter in a virtually unlit, unheated prison, on sparse, unpalatable food, although they were officially entitled to Red Cross parcels like all other Islanders.

Lucille, a finicky eater, always frail and a poor doer generally, spent long periods in hospital, and was in a very low condition on her release. Suzanne, although much more robust, was in quite bad shape also.

Lucille survived only a few years, and on her death Suzanne sold La Rocquaise and moved to a small house at

Beaumont where she died fairly recently. Except for a few close friends, she passed on unknown and unrecognised for her brave attempt to defy the great German Reich.

During the fortnight or so that the two women were too ill to be moved or even interrogated, the channel crossing was still negotiable, but only just, under cover of darkness. The German authorities were anxious to reduce the mouths to be fed and arrangements were made to get rid of a great many foreign workers. While they were about it, they also decided to send over to prison in Germany about fifteen Islanders convicted of various offences.

Among them was the young boy who had been put on probation for socking an officer during the disturbances following the last deportation in 1942. He had not flouted any of the terms of his probation, but the Gestapo were determined to get rid of him.

The whole flotilla consisted of 22 vessels of various sizes, which left after dark, but something happened in mid-channel and they returned in the small hours. The fifteen prisoners and the boy were again shut up in gaol. The following night they set off again and this time made it successfully. The fifteen prisoners were despatched to a concentration camp and few returned alive.

But the young boy managed somehow to mingle with the foreign workers, and boarded the ship with them. As soon as he reached France he slipped away again, and by some means managed to get himself hidden in a French village. Later, after orientating himself to his surroundings, he made his way to the American base at St Lo; the Americans gave him a rousing reception, and sent him safely to England.

All this escaped the attention of the Gestapo. It was reported that the boy had not been with the group sent to the concentration camp, and the Gestapo came to the conclusion that he had managed to elude shipment and was still in the Island. His home was thoroughly searched and his family closely interrogated but they, quite genuinely, had no idea where he was, and the Gestapo finally believed them.

An advertisement appeared in the local paper, with his description and a threat that anyone hiding him would be severely dealt with. Coupled with this were descriptions of one Irishman and thirteen Russians, with a similar threat, but none were recaptured.

With all the activity, both by sea and air around and above the Island, we received captured or wounded every day. A party of Americans were brought in, and most of them admitted to hospital. From the windows they waved and shouted to passers by, and more people than usual took a walk along Gloucester Street just to hear their banter. But this ebullience soon subsided when the novelty of the situation wore off. They missed their home comforts, which were essential to them, even in the firing line, and shouted, asking us to send in ice-cream and candies. Little did they know that we had seen nothing of the sort for many years. They kept yelling that they would rather die than eat what they called "the Nazi hog-swill", but eat it they had to eventually, or do without and die. A little later they were comforted by the regular issue of Red Cross parcels.

The prisoners would have had even less appetite for the hog-swill had they known that its tiny meat content came from very old worn-out horses. Earlier in the Occupation the Germans had brought over a large number of magnificent Belgian horses, but faced with the growing shortage of food they realised that these would have to be sacrificed eventually. This they were understandably reluctant to do, for most of them were young horses, at the peak of their working life. It was very wisely decided to swap these animals for old, worn-out horses belonging to the farming community, with of course a cash adjustment. This was a very good thing for the farmers, but I no longer drew my meat ration, which in any case was only two ounces, and at that chiefly sinew, fat and gristle.

Why one should have this abhorrence of eating horse is difficult to explain logically, seeing that every other nation in Europe does so. I often wonder whether the succulent, tasty ragouts that one consumes with such pleasure in France may not have been trotting along the roads a short time before.

CHAPTER 14

By the late summer it became evident that for most of the German troops in Jersey (there was still 16,000 of them), the War was virtually over. They were to all intents and purposes prisoners themselves, and most of them were glad of it. They no longer carried equipment, were very often sloppily dressed, and slouched about looking gloomy. They were even reduced to picking up cigarette ends from the pavements.

Shortly after this there was great excitement in the community at the news, from German sources, that negotiations for our release had been started.

A destroyer appeared off Guernsey, flying the white flag and asking for an interview with the German commandant. A Canadian major, who was also a member of the Canadian Parliament, was taken by pinnace into St Peter Port. He asked to see the Commandant in order to discuss the military situation. After a considerable period of waiting, he received the curt reply that General Von Schmettow was fully aware of the military situation and there was no conceivable grounds for discussing it.

The general consensus of opinion was that the Commandant felt himself insulted by being asked to parley with a mere major.

Our own morale was now very high, but physically everyone was at a very low ebb, and at this point the gas supply was totally cut off, with the single exception of that to Miss

Frazer's soup kitchen. The electricity also was cut down to two, or three hours a day, which imposed a serious additional hardship on everyone and especially on places like the Maternity Hospital.

A German hospital ship came in bringing almost 200 battle casualties for treatment at the General Hospital which was already full up. Every patient who could conceivably be fit enough (and many who were not) to be sent to billets or barracks was discharged and their beds taken by the freshly wounded. In the wards the beds were moved much closer together and army cots brought in, but this was still nothing like enough. All the hospital corridors had casualties on mattresses, ground sheets, or whatever, lying head to tail. The groaning, shrieking and stench were quite indescribable.

The Germans had three surgeons who started working immediately on an impossible task, and our own two civilian surgeons, who had already observed men dying in the corridors while waiting for attention, went at once to offer their services. They were curtly refused.

The theatres worked at full pressure all night, and next day while chatting to Mr Halliwell (one of our civilian surgeons, in the hall), I saw the senior German surgeon, grey with fatigue after working non-stop for nearly twenty-four hours, pass us. Mr Halliwell at once went up to him and again offered his help and was again refused. This upset Mr Halliwell so much that he announced he was now going home and would not return to the hospital until the carnage was over.

Later in the day the three surgeons broke off for six hours sleep, but resumed again in the early evening and carried on all night.

By this time a number of the waiting wounded had died and been carried off, and perhaps for them it was a blessing in disguise, for the supply of all kinds of anaesthetic gave out in the middle of the morning. We offered what we had, which was little enough, but this was also refused. Nevertheless, sorry as we were for the wounded, we had our own sick to think of, and still did not know how much longer the Occupation would hold out.

Then came something which hardly bears thinking or talking about.

Units of soldiers were brought in and four of them would hold each fully conscious patient while the surgeons operated. Two men waited outside the theatre door to drag out those who fainted, and to take their places. Even some of those waiting outside fainted before their turn came, and although I did not myself see any of this, I heard a great deal of it, and was profoundly grateful not to be involved.

I hope I will never again hear such awful shrieks and groans as were plainly audible to anyone within earshot of the theatre floor. By some quirk of the ventilation or heating systems, rooms quite far away received the full brunt of the horror, and people working in them refused to stay.

In peace-time an amputation is a relatively uncommon occurrence, but one of the nurses told me that bin after bin of severed arms and legs were being brought away from the theatres, not decently shrouded in cloths (which were probably in short supply, anyhow) but just pitched in every which way, till the bins was filled and had to be removed.

At times of catastrophe the Germans were very careful not to leak any sort of information, but in one way or another, stories got about, some of them no doubt exaggerated, and I heard figures of the death-toll which were quite horrifying.

All I can say is that in a few days every survivor was able to find accommodation in beds, and that was not because any living casualties had been removed either to the erstwhile Ladies' College, or the Merton Hotel, which had both become hospitals of sorts.

In the cemetery at St Brelades, there suddenly appeared a forest of white crosses, but as there were always guards on duty there to move us on, we were not able to count them. In any case, there were many funerals every day and more still every night. All who died an honourable death were taken to St Brelades.

The others were dumped in unmarked ground elsewhere but mostly, I think, at Mont à l'Abbé. No one knew when or how they took place, but with the War almost won, there were killings and suicides galore.

A German sailor deserted and went to live with a local woman, where he was captured when the Germans searched her house. He escaped shortly afterwards, but in a few days was discovered with his throat cut.

A gang of sailors started a brawl in a cafe, and one was stabbed to death.

Following the theft of six sacks of Red Cross flour from a bakehouse at First Tower, two soldiers were arrested. One of the sacks had a hole in it, undetected by the thief, as he carried it away on his back. The trail led straight to a blockhouse off Mont Cochon which housed a number of men. It was reported that both the thieves were shot.

A few days later two masked soldiers held up a couple of auxiliary policemen guarding a flour store at bayonet point and got away with two sacks. They were not captured.

Brawling and violence escalated in a most alarming way, and a great many soldiers were on the fiddle.

A German inspector, himself an agriculturalist, detailed for duty in a threshing operation in order to see that all the grain went into the communal store, told the farmers to keep as much as they wanted, provided they allowed him to help himself too.

A young Jersey girl, sheltering her German lover who had deserted, was detected and sentenced to death. But after a vigorous protest by the Bailiff, who was now in a very strong position, it was commuted to ten years, which we all knew might be ten months, ten weeks or even less.

Poor girl, she did not care what sentence she received, for her lover was summarily shot. The Germans magnanimously allowed her and her mother to go to his funeral.

An officer was shot dead while trying to put a stop to a brawl. His killer was executed later.

In an argument between sailors and German officers, one rating was dragged into the Jersey Motor Transport Garage on the front, put up against a wall and shot. This was the last execution of the War.

About the same time Deputy Edward le Quesne was arrested for a wireless offence. He received a sentence of seven months, but because of good behaviour served only two weeks and when released was told that he could do the rest of his time after the War!!

Although all the signs indicated that the War was won, and we lived from day to day expecting something to happen, hope deferred made our hearts very sick.

Wood to keep a small fire flickering in the grate was getting scarcer and scarcer. A weekly ration of tar mixed with saw-dust or any inflammable rubbish was some help, but did not go very far. Empty houses were gutted, floors torn up, rafters removed and the whole building reduced to a shell. The ornamental wooden gates of St Luke's Church were found to be missing one morning and were never recovered. Some elderly friends of mine demolished the back staircase of their large house and burned it to keep themselves warm. Wooden gates disappeared from fields all over the Island, wooden signposts and advertisement hoardings were removed during the night, and high prices were paid for furniture at sales—the bigger the better. These too were intended for the fire-grate, of course.

On 5 February the Bailiff announced that the *Vega* would bring no flour on her second trip. This was a decision made by the British Red Cross in London, and no reason was given. It was certainly not due to shortage, for we heard that there was plenty of flour at Lisbon, waiting to be shipped.

As a result of this, the Island was completely without bread for three weeks, at a time when we needed every ounce of food we could get. Had it not been for the Red Cross parcels, we would have been in desperate straits, for they kept life in our bodies. The potato ration was increased, but more than sixty per cent of them were rotten, and even the so-called good ones turned almost black on cooking.

As some small compensation, we were promised flour on the *Vega's* third trip.

The Germans were now definitely worse off than we were—although it seemed hardly possible. All drill and military exercises were suspended and no football or other games allowed. They were also ordered to take two hours rest each afternoon.

A requisition order for thirty tons of swedes and turnips

was issued and these were made into soup for the troops, thickened and flavoured with limpets.

Parties of soldiers, clambering over slippery rocks in their thick boots, limpeting, became a common sight. There were also raids on tennis courts and poultry runs for netting, and although not conspicuously successful, a certain amount of fish was caught with these. This all went to the troops.

It had come to the stage that no one dared allow a pet dog or cat to wander in the town. I myself saw a soldier in Stopford Road, coax a cat to come up to him, suddenly grab it by the tail, bash its brains out against a wall and cram it into his swag bag. It was all over too quickly for anything to be done about it, and the cat's owner, running out just too late, was terribly upset.

This was a time when the Germans issued an order that no family could keep more than one dog. Anything in excess of this had to be destroyed, and families who had gone to almost any length to preserve their pets were faced with the heartrending decision of which ones to sacrifice.

People with pedigree dogs, which they kept for breeding, could claim exemption on a written official certificate, but even then only two bitches were allowed. As we were so close to the end of the Occupation many people decided to chance their arm, and gave away valuable or much-loved pets on a purely temporary basis, making themselves responsible for their feeding while they were boarded-out.

This in itself was quite an undertaking, as food was becoming scarcer and scarcer. So was everything else. All laundries were closed except one, which had to make itself responsible for most of the hospital linen, so that very little private laundry was dealt with. At the same time the Germans chose a most inopportune moment to send a bill to the States for half a million pounds. This was in addition to a previous bill of one million pounds—all towards the cost of the Occupation. What cheek!

Having cut down thousands of our trees, the Germans now issued a stringent order about unauthorised tree felling. The Island was littered with untidy stumps of fine trees cut at about two feet from the ground. As they no longer felt entitled to cut any new trees, the Germans started blowing up the stumps and chopping them up for fuel. Whatever else it did it tidied up the banks everywhere, and even when they omitted to fill up the craters which were left, we were glad to do it ourselves and have everything shipshape.

For the first time the tail-end of winter really showed us how low our resistence to infection had fallen. Intestinal worms, which had become more and more troublesome, assumed epidemic proportions and we could do little about it till we were liberated. But their presence reduced the general state of health and Dr McKinstry was constantly on the look out for a generalised outbreak of some sort. Skin infections became frequent and any little cut or scratch developed into a nasty septic sore. Poisoned fingers and infected chilblains were rife, and we had to treat them as best we could. We managed to contain these until the spring came and the sun helped them to heal by nature's own remedy.

In the latter part of the morning of 7 March, I was driving my Austin Seven up l'Hermitage Lane when there was a terrific explosion which seemed to lift the little car off the road. This was followed by a series of minor explosions which went on for a considerable time.

The whole of the Palace Hotel was hidden in a cloud of dust and smoke, so instead of turning right at the end of l'Hermitage Lane, I turned left at Bagatelle Road to see what I could see.

Most of the houses I passed had their windows shattered and even roof-tiles had fallen out into the road. This had happened not only in Bagatelle Road, but also in l'Hermitage Lane nearly half a mile away. I found out later that a large plate-glass window of a shop in Bath Street, more than a mile away as the crow flies, had exploded into a thousand pieces, and shot all over the roadway.

At the entrance to what remained of the hotel was a tall tree and a pair of trousers, with jackboots attached, was entangled in its branches. There was a good deal of blood on them and I suspect a pair of legs inside, but the guard at the entrance waved me along at once, and frankly I was not too anxious to remain any longer in the area, on account of the constant fusilade of reports, which I took to be exploding ammunition.

Rumour had it that the top brass had arranged a conference at the hotel, and that some disaffected Austrian Porps men had prepared a reception for them 'à la Guy Fawkes.'

For some inexplicable reason the venue was changed to College House at the last minute, in time to save the participants but too late to prevent the original plan coming into being. The Austrians took refuge among the Island community and a hunt for them was immediately organised, but by no means all of them were captured.

The *Vega* now arrived on her third trip, bringing the long-awaited flour.

People in an affluent society, especially those on a diet, often say that they never eat bread at all, and of course they may not do so, since there are many alternatives at their disposal. But when bread is the main staple of one's diet, its absence causes a feeling of deprivation, which potatoes, filling as they may be, do little or nothing to allay.

But now, after three weeks without bread the flour had arrived, and shelves in baker shops blossomed with serried rows of gorgeous loaves. On that first Sunday, a golden crusty loaf was on show at most of the Island churches, and the gospel of the day was "The feeding of the multitude".

When the first loaves came out of the oven, with the collaboration of a baker patient, I forestalled their appearance in the shops and cycled out to my mama-in-law with one that was almost too hot to hold.

She was just sitting down to a revolting meal of root artichokes in watery bill-poster's paste, and gladly abandoned it for a thick slice of hot, madly indigestible white bread. We had two each of these—no butter, for we had none—but to us it was ambrosia and I regretted it not one whit, in spite of the agonies of indigestion which kept me awake most of the night.

As if to punish us for our good fortune over the bread, shortly after this the milk ration was cut down to half a pint of skim milk, four days a week, and the special milk rations for invalids and children was dropped altogether.

But this worried us less than it might have done, for we felt that we could now hold on until release came, and the sight of German troops now openly begging, especially around the countryside, strengthened our belief.

The younger men were especially pathetic with their too-large uniforms hanging on their bony frames. It said much for their remaining discipline that, though there were numbers of robberies, there was no concerted raid on the stores or shops.

After the capitulation, the British forces found, stashed away in underground stores, enough food to supply all the German forces for six months. This had not been touched even when their troops were literally starving, but were being reserved, we were told, in case they had to defend the Island against a British siege.

As a threat to pilferers and robbers, and because the main prison was inadequate, the Chelsea Hotel was converted to take the overflow, but it proved to have only a short life, as we ourselves could have told the authorities, who were behaving as if they still had a long term of occupation before them.

In the same state of mind, they requisitioned, for billets, a large number of occupied houses, bringing the total so seized to 2,700 over the five years of the Occupation.

On 20 April, the forces celebrated Hitler's birthday, but not with the parades and ceremonies of previous ones. There was a concert, and a military band played in the Royal Square, but no soldier got drunk or roistered noisily around the town.

May Day—which the Germans had been in the habit of celebrating with parades and mass singing—passed off with merely an evening concert, which none of the civilians even bothered to attend.

Late that night came the news of Hitler's death and, even if we had not heard it on our radios, it would have been obvious next morning that some sort of major catastrophe had occurred. Flags were all at half-mast and the troops meandered around the town like lost sheep, with tragic faces and a sloppiness of bearing that was even more marked than what we were becoming used to.

A young soldier shot himself in a lavatory at the hospital, and an officer was found dead in his quarters clutching a photograph of the Fuehrer. Another soldier killed himself by thrusting a bayonet into his throat. Unquestionably there were many other such tragedies which were not divulged.

Later in the day there was a memorial service, which of course only Germans attended, but there must have been a big turn-out for it, because the town was bursting with soldiers. A vast proportion of these certainly came from outlying strong points, and look-out posts, so that had our troops chosen that day to make a landing, they would have done so with little or no opposition.

Mixing with the crowd were Islanders openly sporting red, white and blue favours and calling to each other that there was news of a wholesale surrender of units in north-west Germany.

Those Germans who could speak either French or English seemed intent on engaging in conversation with any Islander who could be induced to listen. According to them they were either Poles, Austrians or Czechs—anything but Germans—conscripted into the German Army and caught up in the machine. Some of this may have been true, but so many had variations on the same theme, that one doubted most of them. Anyhow we had heard it all before.

On the fifth of May everybody who could come into town did so, and the streets were packed. Flags were hoisted everywhere and there was a feeling of intense expectancy.

A number of Gestapo members, who we were used to seeing in mufti, had donned ordinary uniforms, and were trying to mingle with the regular soldiers. Their efforts to be chummy met with a very frosty reception, and those civilians who recognised them, depending on nationality, either hissed or spat. I only hoped that their shabby little ruse to escape identification would be spotted and that they would receive the punishment they so richly deserved.

And yet, while all this was going on, and we were feeling

rather sorry for our enemies, a German, intent on burglary, attacked an elderly woman in her home with such brutality that she was confined to hospital for several weeks.

The sixth of May was a day when little happened. Understandably, only those who genuinely had something wrong with them troubled the doctor, but with all the excitements of the previous days I had a number of arrears on my list and spent the day catching up, for it was evident that something momentous was likely to happen in the next few days.

In the countryside men were painting flagstaffs or, where they had already done so, getting them up and securing stays. Bottles of brandy, hidden against a rainy day, were unearthed and "Just a little one doctor, to celebrate our freedom" punctuated a rather disjointed medical round.

The bubble of this euphoria was badly pricked the next day when, on a country visit, I spotted working parties at various points, either digging holes or building sniper's nests. One gang had strengthened a gun emplacement and was busy dragging up another gun from one of the damaged ships in the harbour. I began to wonder whether they were going to defend the Island after all. That night all posts were manned throughout the hours of darkness and searchlights swept the surrounding sea.

We heard subsequently that General Hufmeyer, a rabid Nazi and fire-eater, had determined to go down fighting, and only gave up the idea when the rest of his staff flatly refused to support him.

The eighth of May started off quietly and there was a feeling of anti-climax in the air when suddenly there was news that all children had been sent back from school and that workmen were putting up loudspeakers in the town.

A statement from the Bailiff announced that at 3pm a message from Mr Churchill would be broadcast, and that afterwards the Bailiff himself would address us in the Royal Square. Everybody who could make it was there, and all the surrounding houses crammed right up to the roof.

There was scarcely a dry eye in the whole concourse when the National Anthem was sung, but the volume of song was not what might have been expected on account of the lumps in so many throats. I myself could hardly sing at all, and indeed have only a very jumbled recollection of the events of that afternoon.

The Bailiff appealed for good behaviour and asked people to remain calm and dignified. He said that political prisoners had been released and that he himself was on his way to visit French colonial prisoners, in their camp. He said that a British Commission was on its way, and that units of the British Navy were already approaching the Island. This news was received with the biggest cheer of all.

As the people began to disperse to meet their friends, organise parties, or just to stand and drink in the scene, church bells everywhere started ringing, owners of radios turned their sets up for the benefit of passers by, and impromptu dances started.

The Electricity Company, who had surreptitiously kept enough fuel for just this occasion, flooded the Island with light, and the Gas Company followed suit.

Motor cars and motor cycles, hidden away for five years, suddenly appeared on the streets and mingled their hooting with the general pandemonium.

I myself, rather bewildered by the noise and conflicting emotions, walked out to High Barn to share the relief and happiness of Bob and Connie Vaynor, with whom I had gone through so many of the vicissitudes of the previous five years.

Completely unknown to me (for he had never breathed a word about it) on the first day of the Occupation, Bob had persuaded a farmer to build a haystack around and on top of a vintage Napier which he had kept, in addition to the modern car which had been requisitioned by the Germans.

The old Napier, which was his baby, had been lovingly restored, and before the War he occasionally drove out in her on sunny days. The possession of such a car was in those times looked upon as a kind of amiable eccentricity, and people laughed and waved as it went past.

Bob had had her towed down to his house by a horse, and he and a young mechanic were busy taking down the engine, while Connie was polishing up the brasswork. Knowing little about the internal arrangements of cars, I helped by doing what I was told, and we carried on till dark when we all had a celebratory dinner together at High Barn.

Next morning I was up early and, after calling at the JMH to make certain that they were unlikely to need me that day, I cycled out to Beaumont for a bite of breakfast with my mama-in-law. My car was empty of petrol, and there was nothing for it but to walk back into the town, which we did together. It was a glorious day, and soon after we set out we saw HMS *Beagle* coming around Noirmont Point.

Our walk into town was something of a royal procession. The sea wall was manned, the whole of the way, by people looking out over the bay, and every few yards patients dashed up to shake my hand, or in some cases to kiss me. Smiles and tears were everywhere.

In the town we quickly became absorbed in the laughing, cheering crowd who were thoroughly enjoying complete freedom after so many years. British Tommies, very smart with special shoulder flashes, and all too conscious of the notice they were attracting, swaggered around, eyeing the girls, and tossing sweets to the children who followed them in droves.

We heard a honk-honk from an old-fashioned bulb horn, and there were Bob and Connie in the Napier, grinning from ear to ear, and calling to us something which we could not possibly hear on account of the noise. Connie pointed to the back seat and we jumped in, to continue our inspection of the proceedings in style.

At one point we came upon Serge, arm in arm with a very young British Tommy on either side. All three had the slightly glazed look of those well gone in liquor, but were blissfully happy and singing at the full stretch of their lungs. What Serge was bawling in Russian meant nothing to me, but what the others were singing was completely familiar. In the days of my innocence, at the village Sunday school, I well remember lifting my reedy treble with great gusto and assurance to those strains. It was *Jesus wants me for a sunbeam*.

At mid-day we called at Bath Street, just long enough to collect a loaf of bread, a tin of spam and two bottles of champagne. Then on to Beaupré, where we sat on the terrace in the sun and shared our lunch with Claude and May Avarne, who lived in half the house.

Claude produced a real cigar, something I had not had for years and, although it was slightly fusty and smelled unquestionably of mice, I thought I had never had anything so good.

I had offered the empty half of Beaupré to Claude and May sometime in 1943 when the Germans completely evacuated Bon Nuit Bay, with the object of mining all the slopes and making it a fortified zone. They were delighted to have it as they were homeless and I was glad to have them, for every unoccupied house soon became a target for wood stealers.

My gardener, Albert Payne, who lived with his family in the other half, disappeared for about half an hour when he heard about my car and came back carrying a full can of petrol with the compliments of a farmer patient and good friend.

When we decided to return, I filled up the car and drove back to Beaumont with mama-in-law for a quiet thanksgiving dinner.

The next day I went down to the Pomme d'Or which had been cleaned and considerably smartened up. The partly butchered carcase of a horse which had been lying in the vestibule on the day of the surrender, had been removed, and the place was full of journalists and all grades of soldiers. One of my friends said that an officer was searching for me, and almost immediately a childhood friend of Ann's, a Major Sykes introduced himself and gave me a fat envelope from her. I was so excited that I am afraid I was only just civil, although it was obvious that he was very ready for a long chat and a drink. All I wanted was to get to the quiet of my own house, open my letter, and be alone with my thoughts for a space.

But, after reading my letter, a guilty feeling about Major Sykes drove me back to the weighbridge, where German arms were being collected and stacked and troops divided into special groups or units. Some were being sent off to internment in England, others were formed into working parties to clear and clean the billets, which were in a shocking state. Still others were put to removing the mines which were dotted all around the coasts, and very often considerably inland. There were a number of fatal casualties in this group, but those who remained when their task was over were sent to join their fellow-prisoners in England.

It transpired that the total number of Germans occupying the Channel Islands numbered nearly 30,000, making the Islands, for their size, the most strongly fortified place in the world.

Major Sykes reappeared and took me around to see a number of things which I would not otherwise have been allowed to see.

Partly as some return for my boorishness over the letter, and partly just to make an opportunity to talk about Ann, I invited Sykes to dinner the following night.

When I announced this to Mrs Ozouf, she reacted like an old war-horse scenting the battle, and immediately started making her plans.

From some source of her own (and Jersey is a remarkable place for knowing someone, who knows someone else, who knows where you can get something you are needing) she produced two fat, fresh Dover soles. One of my bottled chickens, tarted up in a cream sauce with fresh vegetables followed, and sliced bananas, flambé in brandy, completed the meal. As he wiped his lips with a sigh of repletion Michael Sykes said "By Jove, I thought you chaps were on the verge of starvation. I have not had a meal like that for years." I just gave a hollow laugh.

We stayed talking over coffee and brandy till well after midnight, and I walked him back to his billet, through well-lit streets—no curfew, no Germans, and still numbers of happy excited people, reluctant to put paid to what was certainly the most momentous day in their lives.

A short time after, to everyone's relief, came the news that telephone communication had been restored. In the touching belief that mine was the most important call of all, I reached instantly for the telephone. My common sense should have told me what I would find—every line jam-packed for the forseeable future. So the next morning I rang before 7am to a Harpenden number, where Michael Sykes had told me Ann was staying with some lifelong friends.

A familiar voice answered. It was Rosa, an old family retainer, who told me that none of the family were yet down. I dared not ask them to ring me later as the lines were just as congested in the other direction, and while I was hesitating I heard, in the distance, a child's voice ask, "Who is it, Rosa?" All that Rosa replied was "You'd better come and speak", and at once I heard "Hello?"

At this point all my carefully rehearsed opening gambits deserted me. I could only stammer, "You don't know who this is, do you?" The reply was "Oh, yes, I do, it's my daddy. I must go up and tell Mummy." In his excitement he replaced the receiver, ran off and left me standing. I could not get on again, but it was enough. That brief interchange brought home to me as nothing else had done that the family was united once more and that the Occupation was really and truly over.

CHAPTER 15

I hesitate to make my permanent home in Jersey the subject of a separate chapter but, even though I never actually lived there during the Occupation, it influenced me and was so inextricably woven into my life at the time that my narrative would be incomplete without it.

A year or so after we were married Ann and I began to hanker after a home of our own in the country. Living over the shop as it were, was very convenient in some ways, but as we were now expecting a baby we wanted the freedom, fresh air and privacy of somewhere outside the town.

With this idea in mind we began to look out for properties, and as there was no particular urgency about the matter, it gave point and a great deal of interest to our country outings. We saw quite a number of properties but nothing completely fulfilled all the points we thought we required. One large farmhouse, in the centre of the Island, and therefore very suitable for a practising doctor, always appealed to Ann. It was called Beech Farm, and whenever we passed it she would say: "I do so like the look of that place. I am sure I would be happy living there." My reply would be something like: "Not the remotest chance, my sweet. It belongs to a very old Jersey family and will never be on the market."

Events leading up to the Occupation put all such thoughts out of our minds, and the five years' separation began with my living in the house at 105 Bath Street. This was as well, as matters turned out, for when my bicycling days began, I would have found it very difficult to run a practice and the JMH from a house in the country. I still wanted somewhere to occupy my dreams and surplus energy, but for the time being, want had to be my master.

A few weeks later I heard that the house I hoped for was on the market and I went to inspect it at once. At that time there was no rear door to the house; it had an imposing front door but otherwise only a back entrance through the kitchen from the cowshed. I was just knocking on this when it was violently flung open, and a young woman in a considerable state of fright rushed past me. Looking into the kitchen I saw that something was very much on fire, and through the smoke saw a Florence oil stove flaring up to the ceiling from all three burners. I knew better than to throw water on it, and anyway there was none, and not knowing anything about the geography of the place, had no idea where to get sand. Fortunately there was a freshly dug flower bed outside and, grabbing a handy milk bucket, I scooped it full of fresh earth and flung a bucketful on each burner. This did the trick, but not before the fire had left three sets of bad char marks on the fine old pitch-pine rafters of what was destined to be my dining room. They are still there.

Apparently Mrs le Moine, the tenant's daughter-in-law, unable to get paraffin, was attempting to cook with a mixture of diesel oil and petrol—something I knew and had tried myself in a limited way, in a small lamp. Evidently Florence did not like it and reacted violently, with potentially disastrous results.

After a cup of the inevitable sugar beet coffee Mrs le Moine took me over the property. The house would provide all the accommodation I needed, with very little reconstruction, and was very solidly built.

While viewing the upstairs, and going into a back bedroom, where the wheat crop was being stored as a precaution against thieves, I was startled to see an enormous rat staring at me from the far corner of the room, where it had gnawed a hole between wall and ceiling. Otherwise all seemed fine and, subject to an official survey, I decided to buy the house.

After the survey, the agent came to see me and said: "Well, doctor, everything is quite satisfactory. So think about it for a couple of weeks, and let me know what you decide." My reply was: "I don't need a fortnight or even another day. I've decided to have it and would like you to get on with the formalities without delay."

The result was that surprisingly soon I found myself the owner of Beech Farm, which I decided to rename Beaupré, after a property in Wales and as the lease was due to run out at the end of the year I took possession just before Christmas 1941.

Since the house had no electricity, no running water and no inside sanitation, I had to get moving while anything needed for these was still available. Very early, the Germans had ordered that no alterations were to be done to any property for the duration of the Occupation, beyond the figure of 1000 francs. As one of the main attractions of my purchase was to provide an absorbing interest during my loneliness, I obviously had to take the risk. The thought of having the house of our dreams, completed and ready for us to resume our life together, was worth any danger.

Anyone coming up the main St John's Road could, through the double archway, see quite plainly what was going on in the front courtyard, and it was imperative to block it off. In the old press-house I found a pair of massive oak double doors, which had been made for the big arch at least a hundred years before, but had not hung there in living memory. With them was another door for the small arch, and as all were still in good condition we were able, with considerable able-bodied assistance, for they were very heavy, to get them hung.

So far, so good. The whole front of the house, except the roof, was now invisible from the road and the Germans, if they did notice any change, certainly did not comment upon it.

Because of the order, there was practically no civilian building, and therefore no difficulty in getting good craftsmen. Mr Cyril Manger agreed to undertake the reconstruction. As there was not a single architect left on the Island I had to take on the job myself, and spent many happy evenings drawing and redrawing plans.

The original house goes back to 1668 and, as the Jersey houses of that period had very small windows, we decided to enlarge these before tackling the inside of the house. Once we could get them done, the inside work would be dealt with, in still greater secrecy.

It also gave me more time to look for all the inside equipment of a modern house. Providentially, there was only a slow demand for this, and with a careful search of the builders' merchants I was able to get hold of three full-sized baths, four hand-basins and four lavatories, as well as all the requisite piping, drains, etc.

A lady at Fauvic, unable any longer to get fuel for her central heating, and having torn it out to be replaced by gas, sold me everything, including the radiators and a Beeston boiler, for ten pounds. The Aga cooker, by no means new then, is giving excellent service forty-seven years later.

Electric wiring was not so easy, but by buying some here and some there I finally got enough to give a supply throughout the house, although extra points had to be added some years later. The switches were all different from room to room, but that was the least of our troubles.

As the existing water supply was confined to an iron hand-pump over the well, an electric pump was essential; this was provided by a very good patient, an electrician, who agreed to payment after the War.

Wallpaper was difficult, especially as it was impossible to estimate our needs for rooms not yet built, but I bought as much plain or sparsely patterned paper as I could get, and also as much undercoat and gloss paint in white or pale colours as I could find. Most of these were of the same brand, so that when they were needed we could, by mixing, make up colours to suit the wallpapers.

Most of the doors and frames in the house were in good order and re-usable, but the old sash windows no longer fitted the new larger apertures and were replaced by hand-made casements. Fortunately there was enough seasoned wood to be had for these, and they are there still, unwarped and giving good service.

All these stocks were bought and paid for, but left in the stores till required, for there was no point, especially at that time, in leaving them in an empty house, even under lock and key. Furniture, curtains, carpets, etc, posed no problem. I had sold none when I left 100 Bath Street, and stored everything at 105 Bath Street.

I next turned my attention to the garden and, pending a replanning project, decided to buy everything I might possibly need while it was still available. At Mr Percy Jenne's nursery at Five Oaks, although it was much depleted, I managed to get a representative selection of apple, pear, plum, peach and apricot trees, as well as all the soft fruits and many ornamental shrubs. These I paid for, but I left them in the nursery until I had cleaned the tangled land around Beaupré.

There were several visits from German soldiers on one pretext or another, and when the builders saw them in time, they effaced themselves quietly. This was not always possible, and if the soldiers, did recognise what was going on they certainly did not report us to their superiors.

One official visit was for the purpose of examining a row of a dozen magnificent sweet chestnut trees which formed the boundary between my orchard and the adjoining land. The officer who came was a suburban type, a superior clerk, I judged, who knew nothing whatever about firewood or trees. This episode occurred when our fuel began to run short, and the requisition programme had begun not only for this but also to provide beech timber for clog soles. I protested vigorously against the destruction of my beautiful chestnuts, pointing out that their wood merely smouldered, giving out little heat, and was practically useless for burning. On the other hand they yielded many sacks each year of excellent chestnuts, which were a valuable source of food. But to no avail. The young man surveyed me with a bored and jaundiced eye, and said that I would get the Requisition Order in due course. I took it up to higher authority, and made as much fuss as I thought to be safe, but quite soon afterwards a working party, of whom only the leader knew anything about forestry, came and cut them down very untidily. They lay there for about two months before being cut up and carted away, and it was no satisfaction to think that the recipients would curse their log ration, since it would be my own countrymen who would be landed with them.

But by this time we were running short of cement and it looked as if all building would have to stop. Cement at this time was a black-market item, being sold at one shilling a pound and, as well as being ruinously expensive, was extremely hard to come by.

I racked my brain for some way out of this dilemma and suddenly thought of Ray. Ray was a small farmer who, with his own lorry, had been requisitioned to transport cement from the harbour to the various emplacements that were building. He had not been a regular patient of mine, but I had had to take his wife on, at the evacuation, because she was in her last month of pregnancy and her doctor had gone to the mainland. She had already had a stillborn baby, after a difficult confinement, and was very apprehensive. To make matters worse, the first baby had been born at the hospital and she refused point-blank to go into an institution again. I did my best to persuade her, but in the end had to agree to attend her at home.

This time, too, it was a slow difficult job and I did not leave the house for 27 hours, but at last she had a fine boy and Ray, who had sat next door listening to every groan and imagining the very worst, was speechless with relief and joy. With tears in his eyes he wrung my hand and said: "If there is ever anything I can do, and I mean anything, anything at all, you have only to ask."

At the time I did not give it much further thought. During moments of intense emotion we are all rather carried away, but when we calm down are perhaps not quite so rash in our offers. Anyway, I could but ask. I thought that perhaps on a stretch of lonely road a couple of bags of cement might possibly fall off his lorry, and that by a lucky chance I might be passing in my car at the time. I put this to him and without hesitation he said: "Leave it to me, doctor. You'll have your cement somehow. I'll be in touch."

I waited to hear from him, but not with impatience for communications of that sort by telephone were very unsafe. But the very next Tuesday, which happened to be my half-day, I was providentially at Beaupré much earlier than usual, when a lorry drove rapidly into the back courtyard and Ray jumped out. "Here's your cement, doctor," he cried. "We'll have to look slippy". And he pulled three bags of cement off the lorry. I started to thank him—three bags was more than I expected—but he cut me short. "This whole lot is yours," he said. "Is there someone about to lend us a hand?"

Albert Payne, who was always in earshot when anything was afoot, materialised at once, and in a surprisingly short time we had forty bags sitting on the yard. I was too bemused by the suddenness and munificence of the gift to think properly, but the first thing was to get Ray off the premises before his presence from the lorry queue was badly missed. He jumped in, waved a quick goodbye, and left us there, looking at forty heavy bags a pretty hot potato to handle—and wondering where on earth to hide them safely.

The calf stable had an empty corner and we stacked the whole lot into it, making as compact a pile as possible. Arranged like this, forty bags did not look very much, and we then spent the rest of the afternoon throwing down all the hay that I had in the loft—about three tons. Payne built this up into a straight-sided square, bringing it well out on to the floor of the stable, so that there was about six feet of hay in front of the cement in all directions. He then pleached both outer faces thoroughly so that the stack really did look as if it had been there some time.

It was quite dark when I got back to town, but tired as I was I could not sleep for seeing myself in a concentration camp somewhere in Germany. I did not understand how so much cement could fail to be missed, and went to see Ray the next evening to plan our campaign when questions came to be asked. He was completely unconcerned and told me airily that all he had to do was to rejoin the queue of lorries, take on another load, and drive off as if nothing had happened.

The soldier at the other end, who kept tally, had a suspicion that he had made a mistake in his count, but being unable to identify which lorry might be at fault, and fearing a reprimand from his superiors, decided to let the matter drop. Someone, however, had spotted a lorry full of cement racing too fast up Queen's Road and reported it, so a corporal and two soldiers were detailed to investigate. Starting at Cottage Farm they searched all the farm premises on both sides of the road for two miles and were feeling tired and pretty hopeless by the time they got to us.

Again, it was a Tuesday when I happened to be there and a neighbour sent a boy over the fields to give us warning as to what they were looking for, while his own farm was being searched.

My feeling was that they might be too tired to pull the stack to pieces, and instead merely probe it with long rods. I had heard that this was how they sometimes searched for hidden bags of grain. There were a number of rods about, for reinforcing concrete, and they were quite long enough to reach our hidden hoard. These were hastily dumped behind a far hedge, but a bundle about three feet long were left lying about. These the Germans pounced on and proceeded to probe the stack, but of course they were too short to reach the cement. The Germans then made a perfunctory search of the rest of the premises and departed grumbling to each other. My legs felt like cottonwool, and I was very glad of a glass out of a bottle of fiery gin (my own make) which I had given to Payne some time before.

When I had recovered from the nervous trauma of the cement episode and the building was now going swimmingly, I thought it about time that I bought a cow. I found a beautiful fourteen-month heifer at a farm in St Laurence and bought her for fourteen pounds. Her herd-book name was Ultra Beautiful, but to us she was known as Chloe and she carried that name till she had to be put to sleep on the place, at the age of fifteen. She is buried in a corner of the orchard.

In due time she gave birth to a bull calf which, under German order, had to be registered on the day of birth, after which, on the third Monday following registration, it would be collected for slaughter for the benefit of the occupying community. But I was quite determined that no German was going to get a taste of my veal, and laid plans accordingly.

The calf was born on a Sunday, and I delayed registering it until the following Tuesday week, by which time it was nine days old. Three Mondays after that would see my calf about five weeks old and by that time, on unlimited milk, I hoped it would be a sizeable chunk of veal. The calf was housed in a pen in the calf house, apart from its mother, and the Sunday before it was due for collection was the date set for the grand coup. Namely the theft of my own calf.

By this time Payne and his family were housed in one half of Beaupré, but they were in the habit of going early to bed, and we decided that the snatch should take place as soon as they were properly settled down. I did not dare take Payne into my confidence, as he would be no earthly good at pleading innocence unless he was in fact utterly innocent. Also he had a wife and five children, and if any or all of them were in the plot, we would be lost before we started.

My next-door neighbour in the town, Bill Wedgewood, had already discussed the ploy with me, and was game to come in.

It was a long after curfew, and we were already operating outside the law, when at 9.30pm we arrived at Beaupré, shutting off the engine and lights as we turned into the yard, and letting the car run down silently to the calf house. Everything was quiet and there were no lights on in Beaupré. I had previously removed the passenger seat, and I sat in the back while Bill drove.

I slipped noiselessly into the toolshed for a crowbar, which I had left standing ready, and in the car was a large sack and a length of cord.

The door was secured with a short length of chain, running through two stout staples and fastened with a strong padlock. By slipping in the crowbar, and giving a good sharp heave, the door opened without any noise. Working in complete darkness and relying only on feel, we sat the calf into the sack, pulled it up over his head and tied it tightly. In a jiffy he was in the car and we drove off. A light came on, and we heard someone stirring in the house. Paddy, Payne's dog, barked angrily, with a tone of outrage that suggested fury at being caught napping, but we were well down the road by the time anyone could have had a chance to investigate.

We had chosen our route carefully and took the narrowest, least-frequented roads, but there was no way of avoiding the final stretch out of Byron Road, along Stopford Road and down David Place. The last piece of David Place was our area of greatest risk, and as we passed the Cleveland Garage, within twenty-five yards of our objective, we saw a three-man German patrol sheltering in the forecourt. An icy hand gripped my heart, but Bill, without slackening pace, drove on and pulled up before 105 Bath Street.

We heard the footsteps of the patrol coming towards us, and at the same time the calf, which I was holding in the sack, lifted his head and I knew he was about to bawl. I seized his snout and closed it firmly so that the noise was strangled at birth and we sat there, palpitating and waiting for the inevitable to happen. At that very moment came the sound of running footsteps in Gas Lane and the patrol, who had just stopped to investigate us, raced towards the noise. In one movement I was out of the car, had lifted the calf bodily on to the pavement, and was on the steps of 107 (Bill's house). Margaret, who had been waiting behind the door, flung it open and in twenty seconds flat the calf was in the scullery at the back of the house. Bill followed, I took my seat in the car (after all, I was a doctor and as such had every right to be out after curfew) and drove it to the garage in Apsley Road.

The calf was stunned with a club and bled. Then came the skinning and eviscerating and as we dared not leave the carcass in one piece to set, as it was too big to hide easily, we quartered it and hid the quarters in Bill's house and mine separately.

By the time all this was done we were well into the small hours, but after a few hours' sleep we all met together once more and had fresh fried liver for breakfast. It was the best meal we had eaten for many months and, feeling very content, I set out on my round.

In a large plastic sack, packed inside a very professional-looking maternity bag, I had the skin and the entrails, looking for somewhere really safe to deposit them. At a farm which I was visiting in St Peter I caught sight of the husband, re-stacking an untidy heap of manure. On my explaining the problem he at once dug a good hole in the ground, interred the contents of the bag, and by the time I left, after seeing my patient, there was already two feet of manure covering the evidence.

That evening we cut up the quarters into joints, cutlets, etc, and distributed them to our rejoicing friends, many of whom had not tasted a proper piece of meat for years.

Going back to that eventful night, I had scarcely got the calf into the scullery when the telephone went. A distraught Payne, his voice hoarse with indignation, shouted that the calf had been stolen and demanded my presence at Beaupré instantly, or even sooner. As patiently as I could, for I had a job waiting, I asked for details and was informed that the thief had taken the crowbar from the tool shed and 'busted' the lock. He had heard a car start up but had been too late to catch sight of it. He had then informed the Centenier, who very wisely had declined to come out, saying that it was probably the work of Russians or foreign labour. "Russians in a car, my arse!" was Payne's elegant retort. I told him not to worry, that it was not his fault in the slightest, and that we must count ourselves lucky that we still had the cow.

Obviously Payne chewed over the problem all night and came up with an astounding theory. "It's that Dr Bentlif, I'll lay a dollar," he told me. "He was round here the other day, looking for you—or so he said [this rather darkly]." I hurriedly tried to exonerate poor Dr Bentlif, who had a good many sins against the Germans on his record, but not this one. I dared not say too much, unless Payne went off on another tack, so I left him with his mind made up. Bentlif and I often laughed about it, but Payne never spoke to Dr Bentlif again till the day he died, and pointedly ignored him whenever he visited us at Beaupré, which he did frequently after the War, and still does.

With the calf gone we now had lashings of milk; supposedly all this had to go for sale—again by German decree for German consumption—but naturally some was diverted to Payne's family and some to mine. It was impossible for the authorities to control this, provided one was not too greedy, but of course not as easy to cheat with one cow as with twelve. People who had permits for rearing a limited number of heifer calves found many loopholes and took full advantage of them.

But these loopholes were getting too frequent and the Germans clamped down on one-cow owners. Everyone owning single cows had to register them and were informed that they must give them up for slaughter (a) unless they were less than three months from the last calving, when presumably being in full production it was a waste of milk to kill them; (b) unless they were within three months of their next calving, when a fresh calf and subsequent three months of full production would be lost.

Providentially, I had mated Chloe immediately she came into season after her first calf, and she just slipped into category (b) by a few days. Thus I had six months breathing space to plan ahead. I had already determined to give up this next calf, as it would be stretching my luck too far to steal this one, but to my joy she had twins, so I registered only one and kept the other. This I fed till it was more than two months old, and once again my friends had even larger gifts of fresh veal.

Chloe was mated again at the first opportunity and just as she was coming up to the end of the third month and therefore eligible for slaughter, I sold her, by a purely paper transaction, to a farmer friend who had a very big herd. When the requisition came for her, I was able to say that she no longer belonged to me. She stayed with him for just over three months, when she entered category (b) once more and I took her back.

This calf also went to the Germans, as I did not want too many questions asked about the matter. Again I had a further three months grace but my options were running out. We had reached a stage where twenty cows were being slaughtered for the troops each week and every single cow was now on the register. My farmer friend could not help me a second time, but all the same I was determined that she should not go.

The Germans were now almost cut off by sea from France; their morale was failing daily and many men were becoming disaffected, but they still insisted on their twenty cows a week, and hinted that shortly they would need more. Most of the scrub cows had already been sacrificed, and the farmers were at their wits' end to preserve their superior cattle.

Gambling on something happening in our favour soon, I decided that Chloe must be hidden—but where? In the end, with straw bales, scaffolding planks and sacks, we made a ramp up to the loft above the cowshed and, by fixing a pulley to a beam inside and lots of pushing from the other end, we got her into the loft. Hay and water was taken up and daily a large bundle of grass scythed by Payne. She was bedded up to her belly in straw and carefully cleaned out each day.

The Germans came shortly after in search of her, and went through all the buildings in vain. It never occurred to them that she might be on an upper floor, and they got nothing out of Payne, who made himself as unco-operative and stupid as he well knew how to be. He told me afterwards that he was in a cold sweat in case she mooed, but she made no sound at all. The Germans were not completely happy, and he understood them to say that he could expect another visit. But so far so good, and I was feeling moderately hopeful when the blow fell. Her urine started to drip into the shed below. All this in spite of about two feet of straw which we had kept religiously under her. Any German walking into the shed would be bound to see and hear the telltale drip, and I had to admit that the game was up.

Once again the ramp was built and, because the descent was much more difficult than the ascent, she was securely roped and held as we got her down inch by inch. At one stage she nearly fell off and we were all petrified, but finally she reached *terra firma* and was the least disturbed of us all. Thereafter she was grazed as far out of sight of the road as possible, and at odd spots in the garden.

Discipline among the troops worsened daily. Robberies in all parts were a nightly occurrence, mostly without punishment, and cows in remote fields slaughtered by the locals, removed and sold on the black market. Eventually the requisition came for Chloe but I was not there to receive it and, on the pretext that it had never reached me, I decided to ignore it. A second one was handed to me personally and I ignored that too. After that I was bothered no more by the Germans.

Within a matter of weeks the occupying forces capitulated and Chloe survived to provide milk for my family for many years, and to become the friend of all my children.

By this time most of the garden and borders had taken shape, although the area destined for the lawn was filled with a towering crop of tobacco plants. The kitchen garden was also well stocked and flourishing, although fortunately the vegetables were not sufficiently advanced to be worth stealing. For by this time the boot was on the other foot, and the Germans very short of food. Scarcely a day went by without parties of two or three presenting themselves at the door, very civilly asking permission to search the walls for snails, or to cut nettles for soup. The younger ones especially were pitiable objects, hang-dog and haggard, and of course I made no objection to their having whatever they could find. We kept a very close eye on the cats, however, for nothing that moved was safe, and there were rabbit snares in all the hedgerows.

One farmer nearby had bought a large, very fierce-looking Alsatian to protect his premises, but it disappeared during its first night on duty and I myself saw the skinned carcass, with the tail attached, hanging from a small tree outside the bunker which was just over the hedge from Beaupré's southern boundary. This bunker had been there almost from the beginning and housed six men. The inhabitants who had manned it about two years before were all peasant lads from Wurtemburg, who tried very hard to pal up with the nearby farmer. Their hearts were not in soldiering and it was plain that they longed to return to their own peaceful farms.

During the hay season, one large field was full of prime hay, completely dry and ready for carting, when suddenly the sky became leaden in colour and we were obviously going to have a thunderstorm. Without hesitation, all six German lads presented themselves at the farm, grabbing pitchforks and indicating their intention to help all they could. A second wagon was borrowed from a neighbouring farm and, by working like maniacs, the last load got into the barn as the first acorn-sized drops started to fall. They stayed to the best harvest tea the farmer's wife could provide, and no one dared accuse the farmer of fraternising.

In spite of all the setbacks we had, the alterations to Beaupré completed towards the end of 1943, but the house had not been decorated. I had bought all the paints, brushes, etc, but had forgotten one vital thing—wallpaper paste.

When Albert Payne and his family moved into one half of the house, the plaster was scarcely dry and the walls just received a colour wash, but when Claude and May proposed occupying the other half, half a year later, I had to put on my thinking cap again.

In the old days we used to stick on wallpaper with flour and water, but of course one could not possibly devote an essential food to such a purpose at that time. In desperation I went to my baker friend, and he at once said: "No problem. I've got nearly half a sack of flour which got wet somewhere on the journey and is caked solid. I was wondering what to do with it, and if you can use it, you can have it and welcome."

"Caked" was not the word. "Concreted" would have been better. I put Payne on to it with a hammer and chisel and then ground the resulting small chunks in a pestle and mortar. This made an excellent paste and the house was duly papered and painted—to look very smart. Unfortunately Claude and May used an oil lamp with some very peculiar mixture inside which seemed to have given off much more smoke than light, and the paper in both sittingroom and bedroom was ruined.

However, more by good luck than judgment, I had overestimated the wallpaper I had bought and we had enough to re-do both rooms before Ann came back.

When I returned to Jersey with Ann and my young son on 16 July 1945, I was able to present to her a fully decorated, fully furnished house, all ready for occupation—oops, sorry!—for moving into.

My little son, now aged exactly five (for the day he first saw the Island and Beaupré was his fifth birthday) absolutely loved the place and all the freedom of movement it provided. Being of a gregarious nature, he set himself the task of getting to know every family within walking distance of his short legs. Time and again we lost him and, when eventually he was found, would be seen sitting on the edge of a chair, munching a biscuit and talking to the farmer's wife.

Within three years he was joined, first by a sister and then two brothers, so that Beaupré rang with the laughter of children and was the sort of home which helped me to forget the five awful years of isolation.

THE END

Former TV journalist, Roy Mc.Loughlin's fascinating account of the German Occupation of the Channel Islands contains the personal experiences of individuals in the Islands while relating them to the wider perspective of Europe at war.

224 Pages **125 Photos**

Please send me..............copies of "Living with the Enemy" @ £7.85 (£5.95 + £1.90 P&P)

I enclose cheque/P.O. for ....

Name ....

Address..

Telephone ....

Type of credit card: Visa/Mastercard/Switch/Other ....

Card Number ....

Expiry Date ....

Channel Island Publishing, Unit 3B, Barette Commercial Centre,
La Route Du Mont Mado, St John, Jersey, JE3 4DS.
www.channelislandpublishing.com
Tel (01534) 860806